New York Minutiae: An Unofficial and Unauthorized Guide to CSI:NY

Mila Hasan

Contents

Slicing The Apple

"As a rule, TV pilots are busy affairs, charged with the responsibility of introducing an entire cast of characters, their relationships and the world in which they exist." Anthony E Zuiker.

Perhaps *Quincy M.E.* began this whole phenomenon of crime investigation shows. The focus of which wasn't really about whom until the body told you how. Three decades later erupted a whole new era of shows in such a league; this was in the encapsulation of *CSI*. Soon everyone was following suit as other shows cropped up in this realm; spawning 'copycats' like *Crossing Jordan*. Even the UK was getting in on the action with *Silent Witness*, thus the title. As well as *Waking The Dead* starring Trevor Eve. Also on the horizon, but older, were psychological shows like *Profiler* and the Australian, *Halifax F.P.* about the life and work of a forensic psychologist.

Two years after the original *CSI* debut back in 2002 came the second spin-off, *CSI:Miami* and nicely timed, two years later in 2004 came *CSI:NY*. Though I said, they should make a *CSI:Alaska* and be done with it. Each one had a different cast but the sole purpose was the same. These shows had the CSIs mucking in and getting their hands dirty. Striving to find evidence necessary to bring the suspect to book. Almost always made easy on their part – as the suspect happened to leave behind a stray hair or the odd incriminating nail or fibre. [Begging the question, well someone had to ask, didn't any of the CSIs leave something of their own behind leading to contamination of their evidence, surely a tell-tale hair. A piece of their person. To date only Delko in *CSI: Miami* was careless enough to actually sneeze onto vital evidence, deeming it worthless in a season 1 episode and kept this to himself for a long while. Also Stella in season 3.]

Anyhow it's to all the *CSI* shows that this book is a homage, but more so to *CSI-NY* (with the occasional reference to the others.) Written some years ago in 2005, I thought I'd take you back to how it all started for *CSI: NY*. As for the title, *A New York Minutiae*, well because it's a play on a New York minute. Also as *CSI: NY* has always been overlooked where guides are concerned and 'minutiae' means: something always overlooked – not small or trivial.

Now into its sixth season, seems hard to recall how it all began. Plus for me, season 1 was unique and special. It had a new concept and filming style, with its concrete undertones and greys to represent the harshness of the city, hiding the criminal happenings. As well as boasting Vanessa Ferlito, who sadly didn't stick around for the remaining seasons. Also demonstrated by the toughness which accompanied many characters, Flack and Danny. Before the network signalled an all-change and ordered a more subtle lightness to the show.

Crimes are solved, not only with the aid of good ol' fashioned brain power to put the evidence together – and that's your key word – evidence; but also by using a *DELL* or Apple computer or two. The lab is a state-of-the-art-fully functional and equipped forensics lab: containing autopsy room and masses of equipment, just as its predecessor shows.

All the *CSI* shows boast authentic equipment from centrifuges, mass spectrometers, microscopes and so on. In fact everything a real forensics lab lacks. Which brings to mind the supposition: if they did have such equipment, there'd be less criminals roaming around free and the rate of solved crimes would increase. But apparently crime doesn't pay, in the sense that the forensic scientists are the real losers. A sharp indictment of American political and social values, when a TV show can afford vital equipment and real labs miss out.

On the other hand, locations and specific cities are deemed the true stars. Jerry Bruckheimer's movie- making prowess can be seen in his TV shows too. In *CSI,* it's Las Vegas; *CSI: Miami,* of course, it's Miami and *CSI- NY,* it's New York. Each series is filmed in its respective trademark hues. With Vegas and Miami it's orange and red and warm glowing colours. In Miami the earthy tones, cool pastels. In New York, the series is filmed using a blue filter to give the show a more hard-hitting grittier feel of steel – matching the moody skyscrapers and the 'cool' approach to investigating and solving cases. (At least for season 1.)

Although still heavily based on the same premise of 'evidence' i.e. find the evidence, solve the crime.

The show still maximizes the use of being out in the open, gathering and locating evidence; as well as solving and analyzing in the lab. Hence the immaculate white lab coats; the sterile and spotless lab with state-of-the-art equipment. This in stark contrast to the M.E's lab which is more outdated in its décor, tiled and weary-looking. Emphasizing the sort of work carried on here. Also in contrast, is the seamy interrogation room at the police precinct, reflecting the type of work here: questioning suspects, garnering evidence, confessions etc. Conjuring the picture of what future life will be like in a prison cell; when offenders have to face the harsh reality and consequences of their actions. Comments David Caruso, "if we can recover your DNA, it can only be you."

Danny Cannon: "Techniques showing small is important; experimented with small lenses and cameras and making large props so the camera could go in and film." [there is]...nothing like this on TV...nothing behind the scenes and looking inside a microscope on TV." Gary loves the special effects and describes them as coming "to identify *CSI*."

Anthony Zuiker says during season 1 of *CSI:NY* "watch [them] pick up trace evidence, dragged across the carpet, watch [has] fibres from the carpet." These are 3 dramas with forensic mystery.

Says Executive Producer Carol Mendelsohn, "The reality is we don't move an inch forward with the day if the science is a centimeter wrong." This includes actually 'training' the actors – how to handle equipment, strip weapons, put them back together again and the essential element of the show: the pristine and sometimes complex terminology. (Recall Marg Helgenberger getting to grips with the term, 'anaphylactic shock', which just rolls off the tongue for some of us.)

Anthony comments they "set the hook in mystery early in the show." It's how they die and not why, you have to keep guessing. Ann Donahue calls it "the ultimate *"how done it"* [where] "the star is always the star."

So fans couldn't get enough of the endearing close shots of exploding blood vessels, punctured lungs as well as intricate words such as 'hyperplasia', 'epithelial regeneration' providing you with the makings of more gruesome and exciting primetime TV.

On the contrary, to most critics' opinion (at least here in the UK) characters on the whole, do have a sense of direction – as well as back story. Though it's not apparent or revealed in its entirety from day one or the very first episode. The same was the case with the original *CSI*. The show is after all scientific based with the characters' personal history intertwined and getting a mention now and then. Like pieces of a puzzle, it's revealed little by little so you have to put the pieces together, illuminating the bigger picture. This isn't going to happen from the outset.

It's been said the show is more "procedural" than character. It is primarily about the story – the evidence. But in order for it to be part of a whole, character interaction is inevitable as it is necessary. How certain aspects of the case affect the CSIs' reaction to the evidence, personal history...all have an impact on the show and sometimes even goes some way to solving a difficult situation/scenario in the story; providing a clue, observation, fact and sometimes something as brief as a passing comment. Such as the episode of *CSI*, **Unfriendly Skies,** where the team revealed their feelings on how they would have reacted when faced with the situation on the plane and whether they could have taken a life, put into perspective when Gil says that's not the question they should be asking, rather, 'why didn't someone stop to ask how the victim was feeling?'

One aspect that humanizes characters, although not evident is their dedication to the job, ensuring the victim finds justice, missing out on most of their personal lives to do just this. It's all a matter of: "this is who I am; this is what I do..."

Concept

Anthony C Zuiker was a Las Vegas tram driver. After watching a documentary about forensic scientists on the *Discovery Channel*, he chanced upon the idea of a *CSI* show which became a lucrative franchise. "I was watching a show about CSIs with my wife and it seemed like a good idea for a drama series." He pitched his idea of *CSI* to Nina Tassler, Head of Drama Development at CBS: she in turn loved his pitch, told him to get writing and if he could do that, she'd go in and bat for him. Zuiker also had to convince Jerry Bruckheimer and after he read a *Harlem Globetrotters* script he'd written; he pitched his *CSI* idea stating, "I want to do this show about forensics; you walk into a crime scene, there's a dead body on the floor, a plant knocked over and a pink elephant in the backyard and you tell all this through flashbacks [and versions.]"

Says Anthony Zuiker, "The one great thing about the modern day mystery if done correctly, is they've become such visual shows and we are really afforded the opportunities to take storylines that are happening in the here and now and push ourselves not only with science but with technology. I think those are the things that are still essential for an audience and just focusing on compelling storytelling and I believe we're doing that very successfully."

Quoting Jerry Bruckheimer, Anthony continues, he's "famous for saying we're in the transportation business we transport people from one reality to another – that's why the importance of *CSI* is important in terms of entertainment to the world." He also says if he wrote a book about his life, he'd call it, *From Tram to Tinseltown* "because people know what it's like to work for $8 an hour – by me knowing nobody in Hollywood, it really sends out a message that you can have an idea without many contacts, and with pure luck and skill and hard work, something great can happen and I hope that story inspires people." But he did have a contact in Dustin Abraham which put him on the right track. In a separate interview, Anthony also comments, "you know people aren't born to create three big shows. They work for eight bucks an hour on a tram, sweeping up or flipping burgers. Everybody has a specific talent in them and they have a dream, and I hope that people working these menial jobs will be inspired by a story like mine."

Consequently *CSI* premiered 6 October 2000 and became the highest rated series on US TV with 26 million viewers and has amassed a global army of fans. The premiere gathering 17.3 million viewers alone. It is shown in 177 territories around the world and is the number one show in Germany, France, Italy, Spain, Canada and Australia. As Anthony says, it's shown everywhere, but six countries in the world. In China *CSI* is known as *Tracing Crimes*, in the Middle East it's *Investigation of the Crime Place*, Poland: *Criminal Riddles*, France: *The Experts*, in Japan it's known as *Scientific Investigation Group*, Venezuela: *Crime Scene* and in Germany, as *Tracking Down the Perpetrators*, actually in Germany it's just known by *CSI*.

In the UK, all three of the shows are never off air. With some season or another being shown by Five, where the shows found their home, as well as on the other digital Five channel, Five USA. The first episode of *CSI:NY* when it aired on five in 2005 was watched by 2.8 million viewers.

On the bigger question of life after death – he believes we should all end up in a similar place. "I'm hoping there's a greater place for all of us. World peace especially in these times. I'm saddened by these times in the country and in the world. He sits in a hotel room by himself for five days out of seven, every week writing scripts or inventing a boardgame. He believes *CSI* has definitely changed the world and changed television and TV can never go back to what it was after *CSI*.

From Concept to Reality

Zuiker went behind the scenes with real-life investigators. "I got to shadow some real Las Vegas CSIs and one of the first jobs they took me on involved a guy who had been murdered in his hotel room by a prostitute and her pimp; but there was no sign of the prostitute." He had to comb through the carpet to find clues – or as is the job of a CSI – evidence. "So I was down on my hands and knees crawling and as I got over the bed and I looked underneath and there was a prostitute hiding and looking back at me. That was when I realized I was really onto something." [Easy to see where the episodes of *CSI: NY **On** the Job,* and in *CSI* Sara confronting a suspect and Catherine encountered the same; as well as the pilot episode plots arrived from: i.e. not checking or clearing a room properly before any examination is conducted.]

Anthony also watched documentaries on forensic experts as well as shadowing Las Vegas criminalists. Most casino employees are also fingerprinted as a matter of routine and so viewers would easily see how potential criminals could be tracked.

The Las Vegas crime lab is also the second most busiest in the US – after the Quantico FBI lab in Virginia. Add to the mix – real life CSIs as writers with their own stories; special effects, equalling the birth of the procedural show.

His idea was acted upon immediately by TV executives – giving scientists and science a new lease of life. Another walking poster for recruitment into the forensic society. Science made sophistically seductive. With glossy production values, meticulous research, it was guaranteed success.

"When I cracked the show [in 2000, the pilot was watched by over 20 million] says Anthony, all I hoped was that it got on air and did well...ultimately we're educating America and the world about the processes of CSIs, how they go into your homes or to a crime scene, scrutinize evidence and then replicate what happened without being there at the time. We are demonstrating that they are giving peace of mind and closure to the survivors. When a CSI unit meets you on the worst day of your life, there's something out there that's on your side. I think that's an important message to send the world; especially in these trying times."

This sentiment was echoed by David Caruso and Melina Kanakaredes too.

The numbers on the show also increased after 9/11. Anthony: "We thought maybe it would work against us; that people wouldn't want to see blood and destruction after what happened. I think what was happening was the show sort of prepared us for 9/11 and when 9/11 hit, audiences were really rushing to the show and getting their comfort food in terms of having a sense of justice in the world. There were people out there – like our case - helping to solve crimes. Essentially Ground Zero was the world's largest crime scene."

Anthony also says that David Caruso "connected with his TV audience." David told them that, "after 9/11 he would receive phonecalls from people asking him what he was going to do about what just happened. People were actually calling him, still seeing him as a television hero that could fix things and I just found that to be really incredible. He has that kind of connection with the viewers." What can also be said, is that some people may find it really difficult distinguishing between a TV show and a character from the actual actor.

Having created the show, Zuiker was instrumental in bringing the world of forensics to the furor. He has essentially created the CSI Effect. He says, "the upside is the fact that law enforcement officers need to do their jobs properly now and lawyers can't fool jurors with $5 words. The bad part is juries expect too much evidence, they expect the courtroom to run like CSI runs...the technology, the level of awareness of forensic science and educational value are all giving CSIs a voice. They are real people who do these things. This huge public awareness would never have happened if it wasn't for the show. The downside is you're asking the average viewer to be able to realize it's a TV show."

The average jury can't really be expected to have that much knowledge of how forensics work, more importantly that a certain piece of evidence relates to the crime and how. In most trials, juries believe that once a piece of evidence is presented, it automatically means the defendant is in actual fact guilty of the crime. Thereby showing too much reliance on forensics and CSIs; can in turn prove unreliable for the defendant, turning out an unsafe conviction.

Naran Shankar comments on the *CSI* episode **I Like to Watch**, which was about a "reality crime show following an investigation by the CSIs and the questions of shows like ours having an effect on the judicial system put to Grissom — whether or not it teaches criminals to get away with crimes as much as it helps criminalists, it's just a question of how you apply it. You've got to stay 'one step ahead.'" As is true in any area of law enforcement — be it forensics, police investigation or the judicial process. Anticipating the defence's arguments on behalf of the defendant and using your own answers in response, and of course, the all important, evidence.

Danny Cannon commented on how they were finding new ways into the show, like using technical advisors, reading about forensic science. The show has led to an influx in making forensics supercool and even sexy, to a point. Zuiker indicates, "the impact *CSI* has had on the application ratio is astounding. It's gone from 5 applicants per place a year, to 5,000." Colleges have signed on students to study not only forensics, but also criminal justice, in the USA alone. David Caruso also comments on how the shows have affected the application rates to universities, which initself indicates how powerful they are. Ann Donahue comments on *The CSI Effect* and "educating the jury." Which in turn leads to juries practically demanding forensic evidence in a trial. Jerry Bruckheimer comments on how juries react when there's no forensic evidence in the case, and how a trial is not *CSI*. The Vegas crime lab changed its name to include *CSI*. (Also see below.)

CSI is so massively popular that in the season 8 episode **Two and a Half Deaths**, it was mentioned in the show how having pretty people working in a lab could become a hit TV series (already said and done, of course, in *CSI*.) In this episode, the writers of *CSI* were swapped with the writers of *Two and a Half Men* and they came up with the storyline in this episode.

Said William Petersen: "People underestimate the [television] audience in this country constantly – there's no doubt in my mind that anybody in this country can get this show, and knowing that, I think it's our task to make it smarter and make them work harder to get it. Otherwise, they'll flip over and watch Donald Trump."

Pam Veasey comments; "having written sketch comedy where you had to do everything in so few pages and have it be really effective, I managed to do that in writing and particularly here on *CSI:NY* where a lot happens in a little amount of time."

Says Anthony Zuiker, "we cast a great city – we let each city inform us and then we produce to that...we do 45 minute Bruckheimer-esque movies every week with a level of editing and sound and pace unlike anything in motion pictures." He continues, "you go to Las Vegas to escape, you go to Miami to be seen and you go to New York to change. And I think that's really the trinity of the backdrops, the cities."

Why Las Vegas?

Like New York, it's a city that never sleeps: where people come to party, gamble, legally, and participate in conventions. There's an abundance of characters, some cool, some weird or the plain ordinary tourists caught up in the buzz generated by the bright lights and even brighter vibes emanating from the casinos. Where everyone's a suspect and getting your man or woman or sometimes animal, is only an epithelial away.

Says Jerry Bruckheimer: "Anthony Zuiker lives in Las Vegas so he felt it was a great backdrop. So many interesting characters get to Vegas – it's like a melting pot. You can draw on so many stories because of that. There are people from all over the world that come there and make their fortune, so I think you've got a lot to work with. Plus it's a community where people live and work, even though they might work in casinos. It's like any normal town. But underneath it, there's this kind of underbelly that's very interesting."

Ann Donahue sees Vegas as different, it's the nightshift where people do things they wouldn't do anywhere else: there are secrets, the night and not being ashamed. Carol Mendelsohn comments on the stories spinning from here: "the camera veers on the strip, around there...the felon capital of the world."

Gil's character is based on the astronaut Gus Grissom and was originally meant to be called Gil Scheinbaum before William Petersen changed it to Gil Grissom. The characters of Gil and Catherine were based on real life forensic investigators Daniel Holstein and Yolanda McCrery.

The Independent describes Gil as "part *Sherlock Holmes* and part Rupert Giles from *Buffy the Vampire Slayer*, Grissom is a monk-like scientist given to lofty statements which, surprisingly or not, don't stop him being a bit of a hit with female viewers."

When storyboarding *CSI* shows do they begin with the effects and then work the scenes around them or come up with the stories and then think of what special effects can be used?

At any rate, Miami and New York followed as the next cities covered.

Why Miami?

The city that never stops partying: - the weather, the beaches, the cultures that all combine to give Miami its uniqueness. An opportunity to delve into storylines that just couldn't be done in Las Vegas. Or if they could wouldn't seem that kooky or out of place.

Spring breaks, fires in the Everglades, crocodiles with their own DNA database, where even the alligators know Miami is their personal hotbed swimming pool. The first port of call for escaping Cuban exiles and immigrants; not to mention the hurricanes.

CSI is huger than *Friends* (no surprise there then) and *CSI:Miami* gets in excess of 20 million viewers. In the same mould as *CSI,* it followed the forensic investigations linked to the Miami Dade Police Department. Crimes are solved with high-ended equipment, AV studio and comes with its own technical advisors, one of whom is a former bomb squad officer, in the character of Lt. Horatio Caine.

H is named for nineteenth century writer Horatio Alger, the only *CSI* character to be named after a famous American historical figure!

Says David, "maybe it sounds creepy but Horatio Caine does exist. The sense of responsibility he projects in the world is very real and when fans run up to me and say – 'hey you make me feel safe' – that's as real as real gets. In those moments, those people aren't talking to me, they're talking to Horatio."

CSI:Miami was created because the producers had concerns other *CSI* copycats would grace the scene (as they did) so they wanted *Miami* to be the first of the lot! So what of *NY* then? The spin offs were due to the popularity of the show, hence *Miami* and also thus *NY* too.

Danny Cannon says it was Jerry Bruckheimer's idea to focus on Miami. Carol Mendelsohn: "bright, light, sand, sunshine, brightly-coloured clothes. Miami is the place to go to be seen." Jonathan Littman comments on the fantasy element and the larger than life crimes committed in Miami.

The set has everything including: fully equipped forensics lab; autopsy room, full firing range to scale. The centrifuge equipment, mass spectrometers and the $750,000 worth of microscopes which are all authentic equipment.

Even the cast will have become fully fledged forensics experts. Emily Proctor who plays CSI Calleigh Duquesne can strip a gun, resulting in her "man's hands." She commented on how using guns, she found her arms became more muscled.

Khandi Alexander: formerly, M.E Alexx Woods in *CSI:Miami*, commented, "today my lines were anti-mortem abrasions have four stages of healing: scab formation, epithelial regeneration, hyperplasia and regressive granulation tissue. That means a scab on your knee."

It too has its cases based on real life stories and events as well as fictional. In October 2002 the Washington sniper hit the headlines, resulting in season 1's sniper episode **Kill Zone.**

David Caruso said, "One of the things about all three shows is that the CSIs meet people on the worst day of their lives and I think H is very aware of that. He knows how fragile and damaged people are and it's not only about the completion of the case and being able to shut the folder. He knows it's not only about the victim but the victim's family and the aftermath because for them this event now is going to last forever. There is a sense in *CSI:Miami* that we are treading on a very fragile set of events."

Also H's trademark sunglasses, which as well as making quite the fashion statement, are also there to define his character. The glasses come off, go on and then stay off, until the case is solved. At least in the early seasons of the show. Anthony developed the character of H further and he comments, "what was really interesting about that is there would be times where he would kind of come into frame and leave frame, almost as if he had this ghostly presence that could be everywhere – almost like a guardian angel."

Ann Donahue says of David, "the show rises and falls on David's back and I will say with modesty, that it's sometimes the number 1 show in the world and I think that has to do with David. People adore him. I cannot imagine the show without him and I wouldn't want to." On the show in general, she continues, "Anthony Zuiker came up with something so fresh and I very often feel it was the last tram out in terms of a true mass television hit so I don't ever sit here and pine."

Though the shows are based on similar premises, David comments, "We are very different and I think a lot of that has to do with the location. You couldn't do a show about Miami and not have vibrancy and passion and all of the things that the city is about. Even the way the light hits the negative when we film in Miami is totally different to the way the light hits the negative in California; so the footage we get down there is electric and vibrant." He also thinks that, "we have a slightly different licence. We're more police-orientated so we're able to discharge our weapons on occasion and get into some of the action. Miami is an exciting town. If you're doing a show with Miami in the title, and you don't have an exciting show, something's not right." As I said, think *Miami Vice*.

He knows *CSI:Miami* will never be able to achieve the ratings pull and success of its predecessor. "You can't compete with a show that successful." At the time of season 1, David moved to Miami and bought a boutique with his then wife. Whilst he was writing his own drama set in Miami, he was offered the role of H. "It was crucial to get the city's endorsement because I have to live there. But I got invited to a party with a powerful family who live there and it was an important moment to see whether we were going to be rejected or not...some intelligent, sophisticated and educated people were watching the show. I think the stories have captured this very specific tone which is cerebral in nature. The perspective the stories are told from means you are almost in somebody's head when you're watching an episode...for Horatio, it's not only about the victim, but the victim's family and the aftermath of the crime – for them this event is going to last forever."

David has had his own brush of reality with CSIs. There was a mugging near his home and they were searching the scene and he was tempted to offer them help. However playing the role of a forensic scientist is more difficult than he imagined. It's down to the actual CSIs to say what finally stays or goes in a scene and how it's done, and not the producer. He says, "I had a day where I had done, in my opinion, a pretty good take on the shot, it felt good to me, but the advisor wanted to examine my latex gloves because he thought he'd seen a pinhole in the monitor." He was right and they had to film the entire scene again "because technically a pinhole in the latex glove would have compromised the evidence. They are meticulous about protecting the authenticity of the show."

Telling real stories becomes a fine art as they too are played around with and are given a new perspective than how they are actually reported, adding a new dimension of drama and science.

David's father was a journalist and "he said, 'if you want to find out the truth about a subject, read the fiction that's been written about it. There is a lot of truth to that. We have the opportunity to explore a current event by implication in a way that the news media doesn't have. We did a show about a rock and roll club that catches on fire, in season 1 [**Tinder Box**], and that was very specific to Rhode Island when something similar really happened. We eventually kind of told a different story and that didn't really choose to comment on that particular event. But I think they wanted to capture the terror of being in an environment that hadn't been properly protected."

David played Det. John Kelly in *NYPD Blue* when a pay row broke out and he left to pursue a movie career. Even after episode 4 of *NYPD Blue* he was being offered lead roles in movies. After some publically documented scenes he had a falling out with creator Steven Bochco. Thus *CSI:Miami* gave him the second bite at the apple (well if he was in *CSINY* – that is!) and the chance to achieve success. A second chance to cruise the high seas of Miami. "If the press are trying to get your attention you got two choices: you can play the victim or you can listen because maybe they're trying to tell you something that can save your life." He didn't expect to be cast in another major TV show/series. "My first go around ten years ago and leaving was such a public moment I didn't even let myself kind of dream about a second chance. It's kind of like a miracle to get an opportunity to be a part of something like this…I think I represent to people how not to handle your career on television. I didn't handle success first time round but that came from inexperience. Ten years later I have a different appreciation and perspective."

As for being a sex symbol, he said, "I'm a 49 year old [back in 2005] with red hair – think about it!" *The Independent* in the UK described David Caruso as a "weedy-looking redhead…famously given to removing his sunglasses to emphasize a point and breaking up his sentences with dramatic pause."

As everyone knows even though the shows are set in different cities, most of the filming is in LA. *CSI:Miami* films at Raleigh Manhattan Studios. The outdoor shots include filming at Long Beach, California; Manhattan Beach, California; Redondo Beach, California. Other locations include Downtown Long Beach at Marina Creek Park and Naples Lagoon Park. The Naples District.

We all love the cool exterior of the Miami Dade crime lab building. This is actually The Federal Aviation Administration Federal Credit Union building in Hawthorne. (Located on Aviation Boulevard, between Marine Avenue & Rosecarns Avenue, for anyone who might be visiting.)

Why NY?

The Statue of liberty standing watch over the city – a shimmering beacon of truth and democracy. So it is with CSIs effortlessly fighting for the underdog – ridding their city of crime and predators who seek to permeate an air of dishonesty, danger and dilemmas in one of the greatest cities of the world; made all the more poignant by 9/11 and the aftermath of identifying victims. Forensic teams have a DNA database of samples taken from victims who have yet to be identified still.

Jonathan Littman says "it can only happen in New York." Whereas Ann Donahue comments on letting each "city inform us." Executive Producer Andrew Lipsitz tells us "New York is a microcosm of the world – it gives a wide range of access to people, ethnicities and motives." Executive Producer Peter Lenkov says that they attempt to make New York a character in the story and not just a city or backdrop. Whereas Anthony Zuiker comments that "when you shoot New York from the air it has a very raw, steely, monolithic look and it makes for really interesting drama."

In the words of the song, "If I can make it here, I can make it anywhere..." a bit like the series!

Pam Veasey comments on how New York is great since they have all four seasons of the year. "New York is a constantly moving, triple-layered intense dense city. You can have three murders in one building because people live stacked on top of each other....our crime scenes aren't wide and spread out. You see those beautiful shots on *CSI* where they walk through the desert...ours could be a murder at a bodega where the crime scene tape is right outside the door and people who need to get to work are walking past the crime scene and there are cops in front of it. New York doesn't have much room." Almost like London – wait – exactly like London. Only we don't have so many skyscrapers and people living right on top of each other.

Said Gary Sinise: "We're going to explore what being a crime scene investigator in New York post 9/11 might be like...his [Mac Taylor's] wife died in the WTC, so that's an important part of who he is." Pam Veasey calls Mac "the glue and he's strong in his leadership, in the answers of right and wrong in terms of crime fighting. He is the moral foundation of investigating a crime and putting someone away but when it comes to seeing everyone around you feeling and changing and having reactions to loss. Mac has got to be the emotional foundation..." Gary also said "the city is a big part of our show. Even though we don't live here, we want to incorporate as much of the city as we can."

Gary stated they used to film in New York about twice a year, but in later seasons it increased and they now shoot scenes from at least four different episodes. He loves being back in New York and calls it the best city in the world and that "New York's watching our show quite a bit."

Location shooting has taken place at sites such as Times Square, Columbus and museums, Central park, shooting by the fountain, also where *Ransom* was filmed. Also upper Manhattan, Upper West Side, where the season 3 episode, **3.1** was shot.

The *Independent* sees Gary Sinise as "the most modern and complex and the least archetypal of the trio, his greyness suiting the post-September 11 Manhattan location...the writers gave Sinise's character, Det. Mac Taylor, a shameless back-story; a wife who dies in the Twin Towers. Man and the city as one."
Melina Kanakaredes: "there's still going to be what people love about *CSI* [including] an emphasis on character this time."

Actual forensic scientists add to the reality of the show – not only providing an infinite supply of material but also bringing with them a wealth of expertise and experience. Elizabeth Devine was recruited by the show as a part time consultant and became a permanent member. She even keeps samples of her childrens' DNA in the freezer. She says, "none of the characters are entirely based on me, but I think there's a lot of me in a lot of the characters. I tell them about the experiences I have had and I think that gives it a little bit of a ring of truth because I've been there...there's no limit to what people will do to each other. Every time I think I've seen it all something else will come and surpass it..."

She continues, "...we were called out to a murder of a girl who had been beaten and left for dead. Her head was covered in maggots and the officer thought she was dead. The maggots had kept her alive because they ate all the dead tissue...thanks to them she's still alive to this day." This became the *CSI:Miami* episode **Hard Time** in season 2. This girl became a victim as she turned up at her assailant's parole hearing to prevent him from receiving parole. So he hired a hitman to solve his dilemma. She was found covered in maggots and the CSIs discovered she was still alive. She made it to the parole hearing for another time. In the episode the woman had been a victim of rape by her attacker who had her beaten and killed. Evidence led to him being detained for life for attempted murder.

Other stories are ceased upon by Zuiker taking people out to dinner/drinks to gauge information from them. But he likes to write "stories that inspire and interest us. It can be things we rip out of airline magazines and take to the writers' room that can become a germ of a story." These can include the *CSI* story in season 5 episode **Feeling the Heat**: people leaving their baby in the car in the boiling heat. "I live in Vegas where there can be 145 degree temperatures and I have got out of the car with my wife with groceries, taken one bag and gone, 'oh Dawson's sleeping in the car.' As a writer you can come from a position of experience and from the heart. I think the key is engaging viewers in the episode."

News, information from CSIs around the world provides inspiration and aspiration for more plotlines which will allow the shows to last decades even. Zuiker; "I think a show like this probably has a run of about 7-12 years. I feel like we're a family, we're grooming younger people to work with us and we're getting better. We'll go on a long time." 'Til the cast becomes all grey and wrinkly! Almost there then, at least with *CSI* as it enters its 10th season in 2009. Although the original cast, most of them have left, (William Petersen, Jorga Fox, Gary Dordan) the show still continued on without them, with the addition of Laurence Fishburne and Lauren Lee Smith, who won't be around for season 10. But Jorga makes a return, indefinitely.

Zuiker asks, "can you see yourself living through the episode, or a character's point of view matches yours, or do you think against that point of view?" The answer is always going to be 'yes', in *CSI* episodes and especially *NY,* where you think to yourself at times, where's the sympathy, the tact, understanding, especially with some of the female characters or their reasons for not pursuing certain avenues when it's just staring you in the face, until the very end of the episode or not at all. That is until the show found its feet and the characters seemed to mellow somewhat.

CSI:NY is considered more blood-fest orientated than its predecessors.

Said Anthony Zuiker, that 9/11 was the world's largest crime scene, with so much happening and so many forensic personnel involved, so New York was ultimately the only choice available for another *CSI* show. Also Les Moonves gave the go-ahead for *CSI:NY* after a meeting in which all Anthony had to do was choose a city, commenting, that the franchise is "the linchpin of the resurrection of this network [CBS]."

Background

The show has a myriad of experts around the globe they can call upon for information and help. Such as Nobel Prizewinners who offered their brains to be picked in return for a *CSI* baseball hat. For example Gil's obsession /love of insects is based on the insect expert Dr Goff. William Petersen came across one of his books and contacted him. Many of the bug storylines on the show were due to him.

Hill Harper comments on the process of filming episodes and how the Network in this case, CBS, always has a say. The writers "send drafts to the network, the network approves them and they get notes back. The Networks involved, Bruckheimer's involved and then you have actors on the show that want to have some say in what goes down. So there's a lot of people that you're trying to [satisfy] as a writer; find something for and still have your vision on the page. That's a tough, tough challenge. Writers on our show could probably be elected to political office because they're able to satisfy a lot of different interests and that's what politicians do. So, Pam Veasey for President."

Anthony is excited and motivated and to him, "the sky's the limit...if it's happened once and it's cool, it goes in the show!" Carol Mendelsohn talks of looking at close-ups in the shows, how things happen, such as the *CSI:Miami* episode where a blow torch reveals a tattoo, also in the season 1 *NY* episode, **1.13 Tanglewood**. They have real investigators and they talk to others about bizarre situations or stories for the episodes, some are urban legends, like the scuba diver episode in *CSI,* (**Scuba Doobie Doo**.) They go to the Sheriff's crime lab and investigate crime scenes for their storylines. They look at the style and how not to mess with the crime scenes, such as using latex gloves and torches. Ann also says the prosecution doesn't have to spend time explaining some common terms now, such as explaining what epithelials are for 40 minutes. That's assuming everyone watches the show, some people still don't. Ann

Donohue says they read magazines, books, pop-science and some are "ripped from the headlines."

On the *CSI:Miami* DVD extras, such as commentaries, they focus on how the show affects real life and reflects it too. Ann Donohue on the season **2.2 Blood Brothers** episode commentary stated Miami is at the crossroads of the US and South America. Thus its location is used to focus on crimes committed by certain racial groups: usually black/Latino, overly portrayed as gang members and drug dealers, or deadly arms dealers. The show also highlights the fear of US authorities over such issues of immigration stifling the country. Says Donohue, the show dictates to immigrants that they need to tow the line, viz, the US line. Since "if here, [they] need to play by the rules."

CSI has been accused of advocating violence against women – as well as other shows, such as *Law and Order.* Reasons for showing explicit gory and violent scenes have been put down to excuses such as not being able to glorify sexual scenes. According to Jeffrey Sconce – associate professor at Northwestern University, he puts this down to the US TV system: "you can get away more with amplifying violence than you can with amplifying sexuality. It results in this weird sadistic element. Putting women in these sexual situations is a backdown way of getting more flesh in." TV procedural shows need to compete and one way of doing this is by upping the level of violence coming up with new ways of enticing and titillating, as long as its viewed as being within acceptable boundaries.

Another significant fact is that TV shows will normally appeal to women and be watched by them, especially *CSI*. Demographics reveal two thirds of *CSI* viewers in the age range of 18-49 are women.

Women are also classed as having to watch out for themselves. Always need someone looking out for them on the show. In *The Color of Rape* Sujata Moore argues that TV indicates "how social understandings of gender and race are influenced by historical conceptions as well as institutional discourses such as medicine or the nation state and inscribed onto the female body." *CSI:Miami* reinforces and gives voice to the war on terror as being important and necessary, portraying people in a negative light. But this isn't the only show to do this; others include *Without A Trace* (before it was cancelled) and *NCIS,* to name but a few.

Gary describes Mac Taylor as having "an integrity, an honesty, a directness." Anthony Zuiker says "Mac's theory is: everything's connected. He wants to know the why." Cf Gil Grissom – not so much 'the why' or 'the how'. But perhaps 'the who.' [Bad joke there!]

The show is always six scripts ahead. The cast and crew have one week off for Thanksgiving, three weeks for Christmas and three weeks in May.

Some locations are filmed in New York, whereas for the most part the show is shot in Los Angeles due to cheaper production costs. An episode in season 4 was also filmed in Chicago, part of it, at least. Anthony Zuiker wanted *Behind Blue Eyes* for the theme song, but CBS President, Leslie Moonves wanted *Baba Reilly,* by The Who. Lyrics: Pete Townsend, vocals: Roger Daltrey from the 1971 album, *Who's Next.* Season 4 got a remixed, revamped version: more music, less lyrics. Littman says a large part of the show being a success is the opening title, since no one had used an established rock song in a TV show before, at least not in an opening title.

The more information they have, the more technology, more great twists, adding to a forensic story. He says, *"CSI* is timeless and should be on air for 20 years." In which case, *CSI is* halfway there!

The Following/Fans

Not only is there an aficionado of actual forensics experts who love the show, but equipment manufacturers provide labs with free technical equipment.

Recruitment of CSIs has also skyrocketed: Elizabeth Devine: "one of the things I'm proudest of is that science is cool now. [Science was always cool – it's just that people and their perception of it wasn't!] People say they want to become a scientist." Science was never associated with pretty people. Case in point: geeky science student in season 5 *CSI* episode **Dry Ice** where she used her knowledge of science to exact revenge for being used and dumped by a jock. Also season **5.20 Prey** episode of *CSI:NY* where a girl attending one of Stella's lectures at Chelsea University, uses it as a basis for committing murder. Stella discovers she's the connection between the evidence.

The cast have also been invited to forensic science conventions. One Zuiker attended thanked him for their recognition and providing an outlet to showcase their work – not for fame but for the tireless effort of their chosen vocation. In an interview, William Petersen stated that Leslie Moonves, Jerry Bruckheimer and Peter Sussman, as they got wealthy from the show, "they should spend a day on the slab while we poke and prod them."

The new show promised to be hard hitting and just as exciting as the second spin-off to the *CSI* franchise, *CSI:Miami*. In *NY* there's more high-tech gadgetry; along with crime scene investigators being part of the police department; with bags of street-smarts: some learnt on the job and from their extensive backgrounds, bringing together a wealth of experience and persona.

Along with strong backgrounds of the characters, each one has a past which bears on what they do and how they do it – this series is aimed to be more character driven and orientated than the other two and at least since the early seasons of *CSI:* concentrating not only on character but also characterization in the stories, sub-plots, plots. Take, Eddie Cahill, for example, (yes please!) who believes Flack "probably empathisizes with Danny. Danny is Flack's id…Flack keeps a hint of distance between what he wants and what should be done. What I want to do and what's best for the outcome might be two different things – in some respects he's just as much of a hothead but he does something else. There's something there that keeps him practical or keeps him focused. I don't think [dealing with Danny] is ever frustrating – I think he understands it. That's the way I've always taken it, working with Carmine, I get it."

Flack's character and indeed everyone else's, will build over the course of the seasons and especially when Flack faces his greatest heartache in the season 5 finale, after Angell is killed off. He really will take matters into his own hands when he comes face to face with her killer. For now though, on Vanessa Ferlito's character, Aiden being killed off, Eddie feels it was expressed by all at the end and especially by what Danny said about her and his reaction was mentioned, as he spent the most time with her [cf **2.2 Grand Murder**

at Central Station.] Especially when she's killed off to round off her character from season 1.

Only in season 5 has the original *CSI* begun to be more character orientated with its main cast and aims to follow this through into season 6 and onwards. We had snippets of information about the characters (Gil's team) in the context of the investigation or case and only if and when the subject matter called for it. Now as the show finally gets its feet/foothold firmly established in the ratings as a winner – will we get more on our fave characters.

In contrast, *CSI:NY* claims to be more character-driven, emotional, heart wrenching from the outset. That it was with its first episode but also showed, to some extent how you would not want to get on the wrong side of some of the characters. Anthony Zuiker promised to tell stories that could only be told in New York. And was also the first show to have a permit issued to allow filming at Ground Zero. (The end of the first episode when Mac goes there.)

Like the rest of the *CSI* cast, Jorja doubted the spin-off shows: meaning three similar shows, all competing for viewers would work. Die hard fans will stick to their favourites, but most of us watch all three. Jorga: "I think if you're going to offer somebody a really great big piece of cake, they're going to love it. But then if they're offered cake everyday you might start to want ice cream. I would have wished they weren't any spin-offs of *CSI* but I think that all the shows have been able to sort of find their own legs."

William Petersen wanted to keep *CSI* fresh since there were so many other forensic shows on television. Regarding the spin-offs, he commented, "you risk becoming McDonald's – it either changes or grows, or it stays the same and then you can pretty much tune in on any night and get a forensics drama that's the same." He feels the spin-offs could have had a more interesting spin on them – who feels they were just created as a result they can't do certain stories."

Gary Dourdan said "if your team comes home with the winning ring five years in a row, you take care of them you look after your original team, you don't buy a new one." This comment was directly aimed at CBS' new spin-offs and the cast were very vocal in their objections. Marg Helgenberger was in agreement too, when she said, "one moment you are on something inspired and innovative, and the next minute you are the quasi-innovative blond chick on one of those crime-solving shows." Clearly the cast of the original *CSI* were not fully behind any of the two shows. (Yet Marg and Gary from *CSI* appeared in the mini-cross over, opening episode.) William Petersen put this down to network greed. "They can do the show five nights a week with five different casts, but as long as they don't have my guys, they're not going to do it well. *CSI:Miami* doesn't have our chemistry. Taking a blueprint of something that was organically conceived and trying to synthesize it is the difference between organic chicken and chicken jerky. There's nothing I can do about that. That's Viacom, big American capitalism and ratings."

Carmine Giovinazzo on *CSI:Miami*: "...it seems they've got some really big productions going on over there. David [Caruso] – always on the street with his gun chasing people. I'm seeing Adam Rodriguez coming round the corner – he's got people at gunpoint...which is awesome. I think it's great. It's moving. It's live. That's a good way to go, but I think ours is a little bit more contained. It would be nice to get a little bit more into the minds of everybody and have this kind of specific thing that needs to be played between us."

Apparently Jerry O'Connell was to have starred in a role in the show but turned it down. He said, "I have a lot of choices in TV – *CSI:NY* was a choice for me – not to play the Gary Sinise role, but the guy under him. But they wanted me to sign [a contract for a number of years] and I thought, 'do I want to be holding fibres and hairs for seven years?' As an actor on *Crossing Jordan*, I have a character who can goof around and make jokes – I hardly ever say a word that's written for me by the writers, I play a fun, young cop. It's so much more fun than *CSI* would be. I'm not frowning upon it, it's just not what I wanna do. I gotta talk a little more than they do." Seems he would have played either the role of Danny, or Flack, which are much better portrayed as they are with the actors who got to play them.

When the stars of the shows aren't filming a scene, they have to wear their police jackets inside out and their police hats back to front, so as to not be confused with real police. The precinct numbers on the jackets aren't real. When filming, they don't know what the entire story is about and they sometimes shoot when a complete script hasn't been written yet.

CSI vs Law and Order

Law & Order is the highest ratings puller on a Wednesday night slot (aka the midweek slump.) For 12 out of the 15 years it's been on air. In fact, *Law & Order* has put paid to a host of rival shows running in the same time slot on opposing Networks – such as *Chicago Hope, Karen Sisco, Gideon's Crossing. CSI:NY* was anticipated with baited breath and could be in with the prospect of taking the mantel long thrown down by *Law & Order* with the premiere of *CSI:NY* on 22 September 2004: neither CBS nor NBC was willing to gamble or hedge their bets as to which show would be the winner.

Creator of *Law & Order*, Dick Wolf said *CSI* "is the strongest competition we've faced. I don't know what the numbers are going to show." The President of NBC Universal Television Group, Jeff Zucker commented, on *Law & Order* as "the underdog, given the youth and strength of the franchise." Leslie Moonves, the Co-president of Viacom (the media company that owns CBS) in reply said, "calling *Law & Order* an underdog is like calling Muhammed Ali the underdog after he'd won 29 fights. *Law & Order* is still going to be the incumbent champion. For a while."

JJ Abrams said, "if you have three *CSIs* and three *Law and Orders* on the air, people will start to say, 'what else is there?'"

Matt Roush of US TV Guide's verdict: " *CSI:NY* has the advantage of youth. On the other hand the *CSI* franchise might be growing too quickly. *Law & Order* was in series 10 when it received a spin-off series: *Law & Order Special Victims Unit*. "*CSI* has greedily grown an extension every two years." *Law & Order's* spin-offs all differ in content: from investigation of sex related crimes in *SVU*; to the motivation behind the killer's actions in *Law & Order:Criminal Intent*: hence the title: probing the killer's mindset and borders on the edges of using 'entrapment' to catch out the suspect; as do some of the *CSI* episodes.

Law & Order's storylines also feature from the news; "ripped from the headlines, 'promos'. *CSI* is more sensational and more visceral in its depiction of bizarre murders." But also uses real stories, events and even some real methods of crime scene detection to solve cases. Though it uses the equipment available to analyze and help them out – the *NY* lot seem attached to their computers like life-lines or surgical grafts. More so than the other two series. Since *Law and Order* moved to Friday nights *CSI:NY*'s ratings have increased to approximately 16.8 million viewers.

Anthony Zuiker – creator, executive producer, occasional writer for the *CSI* shows isn't too concerned about using a formulaic approach to his three babies, with just a dash of "tweaking" to avoid copy-catting episodes; including briefer storylines with added music. "We'll push the envelope to find the latest technology in forensic science." He's not deterred or put off by the critics. "We're going to attempt to write great forensic mysteries that are grounded, human, emotional and real."

This includes having Mac Taylor as his fearless leader: an ex-marine who lost his wife during 9/11 and has never recovered from this trauma (who could recover so quickly.) This gives *NY* a much more serious and graver tone than the other two shows. As well as a chance to delve deeper into the human psyche and psychological aspects. *CSI:NY* is concerned with living characters than the 'clinical' procedures of its predecessors.

This is demonstrated in its lead character – not only does he have this huge emotional 'impediment'; some may term it, from his past; but he has to incorporate that into his living, working, everyday life too. This in past, his loss, brought home all the time by the nature of some of his investigations. As well as vulnerability to play such a role; the actor would also need a strong presence of authority balanced with maturity, understanding and strength of character to do the job and to make those he leads follow his commands. His lead.

Hence adding a further dimension of emotion to balance the science bit: mixing character with procedure or sometimes with some of the other characters providing a sense of character v procedural...

Gary Sinise says, "I never did a series." He eventually came on board because of the excellent writing. Explains Anthony Zuiker, "we had a four hour meeting. I told him, 'I can't tell you how Mac Taylor takes his eggs, but I can tell you he's a soulful character'." Says Gary, *CSI:NY* is the movie that won't end. "Gary told the *LA Times* "Anthony Zuiker was committed to allowing the characters to live a little more on this show – I came up with a few things I think are important to who [Taylor] is."

Also brought onboard was Melina Kanakaredes as Detective Stella Bonasara, to provide a "warmer" contrast to Mac. They have chemistry but it's purely platonic. Zuiker, "romance is not what we do." (Not until later seasons that is.) Stella was meant to be obsessed to the point of being haunted by the murder of her father – but this was never mentioned or hinted at in season 1 or remaining seasons. However, her mother was mentioned in the season 5 finale.

CSI:NY will be filmed on location in New York, but like the other two will be almost entirely filmed in LA. Zuiker's decision to go with New York as a backdrop city with its gritty feel in contrast to its past tragedy. This may seem exploitation, after all, a show about men and women who, before we meet them, have already had to identify the body parts of those slaughtered on 9/11. Says Hill Harper, "you are talking about people who are shell shocked."

Comments Zuiker, "it is a violent world, on the worst days of their lives, there are people who will do their jobs to bring peace of mind and closure to families...a really keen sense of Americans bringing justice."

Perhaps there is an element of exploitation as the series is primarily about science and what is the notion of American justice. Is it any different to justice throughout the world? It's more about CSIs investigating a crime and bringing the offender to book. Justice should be left to courts. American justice implies a notion of patriotism which is not solely associated with justice.

At the end of the day it's all about science – not an absolute science but should be able to balance elements of everything: science, reality, justice, doing your job and operating within the bounds of the law, rather than any CSI's notion of the law or how they should be doing their jobs. Anthony also says that "juries now have a pre-existing knowledge of science." So that means they demand a lot more from their evidence when called for service/duty, so what happened to a jury consisting of the defendant's peers? We all know that juries can be selected using pre-emptive challenge in the US so they're more likely to be a mix of what both the defence and prosecution are looking for, but that right no longer exists in English law.

Reality V Dramatic Licence

Zuiker: "their biggest complaint about the show is that we have to take creative licence in speeding up time. We give the perception that very difficult, gruesome crimes can be solved within 44 minutes, but sometimes these things take years. But this is television." James Gaskill, former director of Utah State Crime lab; now a teacher of Forensic Science and Criminalistics comments: "it's a fun show, but it's entertainment, just like pro wrestling and it's just about as realistic."

Take some *CSI* episodes as examples. Episode **4.11 Eleven Angry Jurors.** A jury member is found dead with a head wound. The juror had been allergic to everything including penicillin and peanuts. COD (Cause of Death) anaphylactic shock from being stung by a bee. The head injury being a consequence of falling.

In Reality. "if the juror had used an epinephrine injector as he did on the show, he'd have been taken to hospital." Dayle Hinman, former homicide detective and forensic profiler and host of Court TV's *Body Of Evidence* says, "he wouldn't have remained on the jury."

Case 2 Episode **4.11 Eleven Angry Jurors**, a woman gives information about a missing person's case from 4 years ago – about her sister and that she was killed by her boyfriend, who placed her in a 55 gallon drum of gasoline, set it on fire with the ash flowing into a river. Her missing sister had been cremated. Nick took soil samples and looked at the misshapenrings of a tree; resulting in the conclusion there was a gasoline fire near the river 4 years ago. The gasoline didn't match the boyfriend's diesel but was a positive match to the unleaded gasoline at her sister's farm.

In Reality, Hinman deduces it is possible to look at the rings of a tree and find it had been exposed to heat on any given year. But the cause of the fire couldn't have been deduced and whether the gasoline was leaded or unleaded.

Case 3. Episode **Grissom Versus the Volcano**. A car explodes in a casino garage and kills two. The car bomb was the attempt of a jealous wife to kill her cheating husband using a pipe bomb connected to the rental car's clock. This conclusion is drawn by Sara reconstructing the bomb from its parts; using the rental car's VIN and matching the marks on the bomb to a wrench belonging to said wife.

In Reality. Former forensic CSI, Thomas P. Mariello says the wrench connected to the bomb and the inspection of the car for evidence was correct – but everything else wasn't. "There were just too many people moving around the scene and too many people touching things – they're doing the wrong things. CSIs don't even talk to witnesses/suspects."

Case 4. Episode **Grissom Versus the Volcano** the wife of a famous R&B singer is found in a hot tub in their penthouse. She committed suicide by drinking wine containing a toxic window cleaner. No strangulation as there was the presence of poisonous hydrochlorides in her system and acid burns on her hands where she had spilt the cleaner.

In Reality. Marinello says the ME would have noticed the presence of poison immediately. The poison in her stomach would have made her bring it back up. It was so strong as to burn her hand; it would've also burnt her throat. "The coroner would've noticed that immediately."

Case 5 Episode **Coming of Rage**. A teenage boy is bludgeoned at a construction site. Blood spatter surrounds the scene. There's a piece of torn cloth in his hand and a solitary bloodied shoe print. Dogs lead to a mall and the cloth belongs to a girl who admits killing him in self defence – he tried to rape her. Blood spatter indicates three killers and the shoeprint belongs to one of her school friends. She lured the boy here and engaged in a "thrill-kill" with her friends.

In Reality. Gaskill says the presence of a single shoeprint is not real. Photos from the crime scene weren't properly labelled.

Case 6 episode **Homebodies**. A woman is shot through her chest in her own front yard. She'd been having issues with her current and former husbands and was shot by a stray bullet fired by a man shooting in the air in another area. This is because the husband shows no signs of GSR or powder burns on his body or hers. The angle of the bullet and how it entered don't show signs of a close-range shooting. Bullets are test-fired with differing amounts of gunpowder into a gel – they conclude for a 9mm bullet to have entered 4 inches at that angle, it had to have been fired from 18,000 feet away.

In Reality. Ballistics gel does exist but wouldn't be used like it was here. "It's nonsense."

A search or trace of any chemicals or its metabolites can be determined in this manner, i.e. using GCMS [=Gas Chromatography/Mass Spectroscopy] for example poisons, therefore no longer virtually untraceable. This is like a fingerprint of a chemical or its compound.

Also strange poisons can't be detected by an ME in a short amount of time. That needed to successfully conclude a 45 minute TV episode. Firstly, the substance/sample/evidence needs to be screened to see if a poison is present. What type it is and then needs to be tested using, eg, GCMS to identify its exact nature. Which is not done in the space of a few minutes. Most commonly available poisons don't cause a sudden loss of life and take time to work, including window cleaners/detergents, cf **1.18 Dove Commission** episode of *CSI:NY*.

Lt. Rick Alba, former Head of CSI Division of Las Vegas Metro PD says romance "would probably be counter-productive. This job is very intense. You're exposed to a lot of extremely violent crimes on a regular basis. Can you imagine two people taking all that home?" Yes and no. Romance would be no different in that aspect to police officers getting close or lawyers and so on.

Actual real-life crime labs don't have beautiful people, top-of-the-range equipment, computers, TVs (though depends on how people describe or see themselves, but not dealing with TV.) Most lab budgets don't extend beyond the essentials with minimal, essential lighting or glass interiors.

Test/trace results aren't delivered in a New York minute (no pun) but takes up to days or even weeks. (Hence in some episodes of *Without A Trace* the lab results/forensics aren't back in time to help them out with a lot of their cases; unlike *CSI*. Hence other tactics like bluff are required! But that was another show with a completely different premise.)

The *CSI:Miami* season 1 episode **Slaughterhouse** demonstrates the presence of too many CSIs and people at the crime scene for any evidence to remain viable.

Preliminary testing can be done in a matter of hours but the end confirmation takes time, otherwise the evidence is useless. At least the *CSI* shows get it right when dealing with the appearance of dead bodies; with the pale blue-gray lividity and swollen faces, especially when it's death in extreme circumstances. Though we can't say about the smell – except for that episode with Sara in *CSI* when she and Nick had to deal with what was left of that smelly dead body.

Blood will not ooze or spurt of a DB (Dead Body) when the DB is first discovered – as DBs do not bleed; since blood clots very soon after being expelled. Cf the Cohen Bros movie *Blood Simple,* which demonstrates that if any blood does ooze out, trickle or gush, then the DB/victim isn't dead.

The Real TOD (Time of Death). Time(s) of death cannot be ascertained – but only an estimated time can be determined by body temperature, lividity, rigour mortis, or Gil's favourite, bugs.
Poisoning can kill instantaneously, for example, acute arsenic poisoning takes many days. Tell-tale signs include: abdominal pain,

nausea, vomiting, bloody diaorriah. Hence this is never portrayed on screen! Who'd want to watch the symptoms?

Metabolic poisons such as cyanide prevent the cells of the body from utilizing oxygen; leading to symptoms such as shortness of breath, constrictions to the chest, throat, thus causing collapsing.

None of the MEs/CSIs wear masks (unless dealing with noxious/toxic substances) or tie their hair back; or even wear goggles (essential in the lab when I was at school/university) when dealing with chemicals/corrosive material and things likely to spill or explode.   They don't use 'Universal Microbiologic Precautions'; everyone in such a profession uses to keep off bacteria and infections at bay. Would you want to be swabbed by them? Eeww! It's not like we don't know how the actor looks under the mask! And it wouldn't be for the entire duration of the episode.

Repetition In Shows Across Episodes and Series

Gerry Conway – writer on *Law & Order* and other shows, including *Murder She Wrote,* as well as a comic's writer in the 1970's (writing *Batman*, *Superman* and *Wonder Woman*). In an interview, said he got complaints from fans of comics that certain stories were repeated and updated for the current market. And said due to market research from the 1970's which is still potent today; longterm readers or fans of comics/TV series have a 4-7 year age span. I.e. they usually stick to a comic or show for this amount of time.

After this, aside from die hard fans, everyone else gets bored and leaves the show. Hence after 5-7 years, writers begin to repeat old storylines because new readers/viewers have entered the scene. Re *CSI* seasons 4 and 5, regurgitating some old storylines, as well as those being used in the other two series – *CSI:Miami* and *CSI:NY*.

Carol Mendelsohn: "It goes with our concept for this season [5 of *CSI*]. We always hear about die hard fans saying the show isn't as good as the first season, so we said, 'let's go back to season 1 and reintroduce the characters.'" Which they also did again in season 9 after William Petersen left the show and Laurence Fishburne replaced him. They started again with him needing to be told on how to broach forensics, which procedures to employ and so on. This was a good way to surge the show with a fresh approach, ensuring the show didn't get too stale. As well as a novel way of making new viewers feel they were learning something new, along with Dr Langston and weren't left out.

Other Shows on the *CSI* Bandwagon

Some new shows getting in on the act were *Crossing Jordan,* in the season 4 episode **What Happens in Vegas Dies in Boston**, Jordan even mentions *CSI* itself when she says, if they "... rely on Vegas CSI to find anything [they'll] be in a bit of trouble." Don't think so!
But some could be seen as half-way indecent attempts at early versions. One such show was *Leaving LA.* This was described as a police drama/comedy. Airing on ABC in 1997 with a short run of six weeks. A series about the LA Coroner's office. Starring Ron Rifkin as Chief ME Dr Neil Bernstein who kept a roof garden and cooked in his office. Chris Meloni as Reed Simms, an investigator and Melina Kanakaredes as Libby Galante, his trainee. Characters also included autopsy examiners playing practical jokes. Lab technicians conversing with corpses and a photographer who enjoyed listening to Vivaldi and photographing nude corpses. As well as a property clerk who had psychic tendencies, predicting accurate outcomes. Working at crime scenes they came across clues missed by other law enforcement officials and swapped photos of celebrity corpses, whilst becoming involved with one another romantically. The forerunner to *CSI* if it wasn't so dire!

Procedural vs Character

When *CSI* made its debut in 2000, it was described as the "godfather of police procedural shows."

CBS Chairman and President Les Moonves said to William Petersen, "let's not go home with these people. We should get to know them on the job, according to how they relate to each other and how they relate to the crimes and that's it."

Marg Helgenberger says Catherine's the most well-rounded of all the *CSI* show characters. She is a single mother, a former stripper, and is CSI 3. (Now a supervisor herself.) In contrast to the women of *New York* who either spend most of their time in the lab or trying to be one of the guys, especially when there's no need to be. In so much as they lose their objectivity and focus. As Sara and Catherine and Calleigh show, it's all right to be feminine and yet compete with the men in getting the job done; to exhibit emotion and understanding if need be; even towards a suspect, as Catherine has demonstrated many times, such as the hypertrichosis episode, **6.11 Werewolves**, where she was so compassionate to the little girl. On Catherine's relationship with Grissom, she comments, there's an "increased chemistry without them doing it."

She showed sympathy and honesty when questioning victims, as does Sara when she's confronted by cases and victims who remind her of her haunting childhood and past. Perhaps because of this some people have commented on the one dimensional aspects of the female leads in *CSI:NY* not being able to relate to them or feel anything towards them. Not everyone can be Catherine, Sara or Calleigh, but writers should aim to give them a bit more humanity and a little less attitude...

Jorga Fox commented, "I am still baffled by her [Sara's] intelligence. That's a fantasy thing for me because she's so much smarter than I am. That's exciting and how authentic and natural it is. It is just something she was born with and then there's the mystery surrounding her. That was never necessarily intentional but there's a whole bunch of stories there that we are just beginning to tell [in season 5.]

Melina Kanakaredes has carried out research for her role and watched investigators in New York and LA. She says, "partners share, finish sentences; fight and have mutual respect." She describes Stella as being tough, committed, intelligent, loves her job and as being very emotionally connected to finding out the truth. Prides herself in her work."

Paul Guilfoyle says "there is no drama that isn't character-driven. Drama, by its nature, by its Aristoelian terms is character-driven. You can't take the people out of the story."

Says Marg: "I'm always telling producers to take me out of the lab. I like doing action as well as emotion. This year [season 5] I think we'll see different sides of Catherine. I think there are many layers to come with her." Take note *NY*. Seeing as the show was supposed to be more character based, there wasn't that much background involved, especially of the women CSIs. When there was, it wasn't all that interesting either. For example, Stella always dating losers, or killers.

A great episode which delved into Nick's life in *CSI* was **Stalker**, where Nick is stalked by a killer who actually wants to become him.

Marg continues, "The fact that we're number 1 and we're beloved throughout the world is unbelievable. It means that all this hard work and long hours is really paying off." Like the other cast members of the spin-offs she too visited morgue and coroners applauded her on not fainting. She finds the stories disturbing because most are reality based and actually happened.

Said Jorga, "Even though the show's not about characters, they still have to be three dimensional people in order for the audience to get hooked." Keeping the show fresh after four seasons, she was all for the changes introduced after the hundredth episode in season 5,

Changes in episode 9 of season 5, **Mea Culpa** when Ecklie broke up Gil's team; promoting Catherine to swingshift supervisor.

On this Jorga said, "I don't know yet, I was opposed to [the division] but I've been opposed to a lot of smart things we've done. Like moving us from Fridays to Thursdays. I thought we were going to get creamed."

Carol Mendelsohn said that there was some "somberness" to season 4 and so they wanted to "create a situation where the characters were not on top of each other [double entendre here] everyday. It's about fresh eyes for everyone." And not just about eyes either.

She continues: "We've also always had this thing with our show where half our audience would like to know more about the characters and half would really like us to stick to the science." Also re private aspects of the characters' lives: Greg and Sara have a chemistry – we've seen since season 2 but she's got the hots for Gil in a big way. "[Greg's] coming into manhood in the character and Sara thinks that's attractive." Jorga, as Sara, was meant to be a love interest for Gil only. They had a prior relationship which hasn't really been resolved or mentioned much during the course of 5 seasons. However, was resolved in season 9 when Jorja left the show, soon followed by Gary Dourdan and William Petersen.

Just like Sara being picked up on a DUI (Driving Under the Influence). Jorga: "there was no foreshadowing at all so I was really shocked and I don't think I liked it rightaway." The writers concentrating more on the ghosts from Sara's past, i.e. that her mother killed her father (revealed in season 5's **Nesting Dolls**). "Sara has a lot of personal arcs – more than some characters on the show. I've been fortunate and blessed but it is scary to do it when the show is so process and story heavy and then they throw a curve ball at you." It was a little strange watching this episode, since if you go back and read Sara's file in *CSI:Crime Scene Investigation Companion* by Mike Flaherty; it describes Sara's parents as hippies so how come her mother killed her father when they were all meant to be about 'peace and love, man.'

Carol Mendelsohn commented, "before this show is over, some CSI will have sex." Wonder if she was referring to season 5 of *CSI* or the entire series? What about the spin offs? A long time to wait for many to see something of this nature! Ha – but Nick already has had sex in the *CSI* episode **Boom**, so do we need to delve into more personal stories and more importantly – must they be of an intimate nature. Gary Dourdan said, "we've come to the understanding that this show is about this group of people and how they solve cases – but also how they interact. It's more fun to do that than pull hair follicles and process them. After five years, you want that."

Do we want the meaning and premise of the show altered to perhaps *Crime Sex Intimacy*. Surely that can't make for interesting viewing, unless of course it's done subtly rather than graphically or 'in your face.' Will we want to see our favourite characters cavorting around on the screen or will that just become a play on office politics becoming more a case of sexual politics or intrigue. As we know, Gil is certainly not one for politics.

Eric would like to see some of Greg's social life on screen, "maybe visit his apartment and perhaps explore his playful nature with women."

Marg clearly is in dire need of some: "Catherine needs to explore her sexuality and have some intimacy in her life. Carol has told me she can't see Catherine kissing just anyone. It has to be the right guy." Her relationships haven't worked in the past so even if she does find love with Warrick or somebody else, where's the guarantee it'll work out. We don't want a neurotic CSI on our hands. Then there's the question of bringing not only the romance to the office but the work home.

Gary: "there's a lot of tension between the characters, sexual and otherwise. Warrick has had ideas about her [Catherine] since their early days on the team. He's not blind you know!...I'm excited to see what happens with them – I'd love to see that scene on the kitchen table. Or maybe on the desk. And then the break room. Not in the morgue though."

On relationships, did you know Nick and Catherine were meant to have been going out with each other in the Pilot. A scene was filmed but was cut and will be contained in the reissued DVD of season 1. Said George Eads: "it didn't fit at the time – I don't see something like that happening again – the character I play is old fashioned to the extent that he would never do anything with a boss. There's some flirtiness there maybe, but that's it." On the contrary being old fashioned didn't stop him from getting it on with a former call girl.

Perhaps Marg said it best when she commented, "as much as it's said 'it's not about the characters' it is about the characters...I'd like to see the word *procedural* eliminated from the vocabulary describing *CSI* because yes – it's procedural, but it's so much more than that. It's a mystery show, a fun, state-of-the-art Sherlock Holmes for the new millennium."

She carries on, "from time to time it gets kind of boring because the whole show is about pushing the plot forward – that's also the challenge – to make it about each of our thought processes, so it's about what do we think about solving the crime and the evidence. Every season is a bit more revelatory about the characters."

All three shows, although having glimpses and flashes of some of the characters personal lives (not all of them) still stick to the procedural formula because it works – don't want to watch a show in which their private lives take over every facet of what the show is meant to be about. Brief references work since then you picture what the characters get up to in their spare time (what spare time?) rather than full-blown romance – especially if it's between the main characters: which actually was indulged in all three shows, eventually: Gil and Sara in season 7 of *CSI*; Mac and Peyton in season 3 of *CSI:NY* as well as Danny and Lindsay, Flack and Angell in season 4/5. Then Calleigh and Delko in season 7 of *CSI:Miami*. With

Catherine and Nick saying you shouldn't really mix pleasure with your colleagues – does it work? When you see the person day in and day out at work and outside of work – possibly – as long as you have other interests and don't take your work home with you, it can work. Until the rest of the team find out about the relationship when it's been hidden for so long.

Such as Gil and Sara in the season 7 finale and Mac and Peyton – not an easy transition at first since Mac didn't want anyone to know he was seeing Peyton outside of work, pushing her hand away from his face, which she found very offensive. Not to mention Clare's son, Reid entered the picture, also we don't really know for sure whether Mac's really over Clare to begin with. It took him a long time to take off his wedding ring.

Even H had a thing for his sister-in-law Yelina but didn't move in on her because of his brother and not even when Ray was out of the picture. Yelina wanted H to get past this. Even IAB Rick wanted Yelina and asked H for his opinion, whereupon H replies he should just ask her and then Rick turns it around when he does speak to her, as if H wanted him to do his. Yelina hated the way Rick leers but they got together, until he started beating her. Then Ray turned up alive for a short while; H got a son and even got married to Marisol, Delko's sister.

CSI spawned a son and a grandson in the form of *CSI:Miami* and *CSI:NY*. In a rare interview executive producer Jerry Bruckheimer stated, "I love the speed of television. It took me almost five years to get *Top Gun* made. It took me eight years to get *Beverly Hills Cop* made. But TV is so wonderful. You need a script, you get notes, and two weeks later it's on the air. I love the process."

Anthony on Mac Taylor and his "moral righteousness – making the proper moral decision, not only for himself, but for his team and for his city. Doing things right by the book without any moral question is really to the point of view that we take with Mac Taylor." The others are also moral, but says Anthony, Gil won't use a gun and

Gary Sinise's character, Mac Taylor will only use a gun when necessary.

William Petersen on his role of Gil Grissom in the original: "One of the problems that I'd always had in my mind about ever doing television was having to do a guy for possibly, if we're lucky, a long time. But I so love this character of Gil Grissom, and I wanted to do this show because it was an opportunity for me to learn stuff and, I figured if I could learn stuff, I would be thrilled by the show each week. I had always watched *Sherlock Holmes* movies with Basil Rathbone (and who hasn't?)...I think [the subject of forensics] is fascinating...the most remarkable thing about the series is working with these real life CSIs who work on the show with us, getting to deal with their stories and the kind of knowledge that they have. I was terrible at science, terrible at math, so it's a real opportunity for me to live another life. That's what keeps it fresh for me."

Gil had a deaf mother; he knows sign language and is comfortable with nature and being by himself and with his dog. Until his feelings for Sara cause him to examine all this being at one with nature bit...he says Grissom cares about the truth, "it's that part of his science, nature, that he's interested in." Gil's "in forensics – the best place to find the truth."

CSI was the most successful drama for CBS 2000 season. Says Anthony Zuiker, "I was watching a [reality based] show called *The New Detectives* and because I love forensics I said to myself 'there may be a series in this.' It's a whole other weird world. So I decided to take it one step further and go to the Criminology Division of the Las Vegas Police Department and see if I could ride along with those guys. They had never been approached, and they were all a little upset because they find their field to be very interesting, and they were wondering why there wasn't a show based on it. So I rode with them for five weeks, and saw the most horrific, exciting, exuberating crazy world – and said to myself 'there is a series here.'"

William Petersen: "Over the years, what with the OJ case, I've had people talk to me about forensics. This is the new world of crime solving. These are the guys who are going to put people away or get people off over the course of the next 25 years. We know they exist. We've known they've existed in the old homicide shows. It's just that they were never covered, because nobody thought that a fingerprint could be interesting. Figuring out how to shoot a fingerprint, how to see a hair fibre or carpet fibre, was the key. If we could figure for how to do that then all of a sudden it could be a thrilling visual level. Another interesting thing about the CSIs is that they're not policemen [or women]. They're civillians that work under a wing of the police department. They have a licence to carry a gun because they go into crimes scenes, but they're not arresting officers."

On Gil Grissom William says, "he, relentlessly pursues the answer to his problem, refuses to be deterred from the end result: the truth...ultimately his weakness is other people."

Jerry Bruckheimer: "I think it's kind of fun, I think it's a tribute to our cast and to William that they've made them so interesting."

David Caruso describes his character of H, as "having a tendency to take the ambulance out of the barn, attracted to distress signals...some situations are healable, some not...strength is his calling and unwavering dedication to the city and to the prosecution and the pursuit of this form of evil."

As for utilizing his sunglasses, "there's a specific method to how those are used, sometimes if H is onto who he believes is the killer or the perpetrator, he might begin to start hiding his eyes from the killer even indoors." David continues, that H came to Miami in pursuit of criminals and ended up staying. He has "a complicated past; different family circumstances, an event changed his life."
Jonathan Littman says H is hiding from and running away from a secret life. Whereas he calls Mac "a morally centered guy in a city of chaos." He's all in for crime and justice.

As for characters past and present being revealed, said Anthony Zuiker, "**Tanglewood** [in *CSI:*NY] was the turning point where we were like, 'Okay, we're going to tell New York stories and we're going to lighten up our characters and go in a character direction, starting with the mysteries.'"

"In **Blink**, I put the mystery in the background, which is what I promised Gary." The show was going to be about him and Melina and the plan changed." Which is just as well, as not only would it have been unfair to focus on two characters out of six, but also it would get boring pretty quickly if reference was made only to Mac and Stella. Seeing as how, they're both characters very similar to each other. Also Mac is a leader and Stella, assumes that position too at times; they're both detectives with a higher grade than Danny, Aiden and Flack is also a detective grade 1 but he's not treated as their equal. Not to mention, Hawkes being stuck in the morgue and he may never have made it out as a CSI. Stella has a sister, but she's not a real sister. (Season 3 episode *Cold Reveal*.)

Anthony sees **Tanglewood** as a "real story in Yonkers; the circus in **Blood, Sweat and Tears**. **The Fall** where we put one of our characters in jeopardy. We decided Mac is a moral man in an immoral city. He's fighting for the little guy. So we give him more...political obstacles." Something which Gil is familiar with in *CSI*, as Catherine was forever telling him that he needs to be more politic!

Stella was going to find the body of her father when he was killed, but that was similar to Sara Sidle in *CSI* episode **Nesting Dolls**, where Sara tells Gil about finding her father after her mother had killed him. That worked so much better for Sara and Jorga really gave her character pain and anguish. True regret and guilt she was feeling at the time and for such a long time too.

Also the Mac/Danny relationship will be more intense and "complicated." Carmine Giovinazzo comments he likes playing Danny since, "he gets to express himself and be the one that people can relate to a bit...he goes through more of the human emotions you don't normally see a cop go through. He doesn't have to keep himself in check like Mac or Flack."

Gary Sinise was not the first choice to play Mac, as Ray Liotta and Andy Garcia both turned down the part. Also the character was to be named Det. Rick Calucci, which was changed to Mac Taylor. Probably would have been too similar to Rick Stetler in *CSI:Miami*.

As for the spin-off shows, the original *CSI* cast was very vocal in their objections: said William Petersen: "You risk becoming *McDonald*'s. You can tune in any night and get a forensics drama that's the same." Yet fans have watched all three shows. We do.

Anthony Zuiker and the cast are asked to speak at forensics conventions and William even testified before a Senate Judiciary Committee for more funding for the real crime labs. Anthony also speaks of how forensic experts like to work on the shows since they're better paid, for starters.

Emily Proctor got so attached to the 'head' that she had to work with on the show that she even named it. To Marg, "the most touching responses I get are from 10 and 11 year old girls who come up to me and say, 'I want to become a criminalist because of you.'

The cast do get involved in the show and their characters. Eric Szmanda says, "it's a very emotional show. There are a lot of arguments between the critics who believe it's about formula and the fans who want to see more personal stuff. You tune into our show for a reason and it does expose the kind of people who do this. What would you be like if you visited crime scenes every single day and interacted with people on the worst day of their lives."

Jorja Fox has nothing but praise for the writers especially, "the really big part of that pressure falls on the writer's shoulders more than us. Those guys have to come up with stories to keep people tuning in from week to week. I'm sure people get really bored of us. In America we're on several times a day now [here in the UK too, on

Five, Five USA and Living] which is a really strange phenomenon, like you think people have got to be 'Eurgh! Change the channel I'm so sick of that person!' [Maybe one or two nameless people but none of the lot from the first two shows, now there's a big hint!!] but it's such a blessing and it's going to get harder and harder every year." Until one day you pick up sticks and leave.

Gary Dourdan mentions the police officers they have on the show and how they'll talk about their case where something happened. He enjoyed talking and listening to their stories and gaining knowledge on something he had thought about doing himself.

Some of the female cast members are derided for being chosen for their roles to showcase their hair! Instead of their acting abilities. *Entertainment Weekly* described Melina Kanakaredes's performance "like a pretty placeholder for some more interesting actress." To which some would be in agreement. Personally Emily Procter had great hair in the early seasons of *CSI:Miami*, especially season 1, as did Jorga Fox. Loved Vanessa Ferlito's hair and since we're on the subject of hair, let's not be sexist, Eddie Cahill sported a better cut in season 2 onwards! And what's with George Eads going more bald than hirsute at every opportunity?!!

The CSI Effect

"...speaking to the law enforcement officer who couldn't catch a guy at first because he wore booties during the murder. He wore booties! Before he killed somebody, it was that premeditated. There's some good and some bad to it. That's what we get from law enforcement all the time. Criminals watch our shows, that is, what to see, what not to do...the most positive '*CSI* effect,' kids wanting to be forensic scientists. I've seen my fair share of DBs and coroner's autopsy visitations. They just stick in your mind forever about what you've done to the human body, figure out what happened to it." Commented Gary Dourdan.

Comments Eric Szmanda, "in the past you relied on the detective to solve the crime and now you rely on science. The show makes you feel a little bit safer – that if something does happen to you there is a way to get back at whoever did it. It's also a deterrent for people who are considering crime."

The CSI Effect was actually coined by Anthony and taken up by legal eagles, where the shows had to demonstrate months, even years of lab work, squeezed into a 42 minute programme. This caused jurors in criminal trials to have unreal expectations, such as wrongly thinking what they've watched on the show, actually occurs in real life. When witnesses are not enough for the prosecution to produce in court to testify to the events at hand, when defence lawyers love such shows so complex forensics need to be produced – juries insist on it, what's a judge to do?

Judges need to inform the jury that they are not watching a *CSI* episode. Anthony says "for the first time in American history, you're not allowed to fool the jury anymore."

Former LA County public defender, Stan Goldman, also professor of law at Loyola and Legal Editor for Fox News, said that decades ago the effect of a show like *Quincy* meant jurors would want fingerprints presented in every criminal trial. Thus the *CSI Effect* is just as influential and massive in courtrooms today.

Robert Hirschhorn, Jury Consultant, comments on the *CSI Effect* as being "real and profound." In November 2003, prosecutors in the Robert Durst murder trial in Galveston, Texas – could not convince the jury that Durst had killed Morris Black (whose head was missing). The jury would not rely and reach its decision based solely on non-forensic evidence. Hence Hirschhorn states he only selected jurors who knew about *CSI* and other similar shows for this trial.

Claims Josh Berman, "as writers we get smarter...and we share that knowledge with the viewer." Also says LAPD former criminalist Richard Catalani, and now technical consultant for CSI, "I used to have to tell juries what I did. Now jurors have such heightened evidentiary expectations that court prosecutors refer to a *CSI Effect*." He continues, "[DAs] District Attorneys can no longer just put smart-looking people up there as experts and expect the jury to say, 'Well that's enough they've done a good job.'"

Also the *CSI Effect* can be equally applied to criminals who pick up "tips" whilst watching the shows, for example, in September 2004 – a woman robbed a bank and put the money in a nappy (diaper) bag, where did she come up with this 'bright' idea, *CSI* of course.

In 2007, ITV in the UK in its *Tonight With Trevor MacDonald* show, reported on the *CSI Effect* demonstrating the effect of the show as well as commenting on other US and British police procedural programmes.

Recent Developments

Level 26: Dark Origins by Anthony E Zuiker with Diane Swierczynski. Out now. Penguin publishers. A digi-novel about investigators assigned to the *Special Circumstances Division (Special Circs)* of the Federal government. Their goal: to find the most wanted serial killers. In this novel they have to find the serial killer known as the most serious – that in Level 26. He's the one who exceeds the twenty-fifth level used to "categorize serial killers". He is known as "*Sqweegel* (sounds similar to Smeegal in *Lord of the Rings*.)

Why can Sqweegel get away with so much dastardly crime? Because he leaves behind no traceable forensic evidence at the crime scene. [See CSI episode **12.4 Butterflied** where the killer cleaned up after himself so as not to leave behind any evidence.] Sqweegel wears a body suit to all of his crimes. The one man who almost caught him: Steve Dark (Daniel Buran) chasing after Sqweegel killed his foster family. Dark left *Special Circs*. Now married to Sibby (Tauvia Dawn) with a baby on the way, he doesn't want to get involved with *Special Circs*...

Other characters include: Tom Riggins (Michael Ironside) whose only motivation is his work.

The digi-novel has an interactive community – *Level 26.com* where you can go whilst reading the book and interact with other readers. As well as illustrations in the book by Marc Ecko. This book is the first of its kind: a digi-novel using video segments, known as *cyber bridges* – which leads people from the book, to the website and then back to the book. Even if you don't want to interact, the story can still be followed just as easily. There are two sequels planned for the novel. Fans can also send in their ideas for stories and new characters on the website.

Also with merchandise widely available on the show, such as the *CSI* forensics lab, a facial reconstruction kit and boardgame, the American Organization of *Parents TV Council (PTC)* were outraged that such products could be advertised as toys, when clearly they were just a way of selling these products to children, unsuitable for them since the content of these shows is more adult orientated. They said, "because the *CSI* franchise often displays graphic images, including close-ups of corpses with gunshot wounds and other bodily injuries – the PTC doesn't think the recreation of blood, guts and gore should be under a child's Christmas tree this year." They urged members to lodge a complaint with the Federal Trades Commission.

This is all good and well but with kits such as the facial reconstruction kit, it doesn't have any such graphics involved. Also when does censorship go too far, not to mention the fact there are much more serious issues dominating the headlines, such as sex education being taught to primary school children, barely 9 and 10. Such things just reflect today's society and today's generation of parents where such a need arises for this to take place. In the same way there are many parents who are unable to determine what is right and proper for their children to be given as a toy and what they should be involved in. Obviously this is not the correct forum for such a discussion to be held.

On another note, *CSI Live* took place at Six Flags Magic Mountain near LA, where investigators examine who committed murder at a magic show, with some of the audience members as suspects. This also took place at Freestyle Music Park, Myrtle Beach, California.

Pam Veasey said recently, "we'll always be a who-dunit and how-did-they-do-it show, but if we can open up windows to the human side of these characters, it makes it more sexy and adventurous for everyone. Plus we'll always have Mac standing tough behind these cases." Also Pam wanted New York to feature in the show, as a city in its own right as it's something they have which the other two shows don't. She printed T-shirts with the new saying:- *Make it a sex, dangerous, fun, adventurous ride with a grounded, believable motive.*

Personally I'd have gone for something along the lines of:

C: Cool
S: Sexy
I: Intellectual
N: Never
Y: Yielding

Season 1 Episodes

Mia/NYC – Nonstop (CSI Miami/CSI NY Crossover)
1. Blink
2. Creatures of the Night
3. American Dreamers
4. Grand Master
5. Man a Mile
6. Outside man
7. Rain
8. Three Generations Are Enough
9. Officer Blue
10. Night Mother
11. Triborough
12. Recycling
13. Tanglewood
14. Blood, Sweat and Tears
15. Til Death Do Us Part
16. Hush
17. The Fall
18. The Dove Commission
19. Crimes and Misdemeanours
20. Supply and Demand
21. On The Job
22. The Closer
23. What You See is What You See

MIA/NYC – Nonstop

Written By Anthony E. Zuiker, Ann Donahue & Carol Mendelsohn
Directed By Danny Cannon

US Airdate 17 May 2004
UK Airdate July 2004

Guest stars: David Caruso (Lt. Horatio Caine) Emily Procter (Calleigh Duquesne) Adam Rodriguez (Eric Delko) Khandi Alexander (Chief ME Alexx Woods) Rory Cochrane (Tim Speedle) Sofia Milos (Det. Yelina Salas) Joseph Lyle Taylor (Doorman Kevin Dowell) Christopher John Fields (Nick Murdoch) Nicole Paggi (Laura Spelman) Marta Martin (Milagra) Chris Meyer (Michael Hanover Jnr) Heidi Marnhout (Renne Rydell) John Mariano (David Penrod) Carol Mendelsohn (Denise Spelaman)

Background

A girl at a party sneaks back home and finds her parents dead. The killer came in through the back. Horatio gives her his jacket. Horatio tells her she has to go into protective custody because she survived and the news will broadcast that. He promises to find the killer. Purple and orange fibres are found on blankets used by Mabach Air. The car is about to be washed. There's a partial blood print on the steering wheel. The licence belongs to Nick Murdoch, he hired the car. Horatio needs to go to New York, the murders were committed in Miami so they've got jurisdiction but he made a promise to a girl.

Crime Scene Evidence

Alexx says the blood pool is dry around the edges so TOD was around 11pm. The mother's throat was slit from left to right. She was decapitated. Calleigh finds saliva near the back door. Horatio notices the point of entry is the back and the origin of blood drops is where the mother was killed; so the killer missed the bedroom where the father was. He survived, as shown by the arterial gushes on the wall and was stabbed with a single edge knife. He was saving his daughter.

Lab Results

Speed finds tyre tracks and a piece of paper with a logo on it.

Calleigh manages to narrow down the geographical area of the suspect by finding mercury, asbestos and lead, kerosene, petroleum: jet fuel in the saliva. There were cases of upper respiratory inhalation where people lived near Ground Zero in New York. So Calleigh deduces the spit/phlegm belongs to their suspect. Delko comments Miami is the sixth borough so he was from New York.

Horatio finds hairs and shed fibres from eg, a blanket. The shoe print on the paper has an icon from a rental car company at Miami International Airport.

Background

New York

Police are called to an apartment with a DB. He was an undercover police officer. He's been dead 24 hours, probably 72. The identity is missing from his wallet. The officer turns to see Horatio behind him and they introduce themselves. "Caine, Miami CSI." Mac introduces himself as Detective First Grade.

The officer was strangled by a belt and the suspect took his ID. Horatio says they have the death penalty in Florida, as do they in New York, but they haven't executed anyone since 1976. Mac calls this "politics" but agrees. The officer was undercover and was probably killed during the buy.

Penrod escapes from the roof and injures his leg when he jumps. They check his apartment. Horatio finds a Miami airline ticket and Mac finds blood in the sink. He carries out a Haema-trace which reveals the blood is fresh and too fresh for the Miami murders.

Horatio finds out Penrod wrote '702' as the house number, whilst the victims' number was '720'. Calleigh does a welfare check and finds the owner was a Michael Hanover Snr, residing at 1526 Fifth Avenue.

Hanover Snr's mistress was in a play. She used a key to the back door and left at 3am. They examine her key and clothes. Horatio is at a clinic in Tribeca where Penrod escaped to.

Mac shows Horatio the DNA test, one of the alleles match 13 loci, so Rene slept with his son, Michael Jnr. He tells them Rene is his girlfriend. His father didn't care about her. They take his key but he doesn't show them his wounds. Mrs Hanover's key was duplicated.

Hawkes finds hilt mark bruising on Hanover Snr but not on Michael Jnr. So there were two different knives used, therefore two different attackers.

Mac checks out their apartment again and notices a police officer drop his gum wrapper down the lift shaft. There he finds the knife and a tassel. There was no hilt on the knife, so there was no mark.

Crime Scene Evidence

Horatio comments they scrape the hands before they transport the DB in Miami. Mac tells him they bag it safe at the scene and they also fume at the scene too. Danny fumes the wallet and gets a partial whorl.

Lab Analysis

Danny liaises with Speed over the partial found in the car and searches on the computer using 9/11 enhancement software to match the partials.

Lab Results

The print is matched to David Penrod.

Danny finds the lock wasn't picked. He says there are nine rats for every person living in Manhattan, five keys per head. There are only a few hours to make a new key. New duplicate keys are now coated in red acrylic so shavings would be left behind if a duplicate was used. Stella thinks it's an inside job. Danny needs the master keys.

Aiden finds the blue substance was stage make up. Stella doesn't find any blood on the underwear.

Medical Exam

Hawkes finds Hanover was dead since 4am. The stab wounds are similar to the Miami victims. Hanover was suffering from progressive heart disease. There's a blue substance on his groin.

Secondary Crime Scene Evidence

DBs are found at the apartment. Blood drops on the carpet leading to the bedroom. The woman's throat is slit with a knife, she was an addict. The husband is in the study. The son is still alive in his room. Stella takes a photo of the son's entry wound. Mac refuses to speak with the press.

Mac finds a blonde hair in the study chair and mentions his theory of "everything's connected."

Stella finds the Hanover's had three keys; the doorman doesn't have his. Danny processes the back door and the stairs. There was no forced entry. Mac tells him to pop the lock, check the keys.

Conclusion

The doorman stabbed Michael Jnr shown by specificity of DNA. The tassel was cut from the left sleeve of his coat when he wiped the blood from the knife. He was in Hanover's will as he saved his life but became impatient. Penrod was his dealer for ten years. Horatio tells Penrod he's going to be charged with murder and conspiracy to commit. The number was '720' not '702.' He's dyslecsic. He flew to Miami and killed the wrong family. The doorman gave him Mrs Hanover's key and killed the son to draw suspicion.

Horatio takes Penrod back to Miami. Mac talks to the press and Horatio disappears. He turns up at the parent's funeral and the girl turns around to thank him.

Notes

The New York parts of the episode were filmed in New York on location the week of 4 April 2004. The scene where Gary Sinise looks out over the New York skyline is similar to the scene where David Caruso looks over at Miami in the opening credits.

On the *CSI:Miami* crossover episode with *CSI*, Danny Cannon said, "if you've got a killer and he ships town, do you just give him up to another jurisdiction?" That's exactly why Catherine and Warrick went to Miami to get their man and also the reason why Horatio came to New York. Though Mac did give up his man to Miami jurisdiction.

We don't get to see Mac's face until he actually enters the apartment and turns around. In contrast to Horatio whom he sees standing behind him when he turns around. There seems to be a sale on leather jackets in the NYPD, everyone seems to be wearing one. {As did Chris Noth in *Law and Order and Law and Order:Criminal Intent*, where he played Det. Mike Logan.}

H introduces himself as CSI whereas Mac introduces himself as CSU. H is a Lieutenant and so has seniority over Mac who is a

Detective First Grade. Mac mentions everything is connected twice in this episode and mentions it once more in the actual CSI:NY episode **1.5 A Man A Mile**.

Even if New York hasn't executed anyone since 1976, Penrod would get the death penalty anyway for the murder of a police officer, this would be automatic. H believes in the death penalty.

Danny defines his seniority over Aiden. Heated superglue fumes are used to isolate fingerprints. Also Danny here mentions there are nine rats for every person in Manhattan, which is mentioned again in **1.2 Creatures of the Night.** *CSI* shows appear to be obsessed with rats, though we haven't seen any in Miami (yet.) But why did Danny make that comment here?

A lot of references were made to 9/11 in this opener just as they were in the first episode of NY. Enhancement software was developed to identify the victims of 9/11.

Allowing Penrod to escape, didn't anyone think about covering the fire escape both up and down. (No, that's why they needed the addition of Flack!)

OR =owner.

There are similarities to where the DBs were found in Miami and here, only the mother was found in the lounge and here she was in the bedroom.

Stella is introduced; hastily wanting to take a photo of the son's wound when they are trying to save his life. Sums up her entire character really: just doing her job. She also did say this in the first episode proper, about how the job never stops.

H disappears like he appeared without even so much as a hello or goodbye. Though of course it's not as though Mac can't call him!

Mac likes to speak with the press on occasion. (See also **1.3 American Dreamers**.) This was also the first and last time we saw this happen. As he didn't in the remainder of the season, until later episodes.

As we all know, H doesn't put his glasses back on until he solves his case.

The way they entered Penrod's apartment building carrying guns was very gung ho.

Why all the fuss at the hospital over the lawyer not allowing them to see Michael Jnr's stab wound, when Stella already photographed it?

Lots of changes in this to the actual episode of *NY*: Danny wore a tie and no glasses in this and later wore glasses and no tie. Aiden had a very small opening part. Mac didn't wear leather jackets anymore. Hawkes got his hair cut and no longer sported a pony tail.

They mention bagging hands at the scene and scrape at the lab, but this was the first and only time they did that. They didn't do that in any of the episodes and later seasons anymore, or hardly ever.

Says Carmine about this episode; "The fun story about that [*CSI* episode] is the director Danny Cannon, who did the pilot for *CSI:NY* after I met him for the role of Danny – he was like 'What episode did you do in *CSI:Las Vegas*,' he was the one who directed that episode and didn't realize it until then." The episode in question was from *CSI* season 3: **Revenge is a Dish Best Served Cold.** Carmine also says that working with David Caruso was "smooth." On Danny and himself, he comments that his character is very alike to Danny in real life, "We're very similar and also extremely different."

On Eddie Cahill he says, it's "like working with an old friend, he's open, interested and a funny guy."

Anthony Zuiker: "When I wrote the cross-over for *Miami to NY*, there was a time where at the very end he was trying to wave bye to Mac Taylor – Gary Sinise – and Gary had microphones in his face and the second Gary looked back Caruso was gone. So sometimes it might seem like he [David] comes out of nowhere, sometimes he may just walk out of frame – he's there to protect...and we followed that story he told us in real life [about the 9/11 calls] and just metaphorically made it a part of his character and that's why it had to feel that way."

David Caruso loved being in this episode and wanted to do more. Saying, "Gary Sinise has a great presence. People don't know how funny he is." Their paths did cross again in another cross-over episode between the two shows later on. For Carmine, Gary is a great person, he "respects me and I respect him...he's where I want to be in ten years."

Carmine on season 1 also stated, "because it [*CSI:NY*] the stories are of a more personal nature...we can't help but be more gritty, darker..."

Quotes

Horatio: "He's about to know ours [strength.]"

Horatio: "Next time you see my face, you're gonna know that you're safe."

Mac: "One way or another, everything's connected, brought you to me."

Mac: "Different process, same principle."

Danny: "Cleaning bill's murder."

Mac: "New York...they think it, it's news."

Mac: "Until evidence told us a different story."

A Danny Moment

Danny: "Figured you could use a guy like me."

CSI Déjà Vu

In the *CSI:NY* episode **1.7 Rain** this method was also used to find the location of a suspect, by using the substances he had inhaled from Ground Zero but was changed to construction workers working on the site.

CSI season 1 episode **$35K O.B.O.** there were wounds from two different weapons, two knives, however it turned out there was only one weapon and two assailants.

CSI season 2 episode **Overload** where Gil does a glue fuming to keep prints intact, as Danny did here.

CSI:Miami season 1 episode **Bunk** the doctor hands over a knife willingly and the hilt marks from it match the wound.

The *CSI:Miami* crossover episode with *CSI* entitled **Cross Jurisdictions** had a showgirl at a party and here the mistress was an actress.
In the *CSI:Miami* season 1 episode **Wet Foot Dry Foot** Horatio looks out over the Miami skyline just as Mac looks over the New York skyline.

Music

Born Too Slow by Crystal Method; *The Further We Go* by Futique; *Teardrop* by Massive Attack; *One Day My Soul Opened Up* by Millie Jackson; *Fall Into Light* by Lori Carson; *7* by Graeme Revel

Ratings 23.077 million viewers. Rated #2 for the week.
Did You Know

Vanessa Ferlito was the first member of *CSI:NY* to be cast.

1. Blink

Written By Anthony E Zuiker Directed By Deran Sarafian
US Airdate 22 September 2004
UK Airdate 5 February 2005

Regular Cast: Gary Sinise (Det Mac Taylor)
Melina Kanakaredes (Det Stella Bonasara)
Carmine Giovinazzo (Det Danny Messer)
Vanessa   Ferlito   (Det   Aiden   Burn)
 Hill Harper (ME Sheldon Hawkes)
Eddie Cahill (Det Don Flack Jnr)

Guest stars: Conor Michael Dubin (Jason Parnell) Vitali Baganov (Dr Bogdhan Ovanov) Michael Hagerty II (Tim Goodman) Andy Comeau (Carson Silo) Arsha Darbinyan (Nadia Ivanov) Grant Albrecht (Dr Leonard Giles) Ajay Metha (Dr Smythe) Ana K Alexander (Zoya Pavlova) Jewel Christian (Jane Doe) Jennifer Jackson (LeAnn Goodman)

Background

Mac attends church alone. He's beeped and drives to a crime scene.

Mac tells Stella he never went home. Stella says the victim being missing so long, gives her time to be in the system. She wants a 'good morning' from Mac. Hawkes sleeps at the morgue. He was tired by working on the Jane Doe.

The Jane Doe is LeAnn Goodman from Pelham Bay. Her husband doesn't believe it's her. Then he views her with the body coming up on the gurney. They had lunch together and he put her in a taxi.

Stella finds a missing persons report on Zoya Pavlova with an address at 1204 Weyburn. She was a student from Moscow and had a boyfriend, Jason. The Bogdans were her sponsors. Jason is a street vendor. He asks them if they've found her but he wasn't the one she was blowing a kiss to in the photo.

They hear opera music from the building and in the basement find a half dressed woman on life support. Flack looks for the owner. Danny and Aiden process the bedroom and Stella processes the basement. Mac is going to the hospital. He'll rest when he tires.

Flack questions the owner of the building. Danny takes a swab from him by coercion when he opens his mouth to call their behaviour harassment.

Mac tells Dr Giles the blinking wasn't random. He calls it 'Locked-In Syndrome'. She was the victim of a perverted science experiment. All her voluntary muscles in her body were paralyzed except her eyes. She was "locked inside her own body." He sedates them to find arterial pressure points. Mac says the killer was improving his technique. LeAnn was found first but she had bedsores so Zoya died first as she didn't have any bedsores. The third woman was kept because she was a success. She's seen the killer. Mac shows her photos of the victims and the suspects.

She blinks uncontrollably when he shows her the rental man. She suffered another stroke and is in a coma with a Glasgow Coma score of 3.

Mac tells Stella about his 'talk' with the victim. The DNA from the semen didn't match any of the suspects. Stella says they should keep working. Mac wants to know the connection. Why he locked women inside their own bodies? He says his behaviour was intimate. He removed himself from the house when they were onto him. But not from the medical equipment.

Crime Scene Evidence

Flack tells him she's a female in her late '20's with no ID. She was dumped here. No scuff marks on her knees, nails are intact and her body is on the onset of putrefaction. Her belt is two notches off from its usual position. The killer redressed her and took time to do it. Why? Mac notices her wedding ring. He looks beyond the New York skyline, to where the WTC (World Trade Center) used to stand.

Medical Exam

The victim has contusions around her neck. Lividity slats along her back and bed sores. COD was a hemorrhagic stroke, she suffered two of them. An ischemic stroke where the blood is cut off from the cerebrum causing damage to the blood vessels and leading to a hemorrhagic conversion. Her histology shows she inhaled a substance that didn't agree with her. Mac says this was perimortum, smoke inhalation before death. He wants a Tox screen run.

The exam on the second victim shows she doesn't have bed sores. COD was asphyxiation by strangulation. Her neck was broken first. TOD same time. Other features same as LeAnn Goodman; all the arteries to the brain. Mac notices her filling has gold and copper impurities. It's Russian dentistry. He saw it in the Marines.

Lab Analysis

Mac uses a medical bust: skinless and examines how the victims were killed by examining the photos and placing his hands where the killer put his.

Lab Results

The Tox screen shows LeAnn inhaled fire sticks. Aiden says she had a codeine based cough syrup and nicotine bubbles inside her. She inhaled laced cigarettes. Danny says fire sticks are the new date rape drug of New York; all you need are three puffs. Mac says she wasn't raped. So why?

The Russian woman is in the photos, with sites of New York in the background, with a man. Another photo is of an unknown location.

Mac and Stella use photo triangulation to locate the unknown location. Zoya was 5' 9": the primary reference. The secondary reference is the needle on the Chrysler Building which is 1,046'. The tertiary reference is the slant of the Citicorp Building which is 915'. The triangulation points to Queens and Coney Island City.

The medical equipment is sprayed with rhodamin and with a laser. Initials in a Cyrillic alphabet are revealed: 'B.I.' as read by Stella. Mac says 'Bogdan Ivanov.'

Secondary Crime Scene Evidence

A DB is found on a garbage barge. She has neck contusions, lividity slats on her back. Mac determines they're looking for a serial killer. They must sift and isolate the rubbish for evidence. The dimensions of the barge are 140 X 30 feet. Danny says that's half the size of a football pitch.
Aiden finds an empty bag and Danny finds a camera which is still on. The camera contains some black and white film which has been ripped out.

Tertiary Crime Scene evidence

Danny doesn't find any photos or personal items and no partials. Aiden finds semen on the bed.

The woman is in a coma and Mac processes her at the hospital. He scrapes under her fingernails, fingerprints her and takes photos of her trauma to identify her. He apologizes for what he had to do and she blinks.

Conclusion

The killer was a medical doctor in the USSR and was in prison for treason. They matched the reference sample to DNA from the sheets which also had Zoya's DNA. He loved her and took her photo. Mac tells him he's not a doctor but a killer.   He killed Zoya attempting to lock her inside her body. He drives a taxi so picked up his victims. He gave them a cigarette. Mac asks why he locked them in? Bogdan means 'gift from God' in Russian. He wanted them in a cerebral utopia so they could live free. It was a pact. Mac says it was all about control. He lost control when they found him so he left her but she was still alive. The women died because he didn't know when to let go and this led to his capture.

Mac visits the hospital and tells the woman he's tired. He used to sit with his wife, Claire who died on 9/11. He found a beachball in the closet and kept it because it had her breath in it. He visits Ground Zero.

Notes

The plot in this episode could be explained by a David Fincher movie: a gruesome episode for a season opener and is also similar to Mark Gillingham's novel, *Sleepyhead.* The victim is suffering from 'Locked-in Syndrome', which causes complete paralysis of all body muscles except for the eyes. The condition is irreversible; hence she was "locked in her body." Reference to the episode title, all she could do was blink. Still it was more interesting and kept you watching, with some emotion from Mac. An episode of *Law & Order: Criminal Intent* had the same title in season 2. Actual scenes were filmed on location in New York.

The network wanted the show to be more modernized and up-to-date in later seasons. In my opinion it was grittier and better when it had a more darker feel to the city and storylines.

The scene opens with Mac in church. See a later episode where Stella asks him if he still goes? There were many 'firsts' in this episode which didn't happen again: Mac at church. (Though he does go to church in season 4, it's to make an arrest.) You also see him driving to an actual crime scene the one and only time in season 1. The idea to have Mac in church, came from Gary himself, he emailed Anthony Zuiker and they added it in the end of the episode too.

Anthony comments how Gary had a "cadence" about him. Mac didn't wear a suit in the introductory *CSI:Miami* cross-over episode. Also Anthony says he had a call from the NYPD telling him that detectives do wear suits. Gary is a Ronald Reagan supporter and he mentioned how Reagan never removed his suit whilst he was in the Oval Office and that's why Mac doesn't either. Not until later seasons when he did and also doesn't wear a tie anymore. Though he did take his jacket off to wear a lab coat. Ha!

When Mac says that someone is missing a wife, you can almost feel it's a reference to his wife Claire, as he poignantly looks across to the New York skyline across the river. (But we don't know he lost his wife until later in the episode.)

The show also gets a new permanent detective, Donald Flack Jnr, who wasn't in the cross-over, introductory episode with *CSI:Miami*. Flack was very heavy-handed with the tourists, which was uncalled for, as was Stella's questioning of Jason, also it didn't take three of them to question him. This scene was shot in LA.

Flack breaks down his first door when they find the victim alive and promptly disappears to check out the rest of the building, we presume.

Stella asking Mac for 'a good morning', well she wouldn't give him one especially if she was in bad mood mode. Like her sarcastic comment to Danny when he wishes her a 'good morning.'

Danny 'lurks' (!) in this episode. See **1.13 Tanglewood** when he watches Mac and Stella from next door in the interrogation room.

This episode was about sleep, Mac not getting enough and comas. Young women who were given rest against their will. Hawkes sleeping in the morgue, but you don't know why unless you read the official website or interviews, because he doesn't venture out after 9/11.

The body of the man's wife, LeAnn comes up on a gurney in a lift. Said Melina on a visit to a New York morgue whilst researching the role: "When someone goes to view a body, unlike the old *Quincy* shows where they take the sheet off dramatically to show the person, they put the body onto a lift and it rises up into a space behind a glass window with a curtain that gets pulled back. The lift makes this whine and it takes exactly 32 seconds but if you're waiting to see if the body is your husband or your child those seconds must seem like hours."

There was less of a shock factor in how families view the victims/DBs. Also there weren't that many viewings in later seasons.

She also thinks, "that kind of stuff is the icky part for me because you totally feel the emotional connection of what relatives would be going through, but it's also the delicious part for me because the stuff you want to remember when you are doing the scene. [Be good if Stella actually showed emotion like that once in a while on screen. Would Stella put a comforting arm around someone, No] and who is she and what is her connection to other people? My goal is to find clues about Stella that show what compels her to work for the people who are left behind."

Stella looks at Mac as if he's cracked or lost the plot when he tells her he "talked" to the victim.
Mac mentions he was a marine for the first time and thereafter in the series.

Danny has a tattoo on his right arm; which is real as he has it in other shows too; real, and could fit nicely into a tattoo for his part with his gang initiation; see **1.13 Tanglewood.**

Danny and Aiden get garbage detail for the first time and throughout the remainder of the season. This scene was filmed at the New

York Naval yard. It was the first day of shooting and it was boiling hot. Carmine commented on locations and how he lives in New York and had never ever been to the Naval yard. The trash used on this barge was "clean" trash as opposed to the trash in the *CSI:Miami* episode **Blood Brothers**, where the trash was real and a dead rat was found and subsequently used in the scene. Anthony Zuiker managed to get hold of NYPD boats and a Coast Guard helicopter - for free.

Also in later episodes the reconstruction room disappears and is never mentioned again in other seasons either. So much for having it in the first place.

Stella showing her heavy-handedness with a suspect for the first time and again throughout the series. Just as Flack did and Danny taking a swab without consent from the donor. Even if there is 'coercion' in obtaining evidence from a suspect and this happens in other *CSI* shows too – though not as blatantly obvious to remove or take evidence; people can't be so naïve as to believe this doesn't happen in real life. The world is not as perfect as they may like to think. Even if there is a risk of such evidence being obtained illegally or on the boundaries of illegality/legality so as to discredit the entire case against a suspect, the theory or thinking is: if no one knows; no one cares and besides who is going to complain. The closest most of us will ever get to being swabbed is when we are asked to scrape some cheek cells from inside our mouth in biology class, to take a look at animal cells under the microscope. Though that's with a lolly stick and not a proper swab. Swab is such a dirty word in the context of this episode.

Stella knows Russian. She also listens to the police radio in the shower since the job never stops. Danny's not surprised at that. When Stella found the missing persons report with the Queen's address, wouldn't that have been the logical place to start the investigation, after questioning the victim's sponsors.
Mac tells the woman, whom sadly no one claims and we don't find out the identity of, about Claire and 9/11: "nobody saw it coming." A comparison could be made with how the women were caught and

subjected to the will of a mad man. They didn't see what was about to happen to them coming either.

Mac says he kept the ball because her breath is in there; he also kept wearing their wedding ring. He got rid of everything else belonging to Clare, as it was too painful, how about when Clare's son, Reid turns up in later seasons.

The series episode ends as it begins with a poignant view of Ground Zero with the camera panning to the stars and the forever changed skyline.

There were many changes from the cross-over episode too, as mentioned, the addition of Eddie Cahill as Det. Flack and a welcome addition he was too (aside from the eye candy factor. I am not that shallow (!)) But he turned out to be one of my favourite characters, along with Danny, Hawkes and in later episodes, new lab tech, Adam. Also Mac calls Flack 'Detective' Flack here and later he'll call him Flack, or Don.

Eddie Cahill says the series is dark, even admitted by Anthony Zuiker. Eddie says, "in terms of episode 1, which was really dark, physically, I thought it was quite beautiful. As an actor the mistake I made was playing too much into the look of the show and the personality. In **Blink,** I think we all came out a little heavy which I think for TV may be the wrong way to go. I don't think it works for us, but we haven't settled back on the look yet. I think as the personality lightens up, it will be interesting to see how the aesthetic plays out." Though he usually gets most of the witty quips and one liners. Luckily for us.

He also says that the show has found a home for itself. "What distinguishes New York is the city. As we go further and further into the show the city takes more of a leading role. I also think having three of us being from New York helps too. [Himself, Carmine and Vanessa.] New Yorkers have a distinct personality and how they express themselves is highly unique."

Melina on the dynamics of Mac and Stella: "We started the series with him still suffering the loss of his wife that changed him and the dynamics between him and Stella – gradually getting back to their old relationship. They're not in a romantic place but they just understand each other; there's a shorthand between them. It's that respect and camaraderie with a bit of flirting." (What flirting?) Stella just seems to be Mac's favourite. Even after the fights, at the end of the day he will always forgive her. Whereas he treats the others differently, especially, the men on his team, Danny, Flack and Hawkes (and later Adam.) They will always be told, off, disciplined and even humiliated in front of everyone else and most of the time, they don't even suffer an apology from him either. See **1.17** this season in the case of Flack and **1.21** for Danny (and subsequent seasons.)

On Danny, Carmine comments: "The thing I was concerned about was finding the voice for my character and holding up my end of the puzzle while not worrying about the outside. I was more concerned with what I needed to do within the machine of it and not how we were going to compete with the other guys. [From the other *CSI* shows.]

On Flack, Eddie comments: "…there's a real loving sarcasm to the way that city works. So much social activity being a New Yorker is based on breaking balls, and I think, to reduce it to that is interesting…in situations Flack deals with, it's a way of coping and, or, getting his point across. I love that sense of humour…if Flack were faced with somebody [doing wrong such as in **1.17 The Fall**] he's going to do what he thinks is right… he's a pretty good judge of character – so if you do something wrong, you gotta pay the price – and if you didn't do something wrong, you've got nothing to worry about because it will get worked out in the end." Yes, but what of the suspect in this episode being swabbed the way he was and not to mention miscarriages of justice. The evidence is not infallible as many episodes will show!

Anthony Zuiker commented that when he penned this episode, "it was a little too dark for everyone's appetite. I had an idea about a therapist who would be talking to Mac Taylor once an episode and [uncover] what he was going through with his wife. When doing research, almost everyone I talked to had a 9/11 story to tell, and they all wanted to share their story...I thought maybe, we could put Mac Taylor into the identifiable situation of somebody who lost someone in 9/11." He originally thought of finding a part of Mac's wife and he would lay her to rest, before he could move on in season 2.

After the first episode, "CBS felt we were going too dark, too grim, with too much character information about Mac Taylor and we needed to have our own identity and our own stories before we got into the heaviness. It's almost like going on a date...which is too much information. So we wanted to just show where you fall in love with the man (Mac Taylor) and the woman (Stella Bonasera.) [highly likely] we abandoned all the 9/11 stuff." But this show was meant to be about the characters and character-orientated. Whereas the other two predecessors established themselves as forensics shows, procedural; *CSI:NY* could have had the opportunity to become more character orientated from the outset, as planned. It didn't really need to find its feet first and then move onto more personal territory as there was a lot that could be made from the characters and they had masses of backstory to achieve this.

This episode was also a prelude of sorts, to the taxi-cab serial killer arc in season 4, almost!

Gary wanted to do the monologue, such as the penultimate scene in the hospital when he talks about Clare and that's one of the reasons why he agreed to do the show, because of such monologues. (Of which there weren't that many later on.)

Anthony Zuiker said that the message from this episode as far as 9/11 was concerned was "never forget" and this is important for everyone.

It was also said that many police procedurals directly and indirectly report and incorporate stories relating to the events of today, such as 9/11 and the War in Iraq. The *CSI* shows have included stories which have featured topical issues, but the premise remains the same: the fight is still to catch criminals, even if it includes involving criminals in the shape of terrorists and urban terrorists.

Quotes

Mac: "Someone out there is missing a wife."

Aiden: "Black and white film. Are you seeing red?"

Flack: "Let me arrest him for swearing on his grandmother."

Mac: "Murderer with a medical degree."

A Danny Moment

Danny: "Morning dear."
Stella: "Do I have a tail back there?" (So not funny Stella!)

CSI Déjà Vu

Not so much as taking illegal evidence and the like as this has been done in other series anyway, eg the matchbook in the *CSI episode* **Blood Drops.** The envelope Nick asks the security guard to lick, so he can test for his DNA and he unwittingly does (in **Boom**), but ultimately if it's evidence not going to be used in court it isn't illegal and if no one has had their rights violated...

In the *CSI* season 1 episode **Too Tough To Die** Sara does a rape kit on a victim found close to death and Sara promises they'll find her attacker and talks to her as she lies unconscious in her hospital bed. She'll remain in a vegetative state forever as does the Jane Doe that

Mac speaks with in this episode. However in the *CSI* episode they found out the identity of their Jane Doe.

Also in season 5 episode **Harvest** more mention is made of Gil and the church. Where the suspect told Gil that suicide is a sin, in which case Gil asks him why he didn't just kill himself instead of his sister. Gill tells him he was asking his God to forgive murder. Does Gil believe in God? He would then know that what God does is merciful. In the *CSI* season 2 episode **Alter Boys** Gil makes the declaration, "I believe in God. In science. In Sunday supper. I don't believe in rules that tell me how I should live." (What about the law; that's a set of rules?) Anyhow Mac doesn't go so far as to say this, sufficed to say he goes to church and doesn't have problems reconciling religion with science, not that we know of (yet.)

Season 1 episode of *CSI:Miami* **Ashes to Ashes** was the only time Horatio went to church.
In season 2 episode **Blood Brothers** of *CSI:Miami* 9/11 is mentioned as it was mentioned again in the *CSI:NY* season 1 finale **What You See Is What You See.** This episode was also good to show the 'techniques' employed by the US government post 9/11. Even if it was only meant to be fictional, about giving other countries carte blanche to carry out torture on their behalf, whilst maintaining a respectable front in the eyes of the international community. Also how H and the evidence, allows him to bring at least one criminal to book.
Also in this episode, Speed and Delko check the garbage barge for evidence. Delko sees a rat on board and tells Speed it's a long way from his apartment. Calleigh talks to herself in the lab. The suspect spits on Horatio's jacket and so gives his DNA sample freely. Horatio comments, "sure is nice when they help." As opposed to Flack and Danny coercing the suspect to open his mouth for a swab. And in the *CSI:Miami* episode from season 2, **Dead Zone,** Speed is the one who always gets his hand in the toilet searching for evidence.

CSI:Miami season 2 episode **Witness to Murder,** the dead body of a woman was found to have been killed elsewhere shown by double lividity, the blood settled twice.

Ratings

19.258 million viewers. Rated #5 for the week.

Bloops

When they enter the house and find the third victim alive, the record player needle stops and then moves onto another part of the record. The music begins and is heard before the needle touches the record.

2. Creatures of the Night

Written By Pam Veasey Directed By Tim Hunter
US Airdate 29 September 2004
UK Airdate 12 February 2005

Guest Stars: William Russ (Arnold Prescott) Michele Hicks (Robin Prescott) Germaine de Leon (AJ Dalton/AJ Mata) David Marciano (Karl Drewdetski) Fred Koehler (Billy Rendish) Grant Albrecht (Dr Leonard Giles) Joseph Thomas (Donovan Tracey) Josh Hammond (Calvin Montgomery)

Story 1

Background

A girl turns up to a social gathering after being attacked. There are bloody handprints on a car outside belonging to her. Flack questioned her and had to ask what her name was four times before she remembered, Robin Prescott. She was in Central Park. Mac tells Danny to trace her clothes for leads to help them determine the location of the crime scene. Stella takes the victim's clothes at the hospital and processes her.

An employee at the crime scene admits he was there to steal but didn't rape her. Donovan saw her bag and she grabbed him so he ran.

Robin says she went to work and left early. She took a taxi on 3rd and went through the park; she walked but doesn't remember she went out to go north and crossed through the park to the street. Her father tells Stella boys are easier to bring up. She tells him her investigation is ongoing and they can only prove the suspect was at the scene; that Robin fought back and picked herself up to carry on, shown by her blistered fingertips.

Stella tells Mac of her frustration as she can't prove whether the suspect did or didn't do it.

Walnut dust is used to clean statues in Central park: South end of the park east from the bridge, so someone else brought the dust to the crime scene. Danny says they can round up the four men authorized to carry out the cleaning and get swabs. Stella tells him no DNA was left behind. Danny tells her they'll get him so they go over the details once more. Stella thinks they're moving too fast and she returns to Central Park.

She notices flowers by the statues and thinks of the gardener. He says it wasn't him as city maintenance assigned him to the north end. Danny tells her they can match boots to the scene but she says without a confession, they can't prove he did it. It's reasonable doubt to a jury, i.e that 2% of the population fire blanks. Robin misses the line-up.

Mac mentions his nine folders of unsolved cases. Every week he makes calls, dusts off the evidence to see if he finds something not there before. There used to be twelve folders. Stella goes over the evidence again, helped by Danny, Aiden and Mac.

Crime Scene Evidence

Stella processes the scene and finds a wallet, shoe prints and tells Danny he needs to find DNA evidence. She's documenting everything to eliminate what wasn't connected to the crime. Danny notices there were two assailants, one with a heavy work boot who knelt down next to her. Robin fought hard. Stella finds a nose ring with possible blood trace.

Conclusion

Mac looks at photos showing the marks on Robin's body and asks Danny about the note he made concerning sap on her panties from a tree. Mac comments on the intimate nature of finding such a substance there, so it must be secondary transfer. At the north side of the park Calvin was cutting trees due to beetle infestation. The tree sap on his trousers and with her panties shows positional matching.

Story 2

Background

Aiden and Mac are called in to a crime scene involving the shooting of Geordie Thompkins. Aiden comments when she lived in a six story walk up in Brooklyn, could hear rats on the staircase around you. She didn't flinch. Mac tells her rats are creatures of habit and travel 65 feet from the nest and travel the same path home. He says it was too windy in Chicago for rats. He gives her an alloy gun with which she can identify the rat. He finds a hair pulled from right to left, so the rat is moving in one direction. They find a grocery store and the read out is composite for the rat, which is in the attic.

Carl the rat catcher tells them that there are eight rats for every person. Females give birth to about 6-12 rats about five times a year. He and Aiden lay traps with eggs containing poison. There rat's not there. Aiden checks the store and finds the rat, dead.

Crime Scene Evidence

There are no shell casings. Aiden thinks the murder weapon is a revolver. Mac notices blackened gums and singed eyelashes. He was a crack user. There are track marks on his ankles. Mac notices the entry wound is larger than the needle. Tissue at the wound uneven, the fibres are frayed outwards. The gun spatter is unusual as something came out of the wound.

Conclusion

Calvin needed a fix and robbed the deli of $50. Mac believes this wasn't enough so he shot his dealer and tossed the gun. He denies shooting Geordie. Mac comments he thought he didn't know him. He asks, "who ratted me out?"

Notes

Here's Stella being so negative when everyone is giving her so much help and support and all she's doing is saying 'this won't help, that won't help' and true to form Mac comes in and solves her dilemma of no evidence within a few minutes, well, TV seconds. Stella tries to be nice whilst processing the victim and though she genuinely tries to be supportive, you can't really tell where the job ends for her and the emotion or sympathy begins, no wonder Danny summed it up best when he said that this is what she does when there's no one at home for her. Something she'll say to Mac and said in the first episode, **Blink**. She shrugs off Danny's comment/observation and tells him to get on with the job and find evidence. Well, suppose her look said it all.

The scene where the party is being held was shot outside the LA Science Center. Exhibition Park was the substitute for Central Park. The ground shots were filmed in the studio.

When Mac flashes the light, no blood drops are visible to him, they were added later by CGI.

Also the Central Park department knows every single plant or flower which can be found there and where it is located. When Stella returns to the park where the victim, Robin was attacked, the original crime scene; this was filmed in Descanso Gardens, California. A "ghost scene" was shot. The scene with Danny and Stella in the park, after they mention walnut dust was filmed in the night, so night was made into day especially for the scene and also when Stella returns to the park.

The scene between Mac and Stella, when she's frustrated and he tells her to use her head and not her heart was written afterwards and another scene was dropped.

What's unique about all the *CSI* shows is that they use real blood, semen, sperm etc for their samples and for purposes of authenticity.

This episode told us a few too many things about rats. Carl mentions there are eight rats for every person; whilst in **Blink**, Danny said there are nine rats for every person in Manhattan alone.

Carol Mendelsohn said "Liz Devine had told us a story about a body where a rat came out, and then during the autopsy they found baby rats gestating in the victim's stomach!" Gruesome stories featuring rats; or in New York, rather, a case of the rat that ate the bullet!

As usual Stella doesn't give anyone straight answers unless she's trying to pin something on a suspect. Mac telling her to use her head, well she doesn't really use her heart at all. Funny Stella having the shower as though she was the one feeling dirty.

In contrast to the first story where Stella needs a confession to prove guilt or so she thinks, in story two, not only did Mac get his evidence but the suspect actually admitted to the crime. Wonder why Mac didn't handle this case himself as Stella obviously lacked the necessary direction for one reason or another. Even when she had Danny's help. Infact if she had gone over Danny's notes perhaps she may have worked it out for herself.

Anthony Zuiker described Melina as the show's "statue of liberty, the moral guardian of the show" and this is what contributed to her accepting the role.   But she isn't this from the content of this episode/show.   Melina: "[Anthony] has this wonderful infectious energy, when he said the thing about the Statue of Liberty it seemed odd but I still get it.   He had this visualization, a woman who stands for something.   Stella is always the solid person in the room that's committed and will be there for you as a team and will not stop until she gets the job done."   {In contrast to the advice she gave Mac in **1.22 The Closer** when she told him to go home and forget about the case he wanted to reopen and she wasn't there for Danny in **1.21 On the Job**.}   She was about to give up in this episode despite her encouragement from the others.   (See the same thing from her in other seasons.)

Melina comments: "When a girl got raped and my character was obsessed with it, there was a really lovely scene between Mac and Stella where she was like, 'I couldn't fix it'.   Mac's the fact guy and no matter once in a while you've got to have the person who emotionally is that fireball and [the one that] has that calming effect.   I think they really match each other very well and in real life, as friends and co-workers, we just adore each other.   We always have a blast.   He hasn't failed me yet.   He's been a wonderful, wonderful friend and colleague.   It's wonderful working with Gary."

Also because no matter what she does, or fails to do, Stella knows Mac will always forgive her and rally to her side and her defence.   See season 5 and especially the penultimate episode, when Stella got away with so much and Mac gave her so much leeway.   Again, if that had been anyone else in the same position, they'd have hell to pay.   Another thing was the way their scenes together were just between them alone, (see **1.9 Officer Blue**, whereas usually anyone else, Mac will bawl them out in front of the entire lab, such as Hawkes in season 5, Danny on several occasions and even Adam.   Not to mention Flack too.

The DVD commentary for this episode reveals when Stella calls the victim to attend the line-up, this was the last scene as originally written in the script, after everything else was changed. The victim's body was pulled out from the bloody tub in her apartment, however, it was decided not to go with this scene and instead you get Stella in the shower. (Groan, well depending on your point of view, some of you may have liked that.)

When this episode was repeated in the US in December, Gary and Melina sent viewers a "Happy Holidays" message before the episode.

Also notice how Mac's desk gets empty and cleared of files as the episodes and seasons progress, until it eventually becomes devoid of any files for him to solve in seasons 4, 5... He can't have that good a clear up rate. Or rather more conveniently, this was a plot line writers forgot. Especially with all the serial killers, murders and stalkers to come. At least there was some continuity in season 4 when Mac returned to Chicago to solve the **333** caller mystery.

Carmine says: "TV happens quickly but I come from a family of cops so I absorbed that view my whole life. I read a few books on ballistics and forensics. Once I did the pilot it has been an ongoing process and taking what they give me, discussing my character with the creator [Anthony Zuiker] and going over who he was. Then it was putting it into play which we did more than I expected. He's an easy character in one sense because he's sincere about wanting to change things and make them right. He has a strong anger and frustration towards the criminal lifestyle because he came from that world himself and maybe could have gone that way. His family was involved with the wise guys and kids who were really delinquents or coming from Staten Island; 'goons' as I call them.

He went and studied to go against the grain and he really wants to please Gary's character, Mac. He's a bit rebellious which is good because he doesn't always go by the book."

"Stroke the liver" were the directive words of Tim Hunter to Gary Sinise (Mac Taylor) – who had no idea of where the liver is found/located. His response is to ask the director questions. (eg, this episode, the bullet is in the rat.)

The title of course having a double meaning or two meanings: rats and lowlifes! Those that prey on others in the night.

In later seasons, Gary commented that he doesn't do much running in the episodes, since he tore a leg muscle during season 1 and was off work for 3-4 weeks.

Quotes

Mac: "We've got ourselves an 800 square metre crime scene."

Hawkes: "Gunshot wound was main course."
Mac: "...and the dinner guest."

Hawkes: "This is where the story gets tasty."
Mac: "The rat ate the bullet."
Hawkes: "That was dessert."

Mac: "City's the city...use your head and not your heart."

Mac: "Have faith in the evidence, Stella." (Because really not many have faith in you!)

A Danny Moment

Danny: "I guess this is what you do when there's no one to go home to."

CSI Déjà Vu

Calleigh checking guns for bullets as she's a dab hand at this, ballistics being her specialty in *CSI:Miami* as aptly demonstrated in the season 1 episode **Wet Foot Dry Foot** et al. Aiden looked out of place doing this. Perhaps because she was a bit of a novice.

In season 5 *CSI* episode **Mea Culpa,** Sara shows Greg how to bring up the scratched off serial number on a gun: beginning by rubbing polishing compound on the other end of the serial number, then it's filed until smooth. Fry's Reagent is added and eats away at the depressed area exposing the dented metal of the serial number.

Also in the *CSI:Miami* season 1 episode **A Horrible Mind,** H suggests that Delko should try all possible weather conditions on the computer simulation, including wet. Here Mac helps out with the clue, aiding Stella nail the suspect.

The season 2 *CSI* finale **The Hunger Artist**, a rat squeezes out from the teeth of a DB. This case also involved facial reconstruction.

Music

Where's Jack the Ripper? by Grooverider

Ratings

19.474 million viewers. Rated #4 for the week.

Bloops

Robyn's bloody hand is on the car's bonnet on the centre, and no blood spatter is visible. When the CSIs take photos – the handprint moves further left on the bonnet. The handprint resembles a perfect print now. There's visible blood spatter on the bumper and the left headlight now.

3. American Dreamers

Written By Eli Talbert Directed By Rob Bailey
US Airdate 6 October 2004
UK Airdate 19 February 2005

Guest Stars: Grant Albrecht (Dr Leonard Giles) Charles Parks (Mr Moreland) Susan Ruttan (Mrs Moreland) Thomas Kopache (Paul

Danner)   Johnny Speed (Joel/Aaron Moreland)   John Ross Bowie (Lester Jayne) Frank Medrano (Bruno) Julian Cain (John Doe)

Background

A tourist on a tour bus finds a skeleton. Stella thinks it's just an urban legend, a practical joke to scare tourists. The skeleton is probably from a prop shop. Mac tells her a store bought skeleton is bleached with drill marks when it's assembled. This is brown and has no drill marks.

Danny comments on how the New York post will love this story. Mac tells him it's not news. Danny replies it'll still sell papers. Mac comments that's because of where it was found. Aiden is impatient to get to work on the skull.

Mac thinks he's been dead at least ten years. Stella tells him from 1990-1993 the murder rate in New York City was 2,000 a year. She finds six prints; one of them belongs to Lester Jayne at Times Square. He's found at the New York bus terminal. Mac notices exhaust fumes from a bus which leads him to a vent. Here he finds clothes and more bones. Decomposing bones. So this is where he died. Mac believes he lived here too so he's probably a runaway.

Mac and Stella talk to the probable parents of John Doe: Aaron. His mother monogrammed his backpack. The knife was his 13th birthday present. He wanted to be a musician and left home in 1987 at 17. They look at the composite and the father believes it's not Aaron.

Danny tells Stella there are 117 arrest records for criminals committed in a three block radius from where the skeleton was found from 1984-1994. Stella doesn't find his fingerprints in AFIS but could be in the NYPD files. Danny should stick with the hard evidence first.

Mac looks at sketches form Grand Central station and Times Square. The last sketch was of an unknown landscape. He's alone in Times Square and Stella says he's lost. The cris-cross beams in another sketch are of the Port Authority building. Mac's looking at it and it's the only building in the city allowing homeless children free range to all the floors.

Crime Scene Evidence

A.M are initials on a backpack. The victim died from a blunt force trauma from a pipe, there's a pocketknife in his shoe and a copy of *Bright Lights, Big City* copyright 1994. Mac thinks he may have been here twenty years. Stella's read the book. It's about a man who gets out of the city before it gets him.

Conclusion

Aaron is the man working at the shelter. He tells them he wasn't ready for New York, he was broke and hooked on drugs. He used to run the racks and saw the boy there. The boy had money and he always needed money. So he sold his knife. Mac says he was at the Port Authority so he could have taken a bus home. He didn't want to. Six years later, he was clean and he changed his life helping others. Mac says he forgot about his past but his parents never stopped looking for him. Stella tells him he killed the boy for $2. The watch connected him to the victim. He doesn't know the boy's name.

Mac reads *Bright, Lights, Big City*. They don't discover his name. Stella asks Mac out for a drink with the others. Stella loosens his tie and Mac fixes it again.

Notes

Stella sees the skeleton and the first thing she does is crack another joke. Mac saying he's not laughing probably meant at her joke too. Aiden making a joke about the human skull too, when it's just not funny!

As for Stella's comment about the skeleton being left on the bus being an urban legend, see season 5 episode **5.16 No Good Deed** when a bird drops an eyeball in Stella's coffee, she's not too pleased about this and everyone calls that an urban legend. She's not too thrilled about jokes being made too, you see when the shoes on the other foot, it just ain't funny!

Also as a CSI, Stella should've known what a real skeleton looks like! Another episode where Stella has to be up on the pop culture (see other episodes too) i.e. she always has to know about the latest trend in bars, clubs etc, but when it comes to solving a case, the evidence stumps her on many occasions and she needs help or prompting from others, eg blood diamonds episode, from season 3, **Not What It Looks Like** where Hawkes had to point her in the direction of the footage on the airport security tapes; as well as season 3 episode **3.6 Open and Shut,** where Flack and Mac mention the video footage they have, which helps her solve her case and on it continues...

An episode all about crime back in the 1990's and how procedures have changed today with technology and databases providing the answers and suspects at the touch of a button. Also how no files were kept and how missing person's files and details were few and far between. The media were no help here either.

This episode would've made a good crossover with Jerry Bruckheimer's other TV series *Without A Trace,* where probably they could've perhaps gone back further into the case and found some missing clues and links, which is after all their specialty.

But that was left for *CSI* to do a cross over with in season 6.

The dental records also turned up nothing. Mac tells Aaron's parents they're not looking for their son but inadvertently find him anyway. Perhaps the landscape was something he remembered from back home. A pity they don't have a database of landscapes from different states as they have a directory of clothes logos, but none on shoes either; as Danny mentioned in **1.17 The Fall.**

The line Stella says about the watch connecting him to the boy, should've been Mac's as he's into the "everything's connected" bit.

In this episode, the CSIs went from photographing crime scene evidence, to practically photographing next to nothing in later seasons.

Aiden ties her hair back when she reconstructs the skull, but not when evidence is examined. Danny bagged the victim's hands to preserve the trace evidence.

This episode shows that the DBs are weighed upon arrival at the morgue. Also '49' means a gurney.

Mac washes the DB himself here, he doesn't do that anymore and this was the first and only time. As was the emergence of their weapons closet with their stash of various weapons to test out. What happened to it later on, did it run out of varieties of weapons?

Mac reads form the book: *"for what you are left with is a premonition of the way your life will fade behind you like the book you have read too quickly, leaving a dwindling trail of images and emotions until all you can remember is a name."*

This summarizes the episode and the boy's life, all he left behind was the book he had read; the images he drew but no name. A poignant episode, but a pity he didn't sign his initials on his sketches. Couldn't they have followed up on his sketches by putting some out in the media, someone may have recognized his work, parents, an old teacher...perhaps they did but nothing panned out.

Stella loosens Mac's tie as she does in the season finale **1.23 What You See Is What You See**. Stella used to work narcotics out of Brooklyn South. Still that didn't help her with the narcotics cases.

Quotes

Stella: "How long is that soda? That was supposed to be funny."

Mac: "A new take on a bitch ride to hell."

Mac: "This is a joke, I'm not laughing. These bones are real."

Danny: "The media don't care."
Mac: "I do."

Aiden: "Human skull. Big fun."

Stella: "Dream with me a city that can be better than the way it is now." Mac recalls Mayor Giuliani's Inauguration speech from 1994.

Flack: "NYPD didn't find it funny." On the contrary, Stella did.

Aiden: "I figured it was one of the few times that us and the media are on the same team." [A little premature here, but see the season 5 episodes with media mogul Dunbrook and how he insinuates himself into Mac's investigations and his life.]

A Danny Moment

Danny: "It's tough being in the bull pen waiting for your nod."

CSI Déjà Vu

CSI episode **Who Are You?** A face is constructed of a Jane Doe. Also in **Too Tough To Die** computer enhancement was used to age a photo of how a person would look today. In the season 3 episode of *CSI* **Snuff** a triangulation of the Las Vegas skyline is used to find the location of a hotel through the window and this episode also involved the facial reconstruction of a victim.

Danny mentions the media and how they've got a good story, Aiden also mentions the media and how they'll be on their side for once. In the *CSI:Miami* season 2 episode **Death Grip,** Horatio tells the reporter at the end to write about the missing girl and the other missing ethnic minorities; as he and Delko mention, the media concentrate on only the white girls with blonde hair who are missing. (Something also touched upon by Jack, Martin and Viv in *Without A Trace*.)

In the season 1 *CSI:Miami* episode **Camp Fear** Det. Adell Sevilla invites H for a beer with them, as Stella does here to Mac. H takes a rain check as does Mac at first, but then accepts.

Ratings

16.887 million viewers. Rated #8 for the week.

Bloops

Aiden's hands do not belong to Vanessa Ferlito, when she's reconstructing the face on the skull.

Stella prints out six photos of six suspects, Mac takes one photo and points him out as the one they're looking for, but only five photos have been printed and the one Mac holds up is of a black man who isn't in there – the suspect is actually white.

Mac asks Hawkes for a COD and he points to a fracture on the skull above the left eye socket, this fracture isn't on the skull when the skeleton is found on the bus.

1.4 Grand Master

Written By Zachery Reiter. Directed By Kevin Bray
US Airdate 27 October 2004
UK Terrestrial Airdate 26 February 2005

Guest Stars: Dorian Missick (Banner's Manager MC Jayden Prince) Billy Aaron Brown (George Thomas Placid) Olivia Burnette (Madison Haynes) Chayton Arvin (Samir Persaud) Ricky Harris (Disco Placid) Shi Ne Nielson (Mitchiko Muzawa) Long Nguyen (Mitsuo Katsui) Master P (Kevin Vick) Ruel (Christopher Marcus/DJ Banner)

Background

Story 1

"Listen all you New Yorkers": A DJ contest is underway to find the winner of the DJ Master Championship 2004, subsequently announced as DJ Banner. He's 17. Aiden calls the championship a Super Bowl for spinners or today it's known as 'Turntablists'. Mac asks what you get for second place. Aiden is from Brooklyn and explains all the kids there wanted to be a Grand Master. Mac prefers krunk.

Mr. François, the opponent in the contest who lost, smoked in the alley. He stepped in the blood. Mac and Aiden visit *Slick Vick Productions.* He had Banner on contract before the contest. His clients are 'hung-out' over the balcony to persuade them to sign with him.

Crime Scene Evidence

Banner was stabbed in the neck, but made it to the door. A tread pattern is also found. A shred of paper is found at the crime scene. Mac finds another bloodstained shred of paper. There's no blood from the neck, i.e. no arterial spray. So perhaps the weapon wasn't removed from his neck. He was stabbed on the fire escape and ended up on the ground. Three days before his murder a message was left on his voicemail, in the form of a vinyl scratching. The file in the toolbox at the club had blood on it. George Thomas, one of the workers has a record for assault; criminal possession of a weapon. Aiden takes photos of his palms. But he doesn't have a motive.

Mac and Aiden return to the crime scene. A shred of paper still hangs from the window. There's a shredder in the office and a bloody shirt in the toilet flush.

Conclusion

Banner's manager says his contract expired the day after the contest. But Banner had already signed with Vick three days previously. He didn't have the chance to explain he was forced into signing. He didn't betray him but was loyal. He wanted to protect Banner from the Vicks of the world. Mac: "In doing that, you became one of them yourself."

Story 2

Debra Gayle, a fashion designer is found dead at her apartment. Her P.A, Madison Haynes says she was dead when she found the body. She came to collect her last paycheque as she quit two weeks ago. Debra didn't have any friends, only acquaintances. Madison let herself in and rescued Debra from the pool. She was dead, called 911. But she tried to save her...

Sushi is served on naked women in the restaurant. Stella's heard of naked sushi parties but not restaurants. Fugue (blowfish) is only served to special clients at $500 a piece.

Crime Scene Evidence

Debra has an abrasion on her forehead. Broken nail by her body and PDA found in the swimming pool.

Returning to her apartment, Stella and Danny collect samples from her fridge, of water as well as other objects such as mouthwash. Danny finds Debra's spring line on the computer which was used two hours after her death.

Conclusion

Madison claims Debra was already dead when she took the designs. Stella says there must be another woman present: i.e. the woman on the table at the restaurant. Debra was one of her regulars. She used to work as an assistant and was fired for not sleeping with her. Debra requested her everytime she ate there. She's wearing socks now and put poison on her toes. She could've killed herself but doesn't regret doing it.

Notes

When Stella sent the nail to trace, along with the things from Debra's apartment, including her nail polish, wouldn't a check have been done for DNA from the nail to determine whether it was from the victim or not. Instead of matching her nail varnish to nail varnish. In which case, Madison could have been eliminated as a suspect.

Aiden misses the solitary blood spot on the shirt which was a vital clue. As did Stella when she knelt besides Debra's body and missed the nail.

As for the *CSI: NY Police Department* jackets, they were custom made for the show, since ordinarily, the jackets would just be marked *CSU. (Crime Scene Unit.)*

This episode was to air on October 20 but a repeat of *CSI* was shown in its place as CBS didn't want to run a new episode of this against Fox's *Major League Baseball's ALCS*

Disco Placid was also in an episode of *CSI: Crime Scene Investigation* titled, **Anonymous**, and was portrayed by the same actor. Also Aiden comments he moved from Las Vegas to New York.

The fashion storyline was used again in the season 5 episode, **5.11 Forbidden Fruit** when a designer is killed and the suspect uses one of her handbag designs as her own.

Quotes

Mac: "If you close your eyes, Aiden sounds like Queen Latifah."

Mac: "It's my job to know a little something about everything."

Danny: "That's just fine sweetheart, cause tox'll do the talking for you."

Danny: "Here we are looking for the murder at the table."
Stella: "Here the murderer is the table."

Most Pointless Line

Stella: "Doesn't this make you wish you would've gone to law school?" (er, no, and I did. Sorry.)

A Danny Moment

Stella: "Oh that can't be sanitary."
Danny: "Who cares if it's sanitary. I wanna see the menu."
Stella: "Are you gonna be able to focus?"
Danny: "I'm all over it." Yeah, all over the table, you mean. Clearly Danny has been living a sheltered life for too long!

CSI Déjà vu

In _CSI_ season 1 **Table Stakes** Catherine finds a red fingernail in the grass. _CSI season 1_ **Evaluation Day**, Warrick finds evidence of a red bloody T-shirt when he finds a prison toilet has stained red water.

Matching the knife or weapon used in a crime was shown in _CSI_ **$/35K O.B.O.** where the body part is boiled to determine the exact nature of the weapon used. Also done by Calleigh in _CSI:Miami_; when she had to find out which tools were used to cause injuries to the victim.

100

CSI season 5 episode **Mea Culpa,** the murder weapon is found in the tool box, possibly a wrench.

CSI:Miami season 2 episode **A Horrible Mind,** Speed puts together a shredded essay. In season **2.22 Rap Sheet** a rapper survives after being shot at in a nightclub. The investigation reveals another rapper claimed his song was stolen.

Music:

An Open letter to NYC (remix) by the Beastie Boys. *Pay Close* by Brother El. *Acetone* by The Crystal Method.

Ratings

12.98 million viewers. Rated #17 for the week.

Did You Know:

Carmine Giovinazzo is the first actor to appear in all three *CSI* shows as he guested in the season 3 episode of *CSI* entitled **Revenge is a Dish Best Served Cold** where he played a character called Thumpy G. As well as being in the *CSI:Miami/CSI:New York* cross-over episode **MIA/NYC – Nonstop,** the introductory episode to *CSI:NY*.

At least at this point in time he was, others have also gone on to guest in all three shows, including Brian Bloom.

1.5 A Man A Mile

Written by Andrew Lipsitz. Directed By David Grossman
US Airdate 5 November 2004
UK Terrestrial Airdate 5 March 2005

Guest Stars: Joe Riggs (Joe Sikora) Melissa (Shashawnee Hall) Matt (Joshua Leonard) Mike Pniewski (Tom Zito) Terry Kinney (DA

Tom Mitford)   Sarah Foret (Tina Paulson)   Mel Rodriguez (Al McGrath) Eric Ritter (Pete Riggs) Vince Donvito (Jeff Wesley)

Story 1

Background

Underground workers: The New York Sandhogs blow up a tunnel. One man was left behind; Pete Riggs and was discovered dead under rubble. He had worked ten years on site. The curtain contained the blast to the area. Sand Hogs are anyone who help build tunnels, because Pete wasn't down there with them, it didn't mean he wasn't one of them. The DA is on the scene and informing Mac and Danny that 1.3 billion gallons of water are used daily in New York. He wants the site cleared and running. The foreman tells them the Sandhogs are the only ones who build tunnels in New York City. He describes it an accident. A Sandhog measures progress by "a man a mile" because that's the death rate. Hence the episode title.

Mike didn't see Pete leave the tunnel. Joe, his brother calls it an accident. Danny gives him his card, if he wants to talk. The Sandhog Code is that 'every man comes out of the tunnel'. Al fought with Pete after work, the day before yesterday. He hit him because he insulted the Rangers. The ring they wear also matters.

Mac feels they're not lying but covering. It's not murder anymore, but a conspiracy. The foreman says he was careless. He's not responsible for Pete but for his men. Mac tells Danny, the Sandhogs are a union. They form a bond like the Marines. Pete was one of them. Danny feels Joe has to come clean. Joe was beaten outside Tunnel 3. No one saw who did it and he's returning to work. Danny thinks he was beaten to silence him and he's not talking. Mac tells him that unlike the Marines, or the NYPD, the Sandhogs don't have an investigative branch.

Crime Scene Evidence

Pete wasn't shot or stabbed before the explosion. There's trace under his fingernails, covered with a paper bag to preserve it. There was no inhaler. Danny finds blood on the tracks and on the walls of the tunnel. He was trying to find a phone. The inhaler is found near the phone, empty. The lift was manually operated. Danny suggests this wasn't an accident. Mac says Pete knew he was going to die alone.

Police Interrogation.

Pete dropped his keys down the tunnel and Tom Zito got hit in the head with them. He was changed by the blow he received and Flack points out his wife also has an Order of Protection against him. He bit Al.

Conclusion

Pete wasn't wearing the ring when he died. Using metal detectors, they find the ring. Mac explains the Sandhogs did their work for them. The explosion was to cover the evidence, not to preserve it. Joe broke their Code and left Pete down there to perhaps teach him a lesson. He threw the ring down after he pulled it forcibly from his finger, which hit him on his head. When they found the body, it looked like an accident caused by the explosion. Joe looked after Pete when he was growing up. This was the only job he'd ever find. He was his responsibility.

Story 2

Background

Stella and Aiden are called in to investigate a washed up body on a water creek. Aiden describes the victim as wearing a Maschera si dress and Mick Leoto shoes. She's approximately 16 years old. Her name is Hannah Rickie and her body is weighed. Her mother's from Bronx Dale and that's where she lived. She attended the prestigious Chase School for girls on the Upper East Side. Leaving home three nights ago for a friend's house to study, she never came back. Her friend is Melissa Westly but she never showed up.

Aiden tells the girls she went to a school like this too. Aiden didn't go to such a school, but says the girls cut through the attitude if they feel you're one of them. She also says that a uniform is a symbol of social equality. The clothes Hannah was wearing when she was found didn't have cut labels and were real designer labels.

Hannah and Tina went to England together with Tina's father. Matt denies Tina was at his club with Hannah. But it was crowded so he didn't see them, if they were here. The surveillance camera doesn't work. Warehouses surround the area, so they find some video footage. Hannah had a crush on Matt. Stella uses the restroom at Tina's house and spots a fox horn strap on the table. Hannah was blooded in the foxhunt.

Conclusion

Hannah was only Tina's friend and was never supposed to be part of her family. Tina was the one who took her travelling. Blooding was a tradition started by James I of England. The fox horn had blood on it. Her father chose Hannah for the honour of being blooded and not Tina. Tina strangled Hannah. She enjoyed watching the life ebb from her like that in an animal's eyes. This story was all about brothers and sisters, the Millers and they saw her as a potential sister. Everyone liked her except for her best friend.

Notes

The two stories are connected in that they're both about siblings and rivalries. In this case, Tina's brother had responsibility over her and she resorted to killing out of jealousy, because he wanted Hannah and chose her over Tina. She didn't want her best friend to be part of the family. Though it was obvious Tina had something to do with Hannah's death, since she was meant to be at her house but didn't seem overly concerned when she never showed up.

In the first story, Joe was responsible for Pete and chose to teach him a lesson, resulting in his death, which he subsequently covered up. So much for families and best friends.

They tie their hair only when they feel like it.

There's this whole connecting thing going on between Mac and Danny as he encourages him to find the evidence instead of looking for clues based on his instinct alone. Says Carmine, this episode, got "me into trouble. So I don't know if that spawned from early on, he [Danny] was that guy that had a very strong view of what he thought happened or what he thought was right. I don't know where it began, but it seems like I'm the guy if somebody's gonna disagree or somebody's gonna stir the pot…I think I've kind of been the writer's tool to be like, 'Okay, that's Danny.' There's going to be a certain level of conflict in certain ways that it just makes sense Danny's the guy to do that."

Surprisingly Stella and Aiden got a very easy case to solve not requiring the help of the others (like they have done so in the past.) You know, someone to point out the vital clue to them.

Carmine: "It's like shooting a movie every night. We have maybe one read through before a scene and it's straight into it. You have to be there and ready to perform. There's nothing glamorous about it. It's eight days a week, 12-16 hours a day. You do get days off but on them you're just working on your stuff for the next day. It's hard."

Quotes

Mac: "Are you bathophobic?"
Danny: "I'm not anything-phobic. Just a few things that shake me up and one of them is 700 feet of granite between me and daylight. I don't know how you guys work down here."
Mac: "Same way we're going to, rock by rock."

Danny: "Brother's got something to say."

Mac: "Based on?"
Danny: "I can just tell he knows something."
Mac: "Danny, you're intuition is great..."
Danny: "But let's see what the evidence has to say first, right?"

Danny: "Somebody had his ear Tyson-ed."

Mac: "We have pieces of evidence – there's nothing conclusive yet."
Danny: "Well, if the evidence isn't talking we gotta fill in the blanks somehow."

Hawkes: "Possibly inconsistent without context." This had a nice ring to it. (No pun!) I.e. the broken finger would not have been relevant if it wasn't for the presence of the missing ring.

Stella: "Noblesse oblige." The haves act nobly for the have nots, until they usurp their position..." thought we were back in the days of the *Scarlett Pimpernel*. Noblesse oblige. Loosely translated meaning, 'noble obligation.'

Most Pointless Line

Stella: (to Aiden) "Easy for you, maybe not so easy for Hannah."

A Danny Moment

Danny: "In my world, a guy's gotta protect himself and his family. I mean who would you back, your brother or some union?" (Relevant for Danny in season 2 when his brother Louie, hits the scene and also in season 5 when he says he'd do the same thing as the killer to protect his sister.)

A Mac & Danny Moment

Mac: "...pieces of evidence."
Danny: "Yeah, you made that clear. I just don't see your point."

106

Mac: "My point is you're not seeing the connection. It's what we all look for."

Danny: "Yeah, but don't you ever just feel it?"

Mac: "All the time. But I don't act on it until I can prove something."

Danny: "I can't do this job your way."

Mac: "Well, you can't do it yours either. You're coming up on your three years. That means you'll be taking your exam to bump you up to Second Grade. When I put you lead in a case, I wanna make sure you're bringing me evidence. Not intuition." (See next episode.)

Though a good reply to Mac when he mentioned not being able to rely on feelings, would have been, "you can't let the evidence cloud your judgement." Since evidence can be wrong, contaminated, planted etc.

CSI: Déjà vu

In the CSI pilot, Nick and Warrick bet on who will solve their one hundredth case – thus leading to promotion as CSI 3. Here Danny needs to take an exam for promotion. Also, in CSI episode **1.3 Crate 'n' Burial** Gil tells Nick he has to work harder before they can arrest one of the main suspects and Nick wonders what he did wrong. Though Warrick is Gil's favourite and to Nick he's more of a mentor – striving and pushing him to deliver his best.

Here Mac tells Danny something along similar lines, in that he needs to concentrate on finding the evidence and can't just concentrate on instinct to lead him to clues.

Andrew Lipsitz commented on the season 1 CSI episode **Sounds of Silence,** "You can't bring your own conclusions and biases to a case. You have to evaluate the evidence and follow what it's telling you, reiterate CSIs operative credo."

In *CSI* season 3 episode **Lucky Strike,** a DB with a bullet hole in the chest was buried under rocks in a mine. The murderer was trying to hide the body and detonated explosives.

1.6 Outside Man

Written By Timothy J Lea Directed By Rob Bailey
US Airdate 10 November 2004
UK Airdate 12 March 2005

Guest Stars: Patrick Bauchau (Dr Willems) Paul Perri (Joe Garfor Kristen Shaw (Deidre Hertzberg) Michael B Silver (EMT) Greg Davis Jnr (Terrell Davenport) De'angelo Wilson (Lamar Adams) David Barrera (Jose Figgueroa) Laurence N Kaldor (Frank Hertzberg)

Story 1

Background

People with plastic bags over their heads beg for their lives before being shot. One survives. Two are dead in the basement, two more; Octavia Figuroa and Teryl Davenport are found upstairs. There's one behind the counter. Danny tells Flack to get the paramedics to preserve the duct tape and bag their hands as well as use gloves. Flack tells him the door was unlocked and the uniforms had to break it. There are two bodies near the counter. The back door to the alley was open and the alarm wasn't set. The diner closed at 11pm. Mac leaves Danny in charge. There's a dumpster upstairs and downstairs. Danny and Aiden process the scene together, double check each other and then move out from the center.

Aiden says Flack identified the waitress as Gina Robeson, the cook was Jared Perkins.

Aiden thinks the shooter needed to be cool. Octavia was putting away the night deposit and planning a trip to Glenmont, near Albany.

He took their wallets, jewellery, from the dead, so it was a robbery but Aiden asks why they were killed? Aidan calls Teryl a hero.

There was a spoon under Octavia's desk with heroin and Jared was a known user. He spent three and a half years in Fishkill for armed robbery.

Octavia dies at the hospital and is visited by her children and her brother. Teryl says he didn't see anything. His print was on the tape because the shooter made him tape the others first and then himself. The man at the hospital in the car was Luis. They are his children. Jose says Octavia let him in before she locked up last night and the back door was open. Teryl has never seen Jose before.

Danny's back at square one regarding the sequence of events and so has to move forward by going back.

The search for the duct tape results in five auto shops using the same duct tape and muffler tape. One is owned by Luis. It's the same car he was driving at the hospital. Danny examines the car and finds a duct tape imprint in the boot on blue carpet. Tyre fibres were from the carpet in the car. Flack says he took it as "informed consent" from Luis and searched his apartment. But found nothing. Danny needs to look at the dumpster from the auto shop.

Crime Scene Evidence

Danny describes the gun as a .32 caliber Magnum, there were no extractor marks and no rim, so the shooter used the revolver and fired five shots. The plastic bags on the victims were identical so Danny deduces the shooter didn't bring any with him. No duct tape was present either so the shooter was aware of the bags beforehand so he just brought what he needed. Danny comments he was cool enough to reload and careless to leave behind casings. So Danny thinks it's an inside job.

Danny finds a single medium shot to the back of the victim in the kitchen, no powder burns, contact head wound, muzzle stamp and burns to the temple. There's misting spatter on the oven so he was shot here. There's blood on the phone where Teryl called 911. A smear pattern, two parallel trails. Teryl was shot in the head, he carried Octavia upstairs and called for help.

Syringes are found in the dumpster.

Lemar was there but didn't see anything. He also wears a blue wristband.

Secondary Crime Scene Evidence

Danny finds a plastic bag in the trash at the garage.

Conclusion

Danny tells Luis he used flowers to get into the diner, there was pollen on the glass door and Gina let him in. He forced Octavia to call everyone downstairs. Najiv ran and was shot in the back. He shot them all. He took the bag from the shop and tried to make it look like a robbery. Aiden tells him Octavia was taking his children to Albany. Danny says it's not easy to shot someone looking into their eyes so he put bags over their heads. Danny looks at the photos of the victims in the lab. Mac looks at his work and has read his preliminary report.

Story 2

Background

A leg is found in an alley. Mac says the lower leg is 15% of the entire body's weight. The serial number identifies the leg as belonging to Frank Herzberg. The surgery was carried out by a doctor who says his gun went off when he was cleaning it. A lesser surgeon would have amputated it. He saw Frank several months ago. Stella and Mac find Frank dead in his apartment. Mac says they've found the other 85% of him. The paramedic talks to one of the police at the scene.

Joe tells them Frank was oppressed by his leg. He wasn't complete until he had it removed. Frank wanted to keep Joe's

110

finger. They're called "wannabees" as they wish they were amputees. To this end some of them have surgery. Frank's wife was visiting in Connecticut. There's a photo of Frank on his honeymoon without his leg, she says that's his version. He was planning on doing this all along. Joe came up with new ideas to remove his leg, such as drilling, cutting, freezing it in dry ice. His condition is known as apitimnalphillia, i.e. Body Integrity Identity Disorder. They hate a part of their body they think is causing them problems. His wife doesn't want to collect his body.

Stella finds the doctor has a history of removing limbs in Holland. He had medication from his leg surgery and the doctor tells them he won't risk his career for Frank. Drugs are stolen from the hospital everyday.

Possible Crime Scene Evidence

Mac says putrefaction shows he was dead about 24 hours ago as gangrene speeds up decomposition. He knew he was dying. Tetracycline pills are found. Luminol reveals the stain on the floor to be blood. He leg was amputated here. Frank was married and a file of people with missing limbs in photos is also found. Stella finds a finger in the fridge and a print on the fusebox at Frank's apartment.

Conclusion

The paramedic is questioned as the print matches him. The clocks all stopped at 10.45. Mac says all the clocks were wrong by the same time as there was a power failure. He carried out the surgery on Frank and had to finish with a handsaw. He took his gloves off and left his print. Frank begged him to do it and he needed the money, $10,000. He's a pre-med student. He responded to the call when Frank shot himself. Mac wonders what happened to the Hippocratic Oath.

Notes

A very 'procedural' episode, if one can use the term. With some nice continuity following on from episode 5 when Mac lectures Danny about needing evidence to prove the facts/crime. As that's exactly what Danny does in this episode when he's made lead on the case. Starting out routinely in a set pattern, then going back on it when the first set of evidence doesn't pan out; until finally going full circle (at least 180) and beginning with the 'outside in.' Also a good episode to demonstrate how a crime scene investigation would be conducted examining all the variables and clues, gathering evidence and taking it to its logical conclusion. (At least a TV investigation.)

In contrast, in the *CSI* episode **Overload** where it's said they need to break their own rules at times, so they begin with a conclusion and then go back. Just like making the evidence fit their theory. Something which H has commented on and should not be done! Though to be fair here, Danny did say they need to work backwards.

There are lots of tell-tale signs and clues in this episode in both stories. From the shooting and the evidence found, such as the flowers, disregarded until later, the blue fibres, the palm prints etc, giving enough suspects. In the second story, the most obvious clue was in the clock as Mac points out. Also the presence of the paramedic on the scene, curiosity getting the better of him.

Mac was obviously proud of the way Danny handled the investigation – confirming a right step towards promotion.

However much this episode was 'procedural' it was also more emotional. Especially the first story, but Danny keeps a cool head under pressure and doesn't let his feelings show until the end of the episode, after solving the crime and only to Mac. A very big character motivation for those who argue that any of the *CSI* shows aren't about or involve characterization. On the other hand there were always many a funny comment made by Danny, Mac, Aiden and Stella to ensure the episode wasn't all doom and gloom. Even if some of the jokes were uncalled for.

Also perhaps a first for a *CSI* show to handle a story which very much contains a real condition – re people who can't live with their whole body intact.

As well as clues throughout the episode there is almost always one in the title which is a big giveaway, i.e. **Outside Man** - Luis was on the outside of the diner looking in: not ascertained until another approach was developed.

Keeping to tradition there were several references to garbage, which held the final piece of evidence (proving that trash is not collected very often in New York.) Aiden and Danny were on garbage detail again as Danny stated, like they were in episode **1. Blink.**

The vital question in this episode for both stories was WHY? More so than How?

Carmine: "We went to the morgue in NYC which I couldn't stomach. It was horrible. We were in the basement where they put a mask over your face because of the smell and you're in with the corpses. We were shown parts of bodies. It's a job I just couldn't do."

On Danny, Carmine comments: "I like the first time he showed some emotion, when they found a bunch of people in a diner. When he got lost in life and how he felt about it and how people just die and people murder people and are just gone. That was a nice episode. Early on, too, we were all kind of innocent. It was sort of a moment with Mac with him coming in and just observing me and letting me be in that place. He was actually okay with me in that kind of place and he kind of got that, that reflection on the real fact of what was going on around us as opposed to being always stoic and always unaffected by it and obviously; in reality, this much doesn't really happen in the way that it does and they all have their own way of [dealing]. I don't know how close detectives get on their investigations]. Of course they do, but how they keep it together is something I'll never know. My father tells me things and my sister and brother-in-law and I don't know how they would actually keep it together seeing all that stuff and being through all that nasty crap and I think that's why I like the end of [this episode]. It's a [revealing] moment. I don't know how often these cats expose themselves and talk about it because that's not what you do because you kind of just have to deal with it. I think that's another thing about Danny – he cries about or he thinks about it or he brings it up when you might not necessarily talk about that stuff."

On the DVD commentary for this episode it's stated they wanted to personalize the show, identifying where, how the crime happens.

In the scene where Aiden smiles, using CGI, they slowed down her smile and stretched it out, as they wanted it to last longer than the amount of time Aiden actually smiled for when she looks at Danny. Also I noticed Aiden's lipstick is more glossy and later becomes matt. Aiden and Danny's scene in the diner was shot at 1am. In the scene when Danny and Aiden are in the lab analyzing the duct tape evidence, the tape got stuck to Vanessa's gloves and she couldn't get it off.

Anthony Zuiker wanted to demonstrate how the evidence follows on from scene to scene. Also how doctors in some countries will actually perform such operations, it's an ethical question to them. These procedures can be carried out in places like Mexico. It's an ethical question since it's viewed as better if they want to lose a hand, they can cut it off and are allowed to do this; or should the law prevent them from doing this. The actual sawing off of the limb was too gory to be left in the scene and had to be lessened.

Bill Haynes is the resident CSI on the show, a police consultant, working on such things as how to take evidence procedurally, brushing powder for prints etc.

The scene with Mac and Stella finding the DB was shot in LA and the bridge was later CGI added, to provide the feel of New York.

When Danny says "nice" this was added in by Carmine himself.

This is one of his favourite episodes. Says Carmine, "Vanessa and I handled the murders in the café – it was our first lead on a case and I remember it being a difficult shoot but worth it and definitely the one where I shoot the cop." (Episode **1.21**.)
Michael B Silver went on to guest star in *CSI Miami* as an FBI agent and potential love interest of Calleigh.

Quotes

Danny: "Sounds like an inside job."
Mac: "Then that's where we'll start. Danny you're in charge. You're three years in, promotion to second grade doesn't come easy."

Aiden: "Why bag the heads at all?"
Danny: "I'd stick to the how...how come they all got shot?"

Danny: "One's a fluke, two's a pattern, three's a suspect."
Aiden: "You think we got enough experience going through other peoples' garbage?"
Danny: "Notice how we always get put on trash detail."
Aiden: "When you make it to second grade, it'll be a thing of the past, my friend."
Danny: "From your lips to God's ear."
Danny: "Next time I say 'keys are in the garbage' remind me of this moment."

Stella: "This place gives a whole new meaning to the term chop shop."

A Danny Moment

Danny: "I can't wrap my head around it Mac. I mean you get up, go to work, you see the people that you know. You talk, you laugh. You're living your life and then suddenly, boom – it's just over. Just like that. You never saw it coming..." Danny can't change the world or people and that's the reality of the real world. There's Danny's 'boom' being mentioned. He goes on to use this in subsequent seasons as an expression of finding the solution or the right answer, akin to "Eureka."

A Mac and Danny Moment

Mac: "Good job Danny. You're on the promotion grid." (Until things go horribly awry for him. See **1.21 On The Job**.)

CSI Déjà Vu

Also in this episode Danny talks to himself whilst working through the evidence analysis. This was done for the first time in *CSI*, episode **7 Formalities**. When Gil tried this out after he heard Sofia.

Danny mentioning how rather than 'why' and 'vice versa' was also mentioned by Nick and Catherine in the *CSI* episode **Pledging Mr Johnson** where fishermen caught an amputated severed leg. They didn't ascertain whether the body was alive or dead when the leg was amputated as they did in *CSI*. Here the amputation was delved into further to reveal the disease/condition afflicting such people. Also in this episode Danny said a line similar to Gil about how the crime was carried out, see the episode **Friends & Lovers**.

CSI:Miami season 1 episode **Breathless** a syringe was found in a garbage bag with a fingerprint.
In the season 1 *CSI:Miami* episode **Ashes to Ashes,** a computer simulation of the shooting was carried out.

The season 2 *CSI* episode, **Burked** Sara and Warrick have a positive match from a roll of duct tape found in the suspect's truck to a piece that was found in the trash; and there's also a reference to fibres.

In the season 2 *CSI:Miami* episode **Death Grip** a smudge from a nose/forehead was found on the window. Also in the season 3 episode **Hell Night** a face print from a glass door had sebaceous oil which was used to trace the skin cells to the suspect.

Mac and the Hippocratic oath seen in *CSI episode* **Primum Non Nocere**....when it was given its Latin name in the title and provided a vital clue to the killer in that episode, i.e that he was a doctor.

Also see the pilot episode of *CSI* where Nick and Warrick bet on who will solve their 100th case – thus leading to promotion as CSI 3.

CSI episode **Sounds of silence** in which Nick and Catherine investigate a coffee shop shooting and laser-string the scene to check for bullet trajectory. Catherine using the laptop finds a ricochet mark by the door, showing another shot was fired. Similar to Danny stringing with a laser in this episode.

In the *CSI episode* **Evaluation Day** Nick questions Gil as to why he can't work alone and here Mac gives Danny the responsibility of working lead on an important case.

CSI:Miami episode 1 season 2 **Blood Brothers**, Speed mentions that trace evidence is important and then turns around and questions the importance of forensics, if no one can be brought to justice by the forensics they collect, process and analyze. H explains to him at the end of the episode what this job is all about, viz, what 'forensics' is all about: closure for the family of the victim, justice and comeuppance for criminals.

Did You Know

CBS had to re run this episode again on November 12th 2004, since CBS on the East Coast omitted the final five minutes of this episode to air their *Breaking News* piece on the death of Yasser Arafat. Due to complaints the network had to show the episode again. Yeah and they missed out the best and crucial five minutes of the episode!

Ratings

15.379 million viewers. Rated #13 for the week.

7. Rain

Written By Pam Veasey Directed By David Grossman
US Airdate 17 November 2004
UK Airdate 19 March 2005

Guest Stars: Samantha Quan (Joanne Cho) Matt Bushell (Marvin Hummel) Alex Sol (Luther Willett) Kym Hoy (Nina Chang) Mark Kelly (Rob Bloom) Andre Ware (Tony Fenn) David Guzzone (Kevin Moretti)

Background

A burning man runs out of a building in Chinatown in the rain. Mac notices his eyebrows and eyelashes are singed. Bruising on his cheek, his face doesn't have the same degree of burns as his other body areas such as his chest. His hairline behind his ear and above his collar line has traces of melted plastic. Mac finds a discarded plastic mask. They were inside the bank vault and cut the safe deposit vault from the wall. Two bank security guards fired shots and the acetylene tank caught fire. One of the security guards, Mark Hummell thinks there were two robbers but he was trying to save his partner's life. A bank worker said the systems weren't connected to the fire department. Mac takes Hummell's gun.

Six months ago the bank was a shoe store, there's no security and stainless steel sheeting. Mac says they cut through the wall. Aiden comments they came in through the empty store. Stella says they wouldn't have entered until after 8.30 when the alarm was switched off. So they had 30 minutes to rob the vault. Mac thinks the security guard disrupted their plans so they had to get out the way they got in. Danny says the first one out knocked the tank. Aiden wonders why they didn't take all the boxes from the same area. Stella agrees, as they took the numbers 38, 58, 28. Mac comments on the lucky number 8 in the Chinese culture, they thought their money would be safe in boxes with an 8. Danny asks why boxes 12, 14, 45 were also opened?

The leasing agent for the empty store got a letter from the owner a week ago saying he didn't want the building rented out. No one duplicated the door key. Mac notices a hole in the door and finds an umbrella shell outside. This was used to break in with.

Since there were over $10,000 in every box. They had to have known what was in the boxes. Joanne keeps the keys. She recognizes the monkey as belonging to her daughter, she's eleven months old. Stella comments on how it took her a while to work out what they were when she first saw them. She doesn't know the robber. Mac says 2004 is the Chinese year of the monkey. A young, female child would be given this for prosperity and good fortune. The charm wasn't taken from the vault but was brought in. Doris was kidnapped and this was proof.

The bank robbery becomes a kidnapping. Joanne was sent a letter with the missing letter 'X'. She said all the robbers looked the same. Flack finds the phone number is a payphone near Madison Square Gardens. The ransom note was left at Joanne's neighbour's mailbox.

Hummel heard the shot and fired. Flack stipulates the first shot from the robber's gun hit Tony. He wasn't there when it happened. Hummel fired at someone he saw through the smoke. Joanne wants to pay the ransom.

Flack can't stop her as the NYPD has to respect her wishes. Stella places the money in the newspaper stand and they wait. A man approaches the newsstand and runs away when he hears sirens. It's a Police Terrorist Response Drill. The money is still inside and there's a mask on the ground. Mac dusts the newsstand for prints.

The message on the notepad was written by Nina Chang she worked on the play. A bag is also found in Nina's apartment. She made the masks. Mac asks her to write the Pledge of Allegiance.

Crime Scene Evidence

Stella finds a blood trail leading to the alley, which means there were three. The trail ends outside the bank and was washed away by the rain. Another mask is found inside. Mac retrieves a bullet from the wall.

Secondary Crime Scene Evidence

There's a hole in the theatre door just like the empty building. Inside is a dead body. Nearby are small handprints in blood. Stella finds hair on the body. Mac tests the paper as positive for cocaine. There's a missing letter 'X' inside the magazine cover. The dead man is Kevin Moretti; he was in jail with Luther. Mac thinks they'll have a possible homicide in six hours.

Conclusion

Hummel shouldn't have fired his gun. Mac tells him this was planned to the smallest detail. Hummel says he tried to stop them. Mac comments he didn't shoot at anything, his casing was found outside the vault. He could have been a hero and returned the baby and no one would have known.

Notes

There were a lot of firsts in this episode too, the first time a bank robbery was featured, the first time Flack got a bigger role. Mac mentions the number 8 being lucky in the Chinese culture and Five (the channel which airs the show in the UK) screened the HSBC ad coincidentally during the ad break about the Chinese lucky number 8. Also did you notice an HSBC ad in the stock footage of New York in this episode too. Cf Scully re Chinese culture, in the *X-Files* season 3 episode **Hell Money** Chinese mythology and numbers were also delved into where burning specially printed paper money was offered to the spirit world for good luck.

Mac's comment about *Six Degrees of Separation*. A play, which states all the people in the world are connected by no more than six people. It's only one degree to be connected to the victim.

An unanswered question, what about locker numbers 12, 45, why were they opened too? Stella was aloof in this episode too and didn't answer Joanne's question about where her baby was. In contrast to Gil or Horatio from the other shows who would have answered and not evaded, even promising to do all they could to get her baby back.

Danny goes all out to catch the suspect at the end of the episode, as he does again in other episodes. Mac asks Flack if he believes the agent's story in the beginning and Flack asks Danny the same thing; if he believes Hummel's story. Flack's use of "boom" in this episode must've rubbed off from Danny in the previous episode, also it became his catchphrase in later seasons. (Flack comes into his own in **1.17 The Fall** whereas in these earlier episodes he doesn't get to do much.)

Danny moving forward from the last episode after Mac tells him to go with the evidence rather than his instinct. Good continuity here.

Stella tells Joanne the first time she saw the charms she didn't know what they were, well she's not exactly Chinese is she. Oh wow, something Stella's not up on. Must be a first for her too! Obviously Joanne'd know what the charms meant, she's Chinese.

Aiden moulds a mask this time.
The letter reads:
At 3pm TODAY
Call 212 555 1045
PUNCH IN THE
2 DIGIT # S of
the $ SAFE DEPOSIT
BOXES

WE HAVE YOUR CHILD

The second ransom note reads:

Release in unmarked bills

Two hundred thousand dollars
4:00
The New York Bystander

Newsstand, South east Corner
Of Central park

Again there's a clue in the title, or rather this time, the title tells you what the episode is about or the reason the bank robbery was foiled.

In a bank vault episode of *Doomwatch* a man in an astronaut suit staggers onto a London street on a hot day. A gang of bank robbers were using liquid nitrogen to cut through a vault, but his spacesuit seal broke. Similar to this episode.

How pathetic was Stella asking Flack if he knew about the terrorist drill, like duh, there're really going to publicize it! Like the fire drills at school and in the workplace, no one told you it was going to happen, otherwise if you knew it was just a drill; you'd just saunter out at your leisure and maybe not even bother to move at all.

The Police terrorist response drill was real and the scenes with Eddie and Melina were added later on, as the background clearly looks like it's a studio street when Stella walks up to the newsstand.

Also in the season 4 finale, **Hostage** there was another bank raid, only this time there were hostages and Mac was involved.

The man Flack and Aiden question when he tells Flack he's pretty too, well what would you say to Flack, me, it'd be something along the lines of "Cuff me, cuff me once, then cuff me again." On second thoughts that sounds a bit rude!

In **1.21 On The Job** Danny's laser stringing for determining the trajectory of the bullet will come back to haunt him, as something similar happens to him. His fate, job and his promotion all depend on one bullet.

When Danny uses the lasers in the scene to work out where the guard was positioned when he fired, Eddie was completely blown away with the forensics; "I think forensic science is absolutely amazing – applied in the real world where oftentimes it can disprove the story of someone who may otherwise have gotten off. I like when science traces pieces of a body to a person, when science can recreate a situation almost exactly. What an asset to law enforcement and what an asset to us citizens, to know there's that ability...we as human beings have a great respect for human life." I.e. that any case can be solved – even cold cases."

Quotes

Stella: "There's something gooey here."
Mac: "Gooey, that's a good forensic word. Gooey, I'll have to use that more."

Flack: "Gotta wear a mask for a bank robbery. It's a rule."

Danny: "Ballistics is gonna be fun on this one." And he gets the task of checking ballistics.

Danny: "I got this stuff on the front of my dishwasher." (Did you notice a dishwasher in his apartment in season 3 and later on? No, neither did I.)

Flack: "You know me; everybody's a suspect 'til you prove otherwise."

Luther: "Wow cops around here just get prettier everyday."

Flack: "Watch it."

Luther: "Hey don't get upset. I just got out of prison; you both look good to me. (Showing even suspects can be funny on a *CSI* show. Though yes, Flack could be described as 'pretty', pretty handsome that is!!)

Mac: "Some sort of gooey residue on the top of the piece of paper."

Stella: "Great choice of words."

Mac: "It's always something, something you didn't expect or count on. Something that always screws everything up...if only it hadn't rained."

Most Pointless Line

Stella: "Did you know about this?"

Flack: "They don't send out a memo."

A Danny Moment

Danny: "Yeah, I do [believe him] but then there's the evidence." (And that never lies. Sorry me being sarcastic here!)

CSI Déjà Vu

CSI season 3 episode 3 **Inside the Box** featured a bank robbery albeit with different motives for robbing the bank. Danny Cannon commented; "I just love the way vaults and safes look and it was more interesting to me that, instead of robbing the bank and taking money, they go for a safe-deposit box." In the same way the robbers in this episode didn't wait to rob the bank when it opened but went for safety deposit boxes — the twist being, they all contained the number 8.

CSI:Miami episode **Crime Wave** also involved a bank robbery with a difference, taking place during a tsunami.

CSI episode **Friends & Lovers** Catherine and Nick string the room to trace blood spatter. Here Danny used lasers to determine the trajectory of the bullets. Then used a computer schematic showing the guard's bullet shouldn't have been where it was and so proved he was lying. Lasers are also used for this in *CSI-Miami* and in the season 2 episode **Witness to Murder.** The bullet trajectory showed where the victim was shot from.

CSI *episode* **$35k O.B.O.** had the team gathering evidence before the rain washed it away. Gil: "Three minutes to process the scene. After that, we lose it all to the gutters." Here they did lose it all.

CSI season 3 episode **Let the Seller Beware** mentions the play *Six Degrees of Separation* where everyone in the world is connected by 6 people. "To connect you to the victim is one degree."
CSI season 4 **Invisible Evidence** Nick reassures Rachel's sister that they're doing everything they can to find the suspect but he's not making any promises. Here Stella does and says nothing to reassure the worried mother that her kidnapped baby will be found.

CSI:Miami episode **2.12 Witness to Murder** about a diamond broker, rain clouds are around so they had to hold off processing trace until they got to the lab.

Did You Know

The producers and cast actually got to film scenes during an authentic terrorist alert drill when filming on location in New York. The crew were also caught in a real storm close to Central Park as was Melina. This drill let producers come up with new scenes and use them in the episode. Seen in the opening credits with the police cars, sirens flashing.

Ratings

17.462 million viewers. Rated #10 for the week.

1.8 Three Generations Are Enough

Written By Andrew Lipsitz Directed By Alex Zakrzweski
US Airdate 24 November 2004
UK Airdate 26 March 2005

Guest Stars: Sonya Walger (Jane) Peter O'Meara (Paul Stryzweski)
Steven Flynn (Luke Sutton) Tom Bresnan (Nick Lawson) Larry Clarke
(Father Tim Murphy) Sarah Aldrich (Emily Dent)

Story 1

Background

Security finds an unidentified briefcase at the Stock Exchange. Everyone is evacuated and Mac sends in a robot. There may be a bomb. X-rays show traces of nitrates. Mac has sixty seconds to get prints from the case and then disarm. The case is safely blown up and Mac finds a message inside: *INCASE SOMETHING HAPPENS TO ME.* Mac gives Danny a DNA sample to search on CODIS and look at the financial data. Danny knows how to work a spreadsheet.

Prints aren't on AFIS but are from the New York Mercantile Stock Exchange; belonging to Luke Sutton who is unaccounted for. They search his apartment and find it trashed. Aiden suspects kidnapping. Mac tells her if a single man is taken in a foreign country the kidnappers demand a ransom but in New York who knows. If he was kidnapped why did his briefcase end up at the Stock Exchange?

Luke was tracking the illegal trading of Nick Lawson. He explains that the New York Mercantile "works in an open outcry system". Sellers offer their products to all. Lawson prearranged trading through local and independent traders selling at below market price. The local trader sells it at an instant profit and the difference is split with Lawson. Regular trades from the Mercantile floor appear normal unless a pattern is found in trading: every Lawson trade was proceeded by a local trade. If caught, this can result in expulsion from the Exchange and loss of career.

Lawson met with Luke two nights ago. Danny already knows Lawson is trading illegally but he won't provide a DNA sample to eliminate him from the blood found in the case.

Luke said Charles was a lawyer.
A car is found registered to Luke. There's a burnt body inside the car.
Luke was Emily's boyfriend, he made her get the gun. He told her Charles had people watching him and she thought Charles was a dealer.

The parking ticket shows where they met. Aiden asks if this is the right place. The ticket had the name and the e-mail said 'Ridgeway'. They find money and Aiden finds a half empty can. Spent casings are also found.
Mac thinks the bullet reloader and gun powder could explain the traces of nitrates outside the case. Danny comments he could buy new rounds with the money he had.

Possible Crime Scene

Mac finds metal shavings and a degausser: a magnet used to erase electronic information and finds papers on the hard drive concerning a Supreme Court decision from the case of *Buck v Bell 274 US 2 274 200 April 27 1927*. Flack wonders why his apartment was wrecked if they knew what they were looking for?

Crime Scene Evidence

The team goes over the evidence so far: traces of cocaine on the case; Emily thought Charles was a dealer. Danny believes it makes more sense if Charles was a dealer because there's no connection to a lawyer named Charles. The New York Mercantile Compliance Department already has a case against Lawson. Then there's the registered gun. Danny will look at the trace evidence and the missing hard drive. Mac says whoever left it behind thought that the fire would destroy it. The temperature needs to be over 700 degrees to melt it. Mac examines the hard drive.

Story 2

Background

A dead woman is found outside a church. Stella examines her in situ and finds no gunshot wounds, stabbing or bruising. Her name is Katrina Roylston and she's a Catholic. She was a counsellor at the church and was found by a handyman patching up the roof. The priest says there was no suicide note and Trina (for short) wasn't married. She worked late at the church.

Father Murphy admits his prints would be on the candlestick as he fixed it. The lines in the letter are from a WB Yeats poem.
Paul admits to kissing Trina and gets angry.

Crime Scene Evidence

Cigarette stubs are found next to her on the ground. Stella estimates the height: 5 stories – 20 metres. There are no signs of struggle or disturbance and no letter except a rosary. Stella concludes it's not suicide. She jumped off the front and not the side and landed on the pavement and not the grass.

Possible Crime Scene Evidence

At the church Stella finds a candlestick and fibres stuck to its base. Also a typed letter in a Prayer book. The name inside reads: Father Tim Murphy.

Conclusion

Mac looks through the evidence boxes and finds the case reference. The opinion of Oliver Wendell Holmes in the *Buck v Bell* case. Luke had a schizophrenic breakdown. The DNA shows they were both brothers. Mac says Charles couldn't be found because he doesn't exist. There were no incoming messages. The partial print on the candlestick belonged to Luke. Luke was in a delusional state and susceptible to Charles's voice. He took Trina to the roof. Danny says the roof was repaired with a substance containing petroleum distillate, including toluene; therefore the accelerant pattern was on the bottom of Luke's shoes. He threw her over. He meets Paul at the Ridgeway Shipping Company and heard Charles telling him to do something. Luke was a third generation schizophrenic and Trina was going to have the fourth.

Paul admits her pregnancy was an accident. The letter wasn't his as he doesn't like Yeats but James Joyce. Mac said Luke went back to the apartment and attempted to destroy everything. He used the glass from the TV to try to erase the serial number. He thought of shooting himself until the message from Charles altered. Paul said Luke left home at 18 but he wasn't strong like Paul.

Notes

A first where separate cases have become one for the team. Notice how the name Nick Lawson of the illegal trader here was similar to Nick Leeson the actual rogue trader at Barings Bank.

The part where Paul 'turned' the tables on Flack and Stella was an unintentional funny moment.

Paul reads James Joyce, Eddie Cahill also reads him too as he mentions in a later interview from 2007.

Also Danny had his question about why there was only one bullet in the gun answered, as questions are sometimes left unanswered in some episodes.

Stella undertook yet more quoting, this time from the Bible.

Anyone who knows the actual case of *Buck v Bell* would have known what this episode was about from the outset. Yet again the episode title provided the clue, for those who didn't and it also popped up about a third of the way through the episode on the computer screen when Mac was examining the hard drive.

The first e-mail reads: *I am aware of your illegal trading pattern – Charles has given me a week to deal with this.*

The e-mail reads: From: Luke Sutton@servicesix.com
To: Charles.Langdon@ctxmail.com *"per your message I will deliver $35,000 at Ridgeway, but this will be my last payment. If you persist I will have no choice but to involve the police.*

So they find out Charles last name was possibly Langdon. If he was a lawyer then the ABA (American Bar Association) would easily have told them if there was such a person or not. As he would have needed a licence to practice law.

The WB Yeats poem reads:
Hearts are not had as a gift but hearts are earned or by those that are not entirely beautiful.

Buck v Bell

The Commonwealth of Virginia in 1924 passed a statute which permitted it to sterilize by force, some particular males with mental problems, so to improve the welfare of the patient and society. In this case, Carrie Buck – plaintiff – did not want this to happen to her. Holmes J begged to differ, along with other justices on the Supreme Court. He described her as being "feeble minded – daughter of a feeble minded mother and ...the mother of an illegitimate, feeble minded child." The three generations are enough.

The decision in *Buck v Bell*: *"...affirming mandatory sterilization of people once referred to as socially inadequate individuals. It is better for all the world instead of waiting to execute degenerate offspring of a crime, were to let them starve for their imbecilities, society can prevent those who are manifestly unfit from continuing their kind. Three generations of imbeciles are enough."*

Dr Albert Sidney Priddy, Superintendent for the Virginia State Colony of Epileptics and Feeble-Minded was the prosecuting counsel. The case was taken over by Dr James Hendren Bell when Priddy died. Hence the 'Bell' in the title.

More recently it has been argued that Carrie Buck was not feeble-minded but was used as a scapegoat to maintain the family reputation, as she was raped by her adoptive mother's nephew. She also had a useless lawyer. This on the lawyer's part was deliberate since he had connections to the institutions lawyer, Priddy, and was part of the governing board of the state institution.

This case was the subject of a TV drama in 1994, *Against Her Will: The Carrie Buck Story* with Marlee Maitlin, Melissa Gilbert and Peter Frechette.

Not only a harsh decision but showing society and the law as it stood in the early twentieth century: that prevention was better than cure and was one of many radical Supreme Court decisions during that period in US legal history. Other more monumental decisions included *Rowe v Wade*. (The abortion case.)

This episode actually answered some of the questions posed during the investigation: such as Danny asking why Luke had one bullet in the gun; answer: because he was going to kill himself with it. Aiden asking why he had the gun and didn't use it; answer: because he was in the car alone.

Issues of work and church were involved in this too for Mac and Stella and how it affects their work. Mac goes to church sometimes. Is it because he lost his wife or for other reasons. As opposed to religion per se.

They don't wear their CSI jackets anymore, but wear bullet-proof vests when apprehending suspects.

Carmine said this episode, "Threw me for a loop when that came out at the end – that disease [schizophrenia] that was kind of a factor behind what was going on...every episode has some sort of interesting way of committing a crime that's always unusual."

Quotes

Mac: "Fear tends to trump logic."

Mac: "Forgiveness isn't part of our job."   (See later episodes for a rebuttal, oh, okay, a u-turn on this.)

Mac: "I got the money."
Danny: "I got the money too."
Aiden: "I'm in."

Flack: "Suicide's a sin."
Stella: "It's viewed as an attempt against the dominion and rights of ownership of the Creator." Catholic Encyclopedia. (Oh here we go again, more 'know it all' antics.)
Stella: "Suicide's not just a sin, it's a statement and I don't see one here."

Flack: "You could probably find two points of reference in common with my print too."
Stella: "True."

CSI Déjà Vu

See CSI **Alter Boys** with a reference to church and religion especially where Gil is concerned.
CSI episode **Spark Of Life** season 5 where the evidence leads to the CSIs investigating the same case, from what starts off as two

separate cases, becoming one. The DNA evidence and the burnt out lighter tip found at the crime scene.

In **Face Lift** at first there seem to be two separate cases when Tammy turns out to be the murderer, but become one with the discovery of a suspect's prints at the store. Also the season 3 *CSI* episode **Blood Lust** where two dissimilar cases are discovered to be one.

Josh Berman commented, "I do love the device, when two cases become one, it ups the stakes and you really, really want the CSIs to solve it."

In the season 3 episode of *CSI* **Play With Fire**: Gil surmises that a toe nail on the clipper places the suspect at the murder scene; his nail (the killer's), her DNA (belonging to the victim) and traces of these are found at both (the location) and these are the "holy trinity"; i.e. killer, victim, location. Just as Mac mentions this in this episode. Gil also mentions the trinity again in season 4 *CSI* **Invisible Evidence** though in this episode it was incomplete.

Also the episode season 5 **Mea Culpa** with Sara instructing Greg on how to make the scratched serial number reappear on the surface of the gun. Sara says a criminal wouldn't leave his gun behind at the scene, but they do. See also *CSI:NY* **1.6 Outside Man** where the gun was left behind (as well as in other episodes.)

In *CSI* season 2 finale **The Hunger Artist,** Cassie is a paranoid schizophrenic.

In season1 *CSI* **Boom** a bomb explodes in an abandoned briefcase after it's picked up. The suitcase also had letters or initials on the surface.

Ratings

13.497 million viewers. Rated #18 for the week.

Bloops

When the robot is near the briefcase, someone can be seen, at the back, such as a crew member, the situation is a bomb threat and no one should be around.

1.9 Officer Blue

Written By Anthony E Zuiker Directed By Deran Sarafian
US Airdate 1 December 2004
UK Airdate 2 April 2005

Guest Stars: Sonya Walger (Jane) Gabriel Casseus (Jerald Brown) Allen Payne (Willie Chancey) Jude Ciccoella (Nick Vicenzo) Jim Metzler (Dr Huff) Paul Carafotes (DA Tom Mitford)

Story 1

Background

A teenager assaults an old man in Central Park. A mounted officer intervenes and is shot. His horse escapes and is run over by a taxi but is still alive. Flack tells Mac he heard the shot from 6th Avenue and it shook the windows of his car. Mac tells him it was the echo from the weapon he heard. The policeman was shot in his back through his vest by a sniper. Flack takes the dead officer's badge.

Smockton had the lease to office number 3 on the ninth floor. His lease was up. His hands shake and Mac notices his goiter. He has hyperthyroidism a symptom of Graves Disease and couldn't be the shooter.

Mac has a visit from the DA, Tom Mitford, who tells him the horse was donated by the widow of Don Como, in memory of her husband. Mac wants six hours to find the weapon. Flacks says they have a signal from the mobile from Elmhurst, Queens, at La Guardia. They call the phone on the plane and it's answered by Brown. He denies knowing Chancey and claims it was a wrong number, just as Chancey did. He denies owning a car.

Stella tells Mac the 3D bullet isn't any good because stria can't be obtained from it. Mac tells her the profile of the bullet will make them understand the shooter; they need the bullet and the weapon to get the shooter. She says the bullet should've been removed first. Stella searches Brown's apartment and finds pieces of the weapon and tests it.

Chancey's body is found in the airport garage in his own car, shot, in the trunk.

Crime Scene Evidence

Danny and Aiden process the scene looking for the bullet. Mac finds a discarded mobile/cell phone but no bullet. Danny examines the footage from the cameras and determines the center of the crime scene is the distance where the officer fell, the taxi and the horse. The naval is where the shooting occurred. He and Aiden scan all sides of Central Park, north, east, south central and westbound.

Secondary Crime Scene Evidence

GSR is found on the window ledge, the sniper was here. Mac notices a fingerprint on the window but is it inside or outside? Flack tells him about the eye witnesses who think it was aliens or he shot himself. The print from the window matches Richard Smockton with a prior record for staging animal protests.

Police Interrogation

Mac explains Brown was in the park and picked a fight with a bag vendor who works the same area. He lost his phone. He tells Mac a tourist was harassing him.

Conclusion

The prints on the gun bullets match Brown, an army sergeant and marksman with a dishonourable discharge for willfully disobeying orders during Desert Storm. The print on the rifle found in the car matched him. He killed his accomplice, Chancey because he was a threat. Chancey talking on the phone was bait. Brown shot the officer using the AR15, confirmed by ballistics. He hates police because his father was falsely arrested for drug possession and killed in jail. He just picked any officer.

Stella apologizes to Mac. They haven't had a fight in ages and he reminds her of the old Mac. He wouldn't do this job without her.

Story 2

Background

Aiden investigates a death at Lex 94th, a possible homicide. A 19 year old, Lenny, has burns on his face.

Mac tells Aiden she should've called for back-up as soon as she found something. The pizza place was taking bookings for sports, a common occurrence in New York. Aiden returns with back up. The cook's finger on the photo of Lenny's face matches the voids on his face. She burned her right hand and held him with the right hand to close the door of the oven with her left.

Possible Crime Scene Evidence

Aiden checks the ovens for blood/burn stain inside. The cook burned her hand, two fingers. Secondary burn and a fresh wound. ALS shows up blue. A man tells Aiden to leave.

Conclusion

Nick slammed Lenny's head with the door. He went three blocks and was stabbed to death. Nick admits hitting him as he owed him money but he didn't stab him. Aiden tells him he wasn't stabbed but died of an epidural haematoma behind his ear. He left him there and he died by experiencing "delayed deterioration."

Notes

Stella really goes over the top when it comes to finding evidence and bringing the suspect to book, no matter what the fall out from her actions or who may get hurt along the way, even innocent people, in this case a horse. If they went ahead and operated, the bullet from the gun at his apartment wouldn't have matched anyway so her eagerness to retrieve the bullet wouldn't have helped anyway. It's no wonder she wasn't cited for insubordination for throwing her weight around, yet again.

Melina: "We've just filmed this big old drag out fight between them [Mac and Stella] and at the end of the episode she says to him, 'Sometimes you're the dog and sometimes you're the fire hydrant.' I think that's really cool." There was a big fight in this episode but she didn't say this to him at the end of this episode but actually in the **Recycling** episode with the dog show, however they were both working on different cases in this episode and she said this to him after he took her to lunch at the dog show.

Anthony Zuiker's favourite scene of this episode was where the taxi hits the horse. They obviously used a fake horse. They went to the Mounted Police area. The horse had to be a 'dummy' in the scene as it was too expensive for them to get the police officer and the horse. There was a debate about whether the horse should live or not in the episode and Jerry Bruckheimer wanted the horse to live. The cat scan of the horse, as Anthony reveals in the DVD commentary, was real, obtained from Cornell University.

The horses are donated by the widows of fallen mounted officers and they also name them, which was actually mentioned in the episode.

CBS wanted them to use more of the science elements, hence the scene with Danny and Aiden in the park. Also they were required to have another story in here, and came up with the one with Aiden.

The rule allowing then to lie to suspects is bordering on entrapment. This isn't really something you'd think Mac would condone but at the end of the episode he makes his feelings known about the death penalty which is something he doesn't normally do. He was a marine and served in Beirut in 1983. He believes that the "chain of command is sacrosanct." Something Stella should do well to remember. (See the penultimate episode of season 5 for more of her insubordination and Mac's failure to discipline her, something he takes great pleasure in doing to everyone else except her and his other favourite, Lindsay, who appears in season 2.)

In real life, the NYPD are legally allowed to 'lie' to suspects to get them to admit their crime, but can't make promises — but are allowed to lie! Not many know this. Aiden here gets him to admit to the injury on the DB's head.
As for finding Nick's prints all over the oven door, he was the owner there and you'd think that when she left they would've cleaned things up a bit. Why are the suspects always so willing to volunteer information as if it's going to do them any good in the end, i.e. when he said he didn't stab him but admitted to beating him, why didn't he just keep quiet. Not too clever.

Flack says all the eye-witnesses think he either shot himself or saw aliens, see **3.8 Consequences**, when he actually comes across people who believe in aliens and have their apartment covered with aluminium foil. The alien aspect coming to light since the paintballs being fired were in luminous paint colours.

On Aiden, Anthony commented, "She got in a little bit of trouble...that was designed to show how new she was. She will sort of redeem herself and be a little tougher in episode **19**, where she will confront a criminal inside of a jail cell. But she is very loyal to

Danny Messer and she will therefore be tarnished with the same brush."

Why were Mac and Stella test firing the weapons in their suits and not wearing lab coats?

Melina loves Flack's ties..."it's just perfect because it is a specific character trait...crazy, insane silly. They're always something unique and they're always something that stands out. It's a little unspoken thing, Stella will grab his tie or Stella will fix his tie – little moments every once in a while. It's just one of those funny things. It's a character.' It's a perfect costume for his character. Stella's got cool tops and he's got great ties." Stella doesn't get hold of Flack's ties that often, if ever. It's Mac's ties she used to grab hold of, loosen and fix, such as in the first episode.

Also you must know Flack's Armani ties – when they're cut to pieces and sold off in trading cards, sell for small fortunes!! Everyone wants a piece of Flack!! Don't we all!! But Stella's tops really aren't "cool." They're too similar in design and also tres unsuitable for the kind of work she does, too low cut and some are even bordering on skimpy. Take the one in season 5 with the sheer sleeves – she's meant to be at work, not out at dinner or a party!

Melina describes Stella as loyal to her friends, those she cares about and she says she'll make choices – in opposition to Mac, whom she just calls "black and white." To her Stella "is grey and who follows her heart and not always walk the line as an ethical cop. She walks that fine line of grey, but does so for all the right reasons."

Alex Payne, who played the suspect and actual killer of the policeman, was originally vying for the part of Warrick Brown in *CSI*.

Again Mac calls Flack 'Det. Flack' and Flack calls him 'Sir.' More references to the media by Mac, re *The New York Post*.

In comparison to episode 1 of this season, the interrogation room here was more lighter as they were getting notes from CBS in relation to this and Anthony said this lightening of the scenes had an impact since they got more viewers for this episode.

Sonya Walger won a Saturn Award for Best Supporting Actress in TV for her role in *The Librian: Quest for the Spear in 2004.* Now in the critically acclaimed *Flashforward,* where she plays Dr Olivia Benford, the wife of FBI Special Agent, Mark Benford. Sonya was born in London, England. She was in *Lost* where she played Penny Widmore who rescued the Oceanic Six. Also she was in the US re-make of the British series, *Coupling* as Sally Harper. As well as previously being in the UK comedy show, *Goodnight Sweetheart* alongside Nicholas Lyndhurst, as Flic.

In the DVD commentary, it's stated Flack has the line, "I'll carry your nuts for you," in the plane scene as they arrest the suspect. This had to be cut out since the line wasn't quite right for network TV for obvious reasons.
Also in the scene with Aiden, Anthony says Vanessa couldn't have touched the oven with her latex gloves because it was too hot, but that mistake slipped by.

Quotes

Flack: "This city's full of nuts."
Mac: "That's why we're scientists."

Jane: "Scientist with a heart." (Disputable where Stella's concerned, as one second she claims to have one and the next, she's as cold as ice.)

Mac: "No one's delaying the case, Stella. We're not forensically there yet...no weapon, the bullet's only half of the puzzle."
Stella: "...should've been removed first."
Mac: "We need the bullet and the weapon to make an arrest. Plain and simple Stella, until then the horse can stay alive a couple of

hours. It's my call, end of conversation." (But this has never stopped her, see later episodes. When Stella wants to do something, she'll do it, regardless.)

Stella; "In Stella-talk 'it's time to get the bullet out of the horse', Mac. End of conversation."

Aiden: "Don't check out my ass when a kid is dead on the street, have some respect."
Mac: "You're processing evidence that could put someone behind bars for life. You take, nothing, no one for granted...it's your first threat, it won't be the last. So you take back up, you go back to the scene, follow the evidence and if for some reason you need a little help with this Nick Vincenzo, don't forget the rule." (Mac condoning lying. Okay, they're allowed to lie, but still.)

Aiden: "You know what one of the greatest rules is of an investigator, we can lie to suspects legally."

A Danny Moment

Danny: "They don't call me the eagle eye for nothing."

CSI-Déjà Vu

CSI:Miami had a sniper episode in season 1, **Kill Zone**, who left behind a lot of evidence. *CSI* season 5 episode **4X4** had a similar burn in the episode when the boy climbed into the washing machine dryer.

CSI season 2 episode **Alter Boys** where Sara finds the flour on the DB is used in baking pizza.
CSI season 3 episode **Forever** was a horse episode. "Where to start? First witness. First suspect. The horse of course."

Did You Know

Mac served in Beirut in 1983 as a marine. (Okay I've mentioned it a few times.)

Ratings

14.915 million viewers. Rated #16 for the week.

1.10 Night Mother

Written By Janet Tomaro Directed By Deran Sarafian
Us Airdate 1 December 2004
UK Airdate 9 April 2005

Guest Stars: Heather Kafka (Ophelia Dichiara) Corin Nemec (Todd Camden) Michael Irby (Eduardo) Scott Valentine (Dr Steven Rydell) Nicholas Pratley (Ryan Mallone) Bradley Stryker (Jason Walder) Grant Albrecht (Dr Leonard Giles) Ranjani Brow (Rachel Camden) Sidney Faison (Dwayne Meade)

Story 1

Background

A night basketball match. One player throws the ball away from the court and finds a woman giving another female heart massage. Flack tells Mac it's an open and shut case. The woman is Rachel Camden, married and lives in 8A. The other woman is divorced and lives in 7F. Flack says she was found covered in blood with the murder weapon beside her. He's positive she killed Rachel. Stella says the victim died instantly. The woman looks at Mac at the hospital. Her name is Ophelia Dichiara. Rachel's husband doesn't know her.

Ophelia doesn't recall the injury on her shins. She tells Mac disposing of a corpse is a misdemeanour in New York City. Mac tells her she wasn't disposing but tampering with evidence: a Class E felony. There's 24 hours between holding time and arrest and arraignment; unless she's a danger to herself and others. Ophelia is a paralegal. She's never met Rachel and apologizes for keeping him up so late.

There's nothing at Ophelia's apartment to show how she got shin injuries. Mac comments she lived in fear as she was trying to stay inside. The door opens to the hallway. Stella finds a children's book with an inscription. Also present are chewed cigarettes but no ashes. There's a step ladder near her bed and blood on the edge. She hit the ladder when she woke up hence her shin bruising. Mac believes she's a sleepwalker.

The doctor examines her and concludes she's a parasomniac; caused by trauma, depression. During stage 4 there's partial arousal. Ophelia wakes up and hits herself on her legs over and over in a stabbing motion.

Rachel's husband pulled her hair when they fought. He suspected her of having an affair. He says she didn't use birth control. Mac concludes Ophelia is not the killer.

Crime Scene Evidence

Stella processes Ophelia and takes photos of her hands. She drinks water and Stella takes the glass.

The video shows Rachel and Ophelia. Mac wonders why the woman stabbed a stranger and then tries to grab her heart. The video also shows shadows next to Ophelia. She saw the killer and didn't know it. Mac looks at a spoon and says the cornea "shaped roughly like this teaspoon, concaves out." Stella says if Ophelia is in a blindspot this will reflect off her cornea. She uses corneal imaging to magnify and reverse the image. Shows a man wearing a T-shirt with a basketball under his arm. Stella arrests the player who found Ophelia and swabs his bag.

Conclusion

Ophelia noticed bruises on her body and weight gain so she put the ladder next to her bed. But she still got around them. The research was between scientists v psychologists. She tells Mac in science any unknown answers equal insanity. She doesn't recall being outside. Mac tells her she subconsciously knew Rachel was dead.

Stella removes a splinter from the basketball player's hand and a condom from his wallet. He had sex with Rachel and grabbed her from behind. She wanted to call off their affair so he killed her with a stake.

Story 2

Background

A DB of a man is found without identification.
Ryan claims to have changed money at JFK. He hasn't seen the victim. Aiden finds a lens belonging to Lenny Cook. They search his apartment.

Danny mentions the School of Seven Beels, a pick-pocket school in South America. Danny notices the torn carpet and finds $20 and blood. When checked it's not blood but ketchup. Danny also finds a NYC train pass and one stain which turns out to be blood.

The train route is staked out and Danny notices a suspect carrying a fake baby. Danny explains to Aiden that the woman with the 'baby' puts ketchup on the mark. The decoys obstruct the mark and the partner picks his pocket. Eduardo is arrested and claims the wallet fell out. He has blood on his knuckles.

Ryan exchanged money and scratches his wrist. Fibres are caught in his watch strap and are left behind on the table in the Interview Room.

Crime Scene Evidence

There's medium velocity blood spatter and Aiden comments on his pockets being inside out. No wallet or keys and Danny says no junkies have taken the change.

Conclusion

The chemical used at the drycleaners is ethylene so can't be used to check DNA but the cuff would have prevented the blood from being cleaned off the dime. The blood belongs to Lenny. The prints on the dime belong to Ryan. He took all the money from under the carpet. There was jute under the carpet and Ryan was allergic to it. Lenny was skimming and so was set up with Ryan as a mark. Eduardo beat Lenny up.

Danny tells Mac he closed the case as an A2. He takes a rain check on the drink with Danny. Mac looks up the *New York News* archives and finds out about Chris. Ophelia's husband and son were killed in a car accident. She was mimicking the actions of trying to save Chris when she tried to save Rachel. She told him his eyes were like Mac's. When they tried to save Chris in the ER they held his heart in their hands just like she did with Rachel.

Notes

An episode all about sleep and lack of. Mac could be described as an insomniac too. Notice how the sleep walking woman was called Ophelia, a little like Ophelia from Shakespeare's *Hamlet*. The two stories relate in the sense that they both involve the use of hands: the first one is about Ophelia using her hands in an attempt to save Rachel and the second one is about using hands to commit crimes, i.e pick-pocketing and murdering.

The conversation Mac has with Ophelia about the penalties for the crimes she's accused of makes you wonder why he pursued this case if it was only a felony class F whereas he argues with Danny about pursuing a misdemeanour in episode **1.19** Though the suspect who killed Rachel committed murder.

The inscription in the book reads: *To Chris*
Mommy loves you a lot. Happy first Grade.

Notice the clock on the wall behind Danny when he's processing the money, it moves forward and then back again by about a minute or half a minute, so it doesn't take him very long to process!

Stella always convicting the suspect before the evidence is even analyzed and the ink dry. The way she roughly treated Ophelia was out of line and unjustified especially since she was only a suspect at this stage and not yet charged with anything or even found guilty.

They don't wear CSI jackets to crime scenes anymore in later episodes.

Melina: "What is most difficult in any loss is not knowing why you lose someone and not having closure in a situation. I think as human beings we need that. That's why mystery has been such a successful entity always in novels, film and TV. It is trying to discover why or what. Our characters are on a constant search for the truth."

The ending to this episode was changed, says Anthony, where "the mother was waving goodbye to her kid and then they got sideswiped and she pulled the kid out, it was so, so jarring. A little too much for TV in that climate." He felt.

Danny worked at the 63rd precinct.

Quotes

Mac: "...crime of passion between two apparent strangers."

Mac: "What's your rush to put this woman away?"
Flack: "You saw her, what's your rush not to?"

Mac: "In all my years of doing this there's one thing I've learned, sometimes the slam dunks are the ones that are the most deceiving."

Stella: "The unconscious mind overrides the conscious self." She's been reading yet more textbooks to quote from.

Dr Giles: "...thy science is after all sadness."
Mac: "Thomas Hardy...Gimme a hand here [literally].

Danny: "Don't take 'em down until they snatch the wallet."
Flack: "You telling me how to do my job now." Well somebody has to, considering he couldn't find out about Ophelia and her son. (Ooh that was harsh of me! Sorry Flack!)

Flack: "Who...he's an owl now."
Danny: "Something's keeping me in suspense, you know there's something going on and I can't figure it out."

A Danny Moment

Danny: "...pick mark without ringing the bell. Why don't you try it...you're such a girl."
Aiden: "Shut up."

CSI Déjà Vu

CSI episode **I-15 Murders** where Sara notices a glass shard in the cuff of a suspects pants, similar to the dime in the cuff of the pants with the blood on it here. Also in the *CSI* episode **Fear and Loathing in Las Vegas** where frozen blood was found in the cuff of jeans by Sara in the shooting of the man in the freezer story. In **Evaluation Day** Nick finds peanut shells in the cuff of some pants.

CSI season 2 episode **Burden Of Proof** where a reflection in the eye of the victim leads to a clue.
CSI:Miami season 3 episode **Under The Influence** the reflection in a

woman's eye in a digital camera photo is turned around to reveal a vital clue as to how the victim met her death.

CSI season 2 episode **Cool Change** fibres are found on a watch.
CSI season 2 episode **Alter Boys** where dry cleaned jeans were too degraded by chemicals to test the stain for blood.

CSI:Miami season 2 episode **Kill Zone** where footage from an ATM showed the reflection in a suspect's sunglasses as the logo of a jacket.

CSI **6.15 Pirates of the Third Reich** where a woman was taking part in a study involving experiments on sleep deprivation. (Though this is more of a déjà vu happening later. See below.)

CSI Déjà Vu also works both ways, as shown by other episodes and season 7 *CSI:Miami* episode **7.12 Headcase** where they also had to investigate a suspect's claim that he was suffering from amnesia after being found with blood on him. Similar to this episode of *NY*, where the suspect was suffering from sleep disorder and was examined in a facility. In *Miami*, the suspect was sent to an FBI facility to monitor his reactions to images on the screen, as Calleigh says, "brainwaves don't lie." The suspect's EEG showed he witnessed his father being murdered and this was the first time he experienced amnesia. In the same way, Ophelia tried to help her son, as she thought she was helping her son by touching his heart.

Also in this episode, Ryan and Delko theorize on whether the suspect is guilty or not, before all the evidence is in. Ryan suggests it's premeditated murder, whereas Delko surmises they must process the evidence before they convict him. Turns out they were both right, if he really was forced into killing. Here Stella and Flack both surmised Ophelia was guilty of murder too.

Tripp's line in this *Miami* episode: "One guy even said he came down in a damn spaceship." Which Flack has said on many occasions in this season and others. As well as Tripp getting to say Flack's other phrase: "You've gotta be kidding me."

Music

Dirt Off Your Shoulder by Jay-Z; *Lean Back* by Terror Squad featuring Fat Joe & Remy.

Ratings

15.6 million viewers. Rated #9 for the week.

1.11 Triborough

Written By Andrew Lipsitz & Eli Talbert Directed By Greg
Yaitanes
Us Airdate 5 January 2005
UK Airdate 16 April 2005

Guest Stars: Kelly Hu (Det Kylie Macca) Ray Abruzzo (Bob Galanis)Jay Acovone (Paul Gianetti) TJ Thyne (Ron Leatham) Peter Giles (John James III) Patrick Brennan (Ryan Brocco) Carter Jenkins (Will Galanis) Kelly Lutz (Alex Hopper)

Story 1

Background

A body is found on the subway track. No wallet, watch, keys. Mac comments the M.O. doesn't match but it may fit the profile. Third rail electrocutions are foot to foot. Stella says the step on the rail current enters from the leg to the other leg and goes up to the ground. Mac replies it's hand to foot here. No evidence of a struggle. Mac and Stella canvas the neighbourhood. The body was found three blocks away. "Houses are on the same transformer and lost power last night." Mac spots one house that has a statue with a finger missing. The owner, Galanis doesn't recognize the victim. The victim was dumped in the only neighbourhod that lost power.

At the Plaza they notice the man on the photos; he leaves behind a newspaper with his fingerprint. The DB's name is Randy Outz and he left him alive. They're into free running.
In Randy's apartment olive oil from the Sparta region of Greece is found. There's a name, *Julie G* on his CD covers; all burned. There's no food in the fridge.

Stella finds the oil is exclusively sold by Galanis & Son. So there's a connection to the same man they questioned at the house with the statue. At the house they find a broken lock on a bedroom door and olive oil on the sheets. A handprint near the window. Randy escaped out the window.

Mac finds a note in his clothes: *GAP NOON* and a finger from a statue. But no print match. He had olive oil on his body and a digital camera. No transformers blow in January.

Crime Scene Evidence

Burnt skin is found on the flagpole. Randy was electrocuted there.

Conclusion

Bob broke down his daughter, Julie's bedroom door. Stella tells him Randy completed the circuit and couldn't let go. The jumper cables had his prints. His dying was an accident, he was protecting Julie, like he's protecting his son now whose fingerprints were the other set on the cables; over his father's prints. His son killed Randy. The wagon gave him away as it had traces of olive oil. The boy confesses it was his idea. Mac tells him his mistake was made earlier as the cables wouldn't have killed him, but he was perspiring.

Story 2

150

Background

Leo Whitfield, an art dealer is found shot to death. He had no priors and there were no signs of a robbery. Ron Latham, owner of the bookstore across the street, called it in. Receipt books show $50,000 cash was given to buy 'Inhumanity' for Paul Gianetti. Whitefield sold him a fake painting. He also asked Paul for the gun.

Danny discovers Reason Street used to be Greenwich Village and was named after Thomas Payne's *The Age of Reason*. The church called this an attack on the Bible. Reason = Raisin Street. In 1809 Raisin Street became Barrow Street, after Thomas Barrow. The painting, ink and document were all forensically checked out but Danny missed what was staring him in the face. There was a Reason Street and a great fire, not in 1814, but 1776. It became Barrow Street in 1809. The street was correct and Barrow Street is where the art gallery is located.

Crime Scene Evidence

Danny finds high velocity blood spatter on another painting. There are powder burns so he was shot at close range. The killer dropped the gun.
He can check the databases for the gun and GSW was through and through. An insurance document is also found. *This is to certify that Inhumanity by Jacque de Sui owned by Charles Dowright of 234 Reason Street, N.Y was destroyed by fire on 6 October 1814.*
Danny also finds the bullet.

Conclusion

Whitefield was therefore a forger. He was making easy money. Paul and John James knew the painting was real but the document wasn't important to either of them. Danny says Whitefield had a clean past so he needs to go back in time. The tools of the forger: he dissolves the shavings in nitric acid, neutralized with water, tannin and gallets.

There's a book called *The History of Ink*. Danny says that's where he got old paper from as the first page in the book is blank. The book is called *The Homicide* By Mary Charlton 1824. Carbon dating put the error of margin at plus or minus ten years. If a page form the book was used then the earliest would be 1840. Letham's books are where Whitefield was using the paper from. He wipes his glasses on his handkerchief. This has evidence of GSR. Blood spatter on the cover and the first page is missing. He lent him the books but he didn't show them at the gallery. They struggled and Whitefield was shot. He took the money since history can't be reproduced.

Story 3

Background

Aiden investigates a DB at a construction site. There's a smell emanating from his clothes. Bill LaMakia was filling in at the site.

Crime Scene Evidence

The toilet was knocked over whilst he was in there. There are prints outside belonging to Brian. He was caught drinking on the job. Flack says Brian's alibi checks out.

Conclusion

Aiden concludes Bill was hit by Blue Ice. Any liquid from a plane freezes when descends, the temperature rises and falls. There are twenty-seven documented cases of this and the site is near La Guardia airport. So Bill was hit on the head from the frozen waste disposal liquid leaking from the plane.

Notes

A first as this episode had three stories instead of the usual two or one. These cases are getting sad and disturbing especially the first story where a child is involved in carrying out murder without remorse or batting an eye. So "it was cool." Of course the prints on the cables would belong to Bob and to a certain extent, his son since it is his house.

Danny's comment in nothing being stolen from the gallery and it's obvious why, could be referring to his own painting. Hey it wasn't that bad! Also Kylie asking him if he likes anything when she first enters as he's looking at his own painting. Which was good to see, but the shot wasn't long enough. Also Kylie says, "no signs of robbery." To which Danny replies, "I can see why." Indicating to his painting! All Danny needs to do is to find the evidence, as Mac said to him in previous episodes.

The Print match reads:
DATE: 11-29-02
SUSPECT   :   PAUL   GIANETTI
MOB RELATIONS: PASTELLI FAMILY

Funny how Danny's mob relations weren't mentioned here nor whether he was familiar with the Pastelli family. Danny saying he's not a rookie could have been an inadvertent way of telling us he's connected too. Though he was really referring to his CSI work.

Also when Mac mentions Raisin, you can't help to think of Grace's quote from *Will & Grace* where she said she loves raisins and went to see *A Raisin in the Sun* because she thought it was about raisins, but wasn't.
Carbon dating we remember from chemistry and biology at school.

Eddie Cahill was raised in the Bronx and comments on his experience of crime. "I was living with my girlfriend once when we were on Kenmore Street. I didn't witness a crime but a guy tried to break into our apartment building and wound up falling off the fire escape and dying right outside our apartment. That was freaky. Then the detective showed up right as I got out of the shower and pointed it out to me. That same week I was at my parent's place downtown and a guy actually jumped off the building next door. So I saw two dead bodies in a week, which was creepy."

Carmine answers the question of why Danny is so popular on the show: "To humbly answer that question – the only reason I can say if people think that what I do is interesting or good is because I work my ass off and that's the only way I look at it. Everything I do, I care about so greatly and that's how I do it...whatever I'm doing, I just have this competitive edge in me and this passionate way that I just want to figure out how it works and how to do it the best way. I think people feel that drive that people can see that." It's also because of Carmine himself. Okay aside from his presence; he's a great actor and really brings out the part of Danny to the fullest when he's filming and on-screen.

My mum says, if you're going to do something, anything, there's no point in doing it half-heartedly. If you don't put the passion, love and attention into something, and give it your all, there's no point in even attempting it! People loving Danny, it's because Danny is different. He's imperfect, flawed and yet perfect at the same time. He makes mistakes because he believes in doing the right thing – gets berated for doing his job and thinking about the victim and/or the underdog. At the same time, he wears his heart on his sleeve. What you see is what you get with him and he will always be there for you, he's a staunch friend and fiercely loyal!

Aiden gets another case to work solo.

Quotes

Mac: "Why did the kid cross the rail?"
Stella: "To get to the other side."

Mac: "One way or another." How unsavory was this scene!

Stella; "One of those connected moments."

Stella: "We have a 'where' and a 'when'."
Mac: "In order to get to a 'what', we need a 'who'."

Mac: "There's no coincidence in crime."

Mac: "That's even worse. Raisin was a colloquial term for slaves."

Aiden: "Anybody see anything?"
Flack: "When does anybody ever see anything."   An oft repeated phrase from Flack in later episodes.

Hawkes: "Down here we call that a James Brown. It's funky."

Flack: "After you, may be evidence."

Flack: "So a crapsical killed him."

A Danny Moment

Danny: "I need to find the evidence."

CSI Déjà Vu

CSI episode **Sex, Lies & Larvae**, where Catherine proved the painting was fake by using ALS (Alternative Light Source) at the scene and also in the lab. But not to the extent of all the thorough tests carried out by Danny.

In *CSI season 2* episode **Caged** the librarian was concerned about rare books. Also this episode was more about book forgeries instead of paintings, or as is the case here, the authenticity of documents accompanying paintings. Which involved stealing books and replacing them with forgeries; here the paper was stolen from authentic books.

CSI season 2 episode **Cats In The Cradle** where a mineral oil was used to treat knives. Here olive oil was found at the scene.

CSI season 2 episode **Overload**, a hard hat comes down from a construction site and then a body follows. Here the victim took off his hard hat to be hit by a crashing object.

Ratings

15.6 million viewers. Rated #9 for the week.

Did You Know

The painting Danny 'admires' in the opening of Story 2 was painted by Carmine Giovinazzo (he has an artistic name, Carmine means *music* in Italian, which also explains his other love, music and his own band, *Ceesau*.) The painting is entitled, *Sister Tight*. It was actually good to see a show using material from its cast for a change. Over the years, Carmine stated he wished the show would use some of his music but so far have declined.

1.12 Recycling

Written By Timothy J Lea & Zachery Reiter
Directed By Alex Zakrzewski
US Airdate 12 January 2005
UK Airdate 23 April 2005

Guest stars: Julia Duffy (Millie Hanford) Zach Grenier (Dr Ross Howell) Robert Constanzo (Frank Meadows) Steve Hytner (Alvin Marbert) Neil Giuntoli (Mark Stutz) Aisha Hinds (Brett Stokes) Brad Greenquist (Theodore Gates) Paul Carafotes (Det. Charlie Thacker) Sonia Walger (Jane Parsons)

Story 1

Background

A bike messenger collapses. He has one prior for assaulting a cab driver. He has a stab wound to his upper right side and is wearing high tech heart monitors. This is the secondary crime scene. From his delivery manifest Danny finds the stabbing took place between Wall Street and 33rd and 8th.

Danny pays a visit to his boss, Michael Stalin. Danny also seems to think a better route would pay more money.

Stella questions Brett and she asks about Danny, i.e. 'Mr Crimelab'. She got his route so he slashed her tyres. They were racing. The knife didn't kill him but the scissors.

Gates doesn't know who Michael is and lost his knife a week ago, he left it behind. He has a receipt to show he was at a model airplane convention.

Primary Crime Scene Evidence

Danny uses his jacket to provide a sequential timeline, cement and red paint shows he rode on the pavement and through wet cement. The tyre marks match his bike. There's red paint on a nearby sign. Stella spots blood on the line markings. There's a news vendor at the scene. This is then identified as the primary crime scene. Stella finds a knife in the gutter.

Conclusion

The news vendor wears woolen gloves. He doesn't use his army knife anymore but a boxcutter. The fibres from his gloves were on the knife and the lotion was on the magazine. He was the sole supplier at the crime scene. Danny tells him he took an innocent life. He raced past him on the street and so he stabbed him.

Story 2

Background

Flack identifies the victim as Elaine Curtis, a dog handler; she shows dogs on behalf of the owners. Ross Howard, the vet found her body. But denies seeing or hearing anything. The dogs have about nine or ten medications. The key to the case is in her hand and this contains the medications. A knitting needle is found in a bag belonging to Milly Cantford. Milly tells Mac Elaine wasn't liked very much, a judge in Cincinnati was taken aback by her and had to recuse himself. She knits for her dog.

The dogs are lined up and paws checked for blood. One of the handlers and Elaine were involved. She had a fetish and he bit her on her leg. The judge is himself a compulsive gambler and was scratched on his hand by a dog. Then admits Elaine scratched him as he offered her a bribe. He was gambling and so pretended he didn't hear her at the scene. His alibi checks out.

Crime Scene Evidence

Aiden uses LTD on the floor and finds bloody paw prints leading away.

Conclusion

Elaine put the dog's depression medication in the bottle. The dog is a West Highland Terrier. Aiden says the bottle was empty before. Milly admits being tired of her dresses and wanted to slow down her dog. Aiden tells her Elaine was on her own medication and the reaction to both made her collapse onto the needle. Milly didn't intend this.

Mac takes Stella for lunch at the dog show and buys her a hot dog. They bet on who wins the show and she wins $10 from Mac.

Notes

This is Danny's second arrest in the series so far, one where he actually apprehends the suspect. As well as flashing...his badge! This episode was intentionally or unintentionally meant to be funny and the first light hearted one of the season. Hence lots of jokes and one liners galore this episode and including lots of references to dogs. Such as Stella getting Danny to fetch and carry for her, more so than usual in this episode and making a real, dare I say it, dog's body out of him.

Also on the scene with Danny and Stella, there's a dog by the fire hydrant which nobody notices. A nice addition to the second story all about dogs and their cagey owners. (No pun.)

The dog scenes were filmed in the LA sports stadium since the studio scenes on the street are obviously shot in a studio.

About Danny's glasses as a character trait, Carmine comments, "That was part of the character. We're creating a character and I think [the addition of the glasses] worked out for the best. They might come off at some point. I've gotten used to them. Once put those on, you know who the guy is. It's not me, although I do wear glasses." Yes, the glasses did disappear at some point in later seasons and now Carmine [and Danny] wears contacts all the time.

As for beauty tips, well I'm sure Stella wouldn't be the first person Danny consults. Danny's line about water proof mascara was actually picked up from *Elle* magazine. Also in the magazine scene with the vendor, the camera pans onto *Trendy* magazine, which was a big clue, as it's also the one Danny reads in the lab and carries the free lotion sample.

This episode also had a real feel of *Dark Angel* about it, especially the bike messenger service, even down to the smarmy boss!

Strangely enough both stories featured victims with trace under their fingernails.

What on earth was Hawkes doing in the freezer; surely his job description doesn't entail fixing pipes.

Having a credit card receipt shows or proves nothing; since you could have been there, left early or disappeared under the guise of using the rest room, especially if no one sees you there and there's no CCTV.

Mac's words will ring true in season **2.2**, after Vanessa Ferlito had made her decision to leave and was written out. She tampered with evidence to bring a suspect to book and paid the ultimate price. She was "processing" (i.e. manufacturing) evidence which could put someone behind bars for life, that's why she tampered with the evidence. Probably Mac's phrase stuck in her mind. (Or as Danny would say, "don't 'Messer' with me!" Bad joke.)

In the UK, the night this episode aired, the movie *Best In show* about a dog show was also screened.

The episode title **Recycling** not only a reference to the bike, but also to the dog's feeder bottle with the water. Eeww.
It was said that real dog show people were used whilst filming and they were so competitive that they had to keep the name of the winning dog secret; otherwise they would've walked off the set.

Bloops

The dog blanket appears to be crocheted and not knitted; as the suspect says she knits. Also when Mac hands Aiden the dog's bottle, she takes the lid off and then he glances at the notebook in the briefcase; Aiden is then shown taking the lid off the bottle again.

Quotes

Danny: "Is that still a crime in New York?" I.e. assaulting a cab driver. (See the episode, where Aiden and Danny investigate the death of a gypsy cab driver; **1.18 The Dove Commission.**)

Danny: "I'm looking for the truth, you don't seem so eager to deliver." (Lots of courier jokes too.)

Danny: "Don't kill the messenger. See what I did there?"

Danny: "What's the matter am I too old for you?"

Stella: "Some days you're the dog, some days you're the hydrant."

A Danny Moment

Danny: "I think I might have spoken to her this morning."
Stella: "Really, she seem suspicious?"
Danny: "I didn't think anything."
Stella: "Cause she's a girl?" Stella's always so eager to accuse people, even without evidence and does it really matter if it was a girl or not, judging from her treatment of suspects and victims alike. (See next episode)

Another Danny Moment

Danny: "Do you know that water mascara dries out your lashes, that's amazing." Thanks for the tip Danny! Albeit from *Elle*.

CSI Déjà Vu

CSI episode **4x4** where someone was also found attempting to fix a leaking pipe.
CSI:Miami season 3 episode **Under The Influence** where box cutters were found in a drawer, covered with blood. The tip of the box cutter matched that found in the rib cage.

CSI Miami episode **7.7 Cheating Death** where the suspect claimed she was at a restaurant and had her credit card receipt to prove she was there, but later turned out to be the actual killer.

CSI:Miami where *Megan's Law* was mentioned by Delko and Megan too. *Megan's Law* is a Federal law which requires states in the US to tell communities if a sex offender is in their neighbourhood: either living there or has been released from prison. Also sex offenders have to register with local police, as well as informing them of their intention to move somewhere else. Also see *CSI* episode **Harvest**.

This law was named after Megan Kanka, a seven year old girl who was sexually assaulted and murdered in 1994, in New Jersey by a neighbour who had been previously convicted for sex offences against children.

Ratings

13.6 million viewers. Rated # 21 for the week.

1.13 Tanglewood

Written By Anthony E Zuiker Directed By Karen Gaviola
US Airdate 26 January 2005
UK Airdate 30 April 2005

Guest stars: Sonya Walger (Jane Parsons) Michael Deluise (Sonny Sassone) Stacy Edwards (Debbie Montenassi) Fredric Lehne (RossLee) Jordana Spiro (Tavia Greenburg) Marco Sanchez (Ramir Santo) Anjul Nigam (Harish Lev) Eamon Behrens (Johnny Lucerno) Irene Tsu (Madame Tuki Song) Nick Di Brizzi Jnr (Paul Montenassi)

Story 1

Background

A boy runs in the park and is chased and beaten with a baseball bat after begging for his life. Paul's mother says he didn't have a tattoo. Mac thinks he had gang connections. She doesn't know what he used to do.

Aiden is called to a homicide of a bogoda owner's brother who was shot. Flack says it's robbery homicide. There is surveillance footage.

Mac doesn't know about the Tanglewood area, but asks Danny. He tells him the Tanglewood boys are bad news. Their rivals are the 'Pelham Boys'. Any run in with them is 'all deadly dangerous'. Danny identifies the tattoo as a 'fugazy,' a fake. As there's no end date = day of joining and out date = leave legitimately, but this doesn't happen.

Later, Danny asks Mac how his case is progressing. Mac keeps thinking about Paul's fake tattoo. Danny tells Mac they hang out at the New Rochelle Mall. Johnny tells them he got hit by a bat outside a bar. He had stitches. The bar is 'Billy Bats' in Yonkers. Stella and Mac notice the shuffleboard at the bar. The bartender asks them if they want to use the ATM for money, above which is a space for a baseball bat. The prints on the case match Sonny Sassone. He is questioned and says he saw Paul around the bar but he denies stealing the bat. Stella notices his truck has a new back window, new tyres and there's a shoeprint in the snow.

The search of the shed leads to a high power cordless sander. Stella finds it's visually positive for blood.

Crime Scene Evidence

There are sets of shoe prints in the snow. Mac 'cooks up' some pure sulphur. Stella spray paints the shoe prints. Mac pours the sulphur in the imprint to get a cast and finds part of a broken baseball bat in one of the prints. Stella finds tyre tracks.

The search of the truck shows it was cleaned with bleach. There's a Derek Jeter bobblehead on the dashboard. The head moves and Mac sees blood inside.

Conclusion

Sonny says he will settle out of court. Stella says not on murder he won't. Mac tells him Paul got drunk and Sonny promised him an affiliation so he tested him. Paul had to shoot the clerk and he hit him with the bat. Paul wasn't going to be part of the Tanglewood

Boys anyway. Sonny had to keep Paul quiet so sanded his tattoo: hence the blood spatter on the doll and killed him in cold blood. Sonny calls it Mafia style. Mac tells him in the heyday the mob killed for business and not sport. Sonny replies Tanglewood are the next generation of mobsters. They have their own set of rules. Sonny says he'll get off and Mac should ask Danny about them since they all know about each other.

Story 2

Background

A woman is found in a car wreck: Marta Santo. Marta's husband identifies her body and loses his temper. He crashes through the glass window, head first. Danny tells her Marta's husband 'wigged' out and got blood all over him. He has priors for domestic violence, six counts within two years. He apologizes to Danny for his behaviour. Marta was a nymphomaniac.

Aiden tells him of the evidence of multiple donors but he says she worked at a hair salon in West Village. Danny says most massage parlours are owned by the Asian mob. Once you're hired, you can't quit. They check out the parlour and Aiden finds a white gem stone on the floor. Using ALS, Danny finds multiple evidence in a towel bin. Her last client was an R Lee.

Ross Lee tells them he's happily married. He was at the parlour but his wife doesn't know. She drives a car.

Flack finds a hit on the database re the paint chips, which were from a silver Lincoln Navigator. Ariana Lee is the registered owner of one. Her nail varnish colour is ruby passion. Her car has red paint on it and she says she hit a fire hydrant.

Ross says his secretary, Tavia signs for him. She denies being there.

Crime Scene Evidence

There are suspicious skid marks on the road and silver paint on the red car, flakes dried in and are just about clinging on so they are recent. Danny calls it a hit and run.

Conclusion

Ross was Tavia's lover and she wanted to keep Marta away from him. She keeps press-on nails in the office which match the stone and owns a silver Navigator which Ross gave her. Ariana told her about his affair. Aiden says Tavia wanted revenge so drove up to her. Tavia says she only wanted to scare her. Danny charges her with vehicular manslaughter 2.

Notes

Stella counts the number of prints in the snow, but how about the shoe prints of whoever found the body, not to mention others at the crime scene.

This episode was actually filmed in California and a snow machine was used for the snow. Anthony Zuiker commented on how this episode became more lighter and gained some *Law and Order* viewers too in the process. Zuiker wanted Mac to have a victim to care about in this episode, so he could express his feelings towards him; but he's had plenty of victims to care about in previous episodes too, so this wasn't the first time. Also Karen Gaviloa was the first female director used on the show.

The part in the beginning where the suspect actually hides out still at the crime scene has been covered before in *CSI* and more recently in *CSI:Miami*, but finding suspects still at a crime scene is the norm in everyday, real lives of CSIs and they have even been there alone, without police or anyone else present at the crime scene; only for the suspect to return or come out of hiding when they think the coast is clear. There have been many documented stories of this.

Notice they show the view through the interrogation room window and then the camera pans out through there at the end, this time revealing Danny; though he could've been creeping about in the shadows all along. Interestingly he wants to find out if Mac learns anything about him.

A real character-orientated episode if ever there was one. Just over halfway through season 1 and it gets better. All about one of our fave CSIs, well, almost all and this was really personal for Danny, as you can see the temperature rising. No wonder Mac didn't have Danny working on the case with him; besides consulting him for information, actually being on the case would've been a little too close for comfort for our Danny boy and a dead cert giveaway, re his background.

Mac didn't realize what this 'case' means or would've meant to Danny or about where he got his first hand information from, other than work and being approached by them to join up and hanging out with them a few times. Even when Sonny mentions Danny at the end, it still doesn't click. Perhaps he thought Sonny was just being vindictive towards Danny.

Also we didn't get any details either and no alarm bells from what he said: they wanted Danny to be a part of the gang, does this mean his father was connected to this gang too, or why else would they have asked him as Danny says, their fathers are all connected. And they just don't ask anyone to become a part of them. (See later seasons when it's revealed Danny's brother Louis was also a gang member, so perhaps that's why Danny was approached too.)
When Danny mentions to Mac about Paul wanting to belong, desperately, wonder if he's also talking about himself too.
Danny seems to be an expert on the mob affiliations of any culture, perhaps put down to his own 'mob' connections. No mention of this in **1.11 Triborough**.

In a way, the two stories overlap: once 'initiated' as a Tanglewood boy you're in for life. Once Marta started at the massage parlour, that was for life too, so both were mob orientated stories in a way. Though one was about jealousy.

When Danny mentions he's proud to be working here, you can't help feeling there should be a "but" there; but it was a tough decision, easy, not what his family wanted etc. Has Danny got a tattoo of his own? He could have been a part of them...but...
Carmine: "I was happy and fortunate. I think it just went that way because of my dynamic with the writers or my intensity and what I brought into it, but it just went naturally." In other words, the writers choosing to write Danny as they did in this episode and indeed his character, generally.

As for his character in this episode; Carmine comments, "What I really dug, that conflict with Mac, has kind of subsided. The first few episodes I didn't really converse with Gary so we were talking about it. Last time, it ended with Mac saying, 'We'll see how we feel about each other', but it seems like we had our time apart and now we're okay."

Until the next time. This was said in the season 1 finale. But Mac wasn't sure about Danny though as he confided in Stella.

Danny uses Buffy's favourite term, she knew all about wigging out and 'the wiggins'.

Another beauty tip for Danny as in **1.12 Recycling**: the stone on the nail, is either already affixed to the false nail like that so there shouldn't be any actual gluing involved or comes in sticker form with adhesive, at least
most of them do.

Oh and the signature part may have been a bit confusing for some: the signature on the list looked like it was just printed in capitals and not signed. What we'd call 'PRINT' here. I.e. you're asked to print (write in capitals) and then sign. The name on the business card looked as though it was just written in normal writing and not a signature. When he gave them his card, obviously he wouldn't have signed the back of it, no one signs business cards, it would just have been his name and details in ordinary writing.

The advertising office where Danny and Aiden questioned Ross was actually the writers' building used for the show.

The line Danny says to Aiden of *Crouching Aiden*...was actually an in-joke between Zuiker and Andrew Lipsitz, when he went into the bathroom and then came out of the front door of the garage, Zuiker wondered how he managed that and so commented about, "Crouching Tiger, Hidden Lipsitz."

In another first for the show, you can actually see the killer in the opening shot.

This episode was all about belonging – for Mac in the marines, for Danny and his job, and for Paul in a gang or out of a gang and for Mac and Danny, doing the right thing for the right reasons. Mac mentions he was a marine again, and twice in the episode, telling Sonny he killed men to protect the likes of Sonny. Mac joined the marines because he wanted to serve his country and he would've done anything to belong. But Paul's sense of belonging was achieved in the wrong way, through a gang.

Their fathers are all connected, as said before, so was Danny's too, or his family? For him to have known them as Sonny knows all about Danny. The question is why or how?
Says Carmine: "...what we discussed in the beginning when we were creating the character that he's a kid that came form the wrong side of the tracks and has kind of a street mentality but enough of an intellectual mind to be in the world that he's in, so that's a conflict. That doesn't usually happen; you don't usually find a golfer who points. It's just a rare thing – certain things don't usually go hand-in-hand, and I think that's what's
good about him. These opposing things are one person and that's human to me. That's what I think makes him interesting."

When Sonny asks how much she gets paid, Stella actually answers his question: $495,746.32 and they earn every penny. See Flack in season 5 episode **Enough** when reference is made to his 'cheap' suits.

Anthony Zuiker describes this episode as the "turning point of the season...I think that's when we really began to put a character off-center. Danny Messer has a secret, that became sort of interesting. The episode scored in the ratings well, pulling in 17.3 million viewers and intriguing fans with a mystery of a different kind; the backstory of one of the characters. This storyline was completed in the season 2 episode, **Run Silent, Run Deep**, where Danny's secret was revealed, Danny Messer had a lot more involvement with the Tanglewood boys than he's leading on." And also they had good ratings for this episode as NBC did not screen *Law and Order* for that week.

Anthony also calls Danny the 'Sonny Corleone' of the show: a hot-head and he wants that to come out and delve into it more. "He's really righteous about things. That stuff gets him into trouble, but it also makes him an interesting character."

Anthony comments, they got lucky with this episode, "We had about five or six bad things happen to us: one was Boston came back four games in a row on a Wednesday, Wednesday had the episode **1.6 Outside Man** cut off for [Yassar] Arafat's death [Wednesday is also known as the mid-week slump anyway.] Our season, in the UK, is aired on a Saturday night, though the timing for each episode keeps changing which sucks!] We had game four of Boston Sweep on a Wednesday; we had the Presidential debate, we had the State of the Union address on a Wednesday...not being consistent in our air schedule because of outside powers we couldn't control. We finally got a break when NBC didn't put on *Law and Order* and we had a chance to air one of our best episodes of the year. That really helped."

N.B: the CBS producer who interrupted the show with the news of Arafat's passing was subsequently fired!

This episode is concluded in the season 2 episode, **Run Silent, Run deep**. Where Danny is linked to a past murder by the inclusion of a cigarette butt found at a crime scene.

Quotes

Mac: "Lucky for us it happened out here. Best investigative tool money can't buy: snow."

Mac: "I haven't spent much time there, but I know someone who has."
Danny: "...all their fathers, they're all connected. These kids, believe me, they're more made than the made guys. Nowadays it ain't the mobsters you've gotta worry about – it's the next generation."
Mac: "What's the difference?"
Danny: "What's the difference – these kids don't give a 'F'..." ooh, Danny on the verge of swearing.

Johnny: "What are you guys, like a couple of homos or something?"
Flack: "I was about to ask you the same thing. NYPD."
Sonny: "We'll see. Ask Danny Messer. He works for you right. When you see him ask him the odds of me going away. He knows all about us and we know all about him."
Mac: "Sure you do." We didn't see that coming and neither did Mac or even Danny. So did Sonny go away?

Danny: "Oh there she is, 'Crouching Aiden, Hidden Burn'. You're on this case; you're on that case, the other case..." We loved the banter between these two, which was missed when Vanessa left!

A Danny Moment

Danny: "I played baseball back with these kids at Roosevelt, hung out with them, here and there. They wanted me to come in at one time actually; but I, well, I didn't wanna get mixed up. I knew what they were all about: women, cars, coke, guns; sleep 'til noon, hang out at New Rochelle Mall at all hours of the day."

Another Danny Moment

Aiden: "Come on act like you haven't been to a place like this before."
Danny: "You kiddin' me. I had girls for that, why would I pay?"
Aiden: "You're payin' in one way or the other, trust me."

A Mac & Danny Moment

Danny: "Made the wrong choice."
Mac: "Yeah, well you had that choice. You could've gone with these kids but you didn't. You were smarter than they are. Look where you are today – you're respected, you're law abiding, you're performing an important civil service for the finest city in the world. You should be proud of that."
Danny: "I am proud of that, I am." (Just didn't sound that convincing here, at least he was trying to convince himself, it felt that way.)

CSI Déjà Vu

All the car paint chip, hit and run episodes. In the *CSI* episode **A Night At The Movies** glass shards from the optical lens of a video camera are found. Also in the *CSI:Miami* season 3 episode **Legal** sheets and towels were swabbed for fluid after being found in the bin at a massage spa.

CSI season 3 episode **Precious Metal** Catherine finds a missing false nail with a gem at a warehouse. Also in the episode **To Halve and To Hold** Warrick and Sara find a cubic zirconia diamond at the crime scene.
CSI episode **Recipe For Murder** where the glass in the victim's hair came from a car windshield. Also the nail polish on the knife the waitress used, showed she was wearing press-on nails.

CSI:Miami season 1 episode **Grave Young Men**, a fingernail is linked to a killer.

CSI:Miami season 2 episode **A Horrible Mind** where a Hawaiian dancer doll/bobblehead was missing from the dashboard.

In *CSI:Miami* season 3 episode **Under The Influence** tempered glass is found without a membrane, possibly from the side window of a car.

Music

Drop It Like It's Hot by Snoop Dogg

Ratings

17.56 million viewers.   Rated #5 for the week.

Did You Know

Michael DeLuise and Marco Sanchez both worked on the series *SeaQuest DSV.*   Michael is the brother of Peter DeLuise and David, who all guest starred in *Stargate SG1* and are the sons of the late veteran actor Dom De Luise.

14. Blood, Sweat & Tears

Written By Eli Talbert & Erica Shelton Directed By Scott
Lautanen
Us Airdate 9 February 2005
UK Airdate 7 May 2005

Guest Stars: Jim Pirri (Bernardo Espargosa) Mark Ivanir (Maxwell Neiman) Anthony Crivello (Ringmaster) Vidtor Browne (Jason Carty) Michael Cornacchia (Rosie)   Sarah Lafleur (Paige Worthy) Katie Chonacas (Anasuya Espargosa)

Story 1

Background

A swimmer finds a box on the beach with a body. It hasn't been in the water long. Mac says he wasn't double jointed but he had very loose tendons and ligaments. He could be an escape artist. Lukas says it was his son. He was 17, Neiman saw him last night. He was a contortionist; the box was part of his act.

Neiman punches Espargosa; he's a trapeze artist from Brooklyn whereas Neiman is a third generation performer: European royalty. His daughter Anasuya is the star of the circus. She has scratches on her hand and a cyclone tag, a gift to her from Lukas. She never went anywhere with him and Mac says she was off-limits. He was Romeo and she was Juliet; the theme of the circus act. She hurt her arm on the trapeze due to a bad release. Her father caught her and they don't use nets.

Jake Lydell the elephant handler wears a coat. The clown admits to touching the box during his act. His cane was used to make the bruises on Lukas's body. The stockade was his props. Lukas spilled his bucket of bubbles so his act failed. He took him to clown court and was punished in the stocks.

Barnardo Espargosa grabbed Lukas five days ago after he attacked Anasuya. Mac comments Barnardo means 'strong as a bear' in Portugese. Mac says he couldn't throw himself into the ocean so why didn't he fight to get out of the box. It's a case of life imitating art, i.e. *Romeo & Juliet* was taking place backstage. Lukas wanted to end his life so why is Juliet still alive?

Crime Scene Evidence

Stella finds twine in the elephant enclosure. Trace material on the dolly is sand. Mac states everything is here but not his costume which is found in the bin.

Conclusion

Anasuya wore a black sweater as there were black fibres on the dolly. The tears on the costume had traces of mascara in the droplets. Stella says Lukas committed suicide and she found him. She's been at the beach before with Lukas and wanted to go even further than Coney Island if they could. She hates the circus, but Lukas got away. She was going to kill herself from the trapeze but changed her mind.

Story 2

Background

Blood in the apartment went through the ceiling. Danny says there's about 4.5 litres average of blood so any loss of about 500ml leads to unconsciousness. The victim's name is Paige Worthy and she hasn't been seen by anyone for a week. The body in the chute doesn't match Paige's photo. Paige is found at a hotel. The woman at her apartment was Lita Carty.

Her husband denies hitting her because she was college educated and pretty, she wouldn't have stayed with him. He was at the apartment but she didn't open the door so he talked outside for 15 minutes. Lita bought food. Flack tells Danny you can have anything delivered in New York at any time. She ordered loomi so who made the delivery?

Crime Scene Evidence

There are no signs of a struggle. Danny notices the shower curtain missing so the body was carried out. There are multiple fingerprints on the door knob and an unknown powdery substance on the floor. The blood is gravitational towards the door and leads to the garbage chute. There's blood on the chute handle.

Conclusion

174

He spilt the loomi on the floor as he was flirting with Lita. Flack tells him he misread the signs, she wasn't into him. Danny agrees and tells him he stabbed her. He says a man was trying to get into the apartment but it was too late when he left. So, adds Danny, he just threw her out.

Notes

Another episode where the title gives the clue to the episode, especially for the first story and possibly for the second too. (A season 2 episode of *Law & Order Criminal Intent* entitled **Cold Comfort** shown here in the UK on the same night had a woman stabbed in the femoral artery of her leg, this time it was her right leg.)

The 15 minutes Lita's husband stood at the door were the wasted 15 in which she lost her life. Wasn't there a phone at the apartment where the killer could have called for help and escaped via the fire escape. No, life is cheap as Danny comments when he says he just disposed of her.

The uncertainty of suicide pacts, one person always gets cold feet. Coincidentally I mentioned *Romeo & Juliet* hours before this episode actually aired.

There was evidence of unidentified powdery substances in both stories.

Everyone talks to themselves in this show, it's like their trait. Until that too was forgotten in future seasons.

Lots of quoting from Shakespeare's *Romeo & Juliet* going on here, like Act 2 Scene 2 "parting is such sweet sorrow..."

Ehlers Danlose Syndrome aka cutis hyperelastica is an inherited connective disorder. Named after the Dutch doctor Edvard Ehlers and French doctor Henri-Alexandre Danlos. There is no cure.

Quotes

Mac: "Not blood, not sweat, I know what they are..." after eliminating the other two it only leaves, tears.

Danny: "You've gotta get outta here without leaving a trail of evidence and that trail starts right here."

A Danny Moment

Danny: "That doesn't mean anything. I've lived in my apartment three years, none of my neighbour's recognize me." (Hey, we'd recognize him!!)
Flack: "Better hope you don't go missing."

A Mac and Danny Moment

Mac: "Danny, breathe."
Danny: "I feel like it's right in front of me, Mac. I just can't see it."
Mac: "Take your eyes out of it. Talk it out."
Danny: "Husband's DNA doesn't match."
Mac: "Husband wasn't in the apartment, but somebody else was. The evidence is right there Messer, you're not."
These two never stop talking about evidence; which is great for this show.

CSI Déjà Vu

CSI **Chaos Theory** where the body was disposed of down the garbage chute, so she was actually in the garbage when Catherine missed the body in the dumpster outside and no one bothered searching it. There was a bloodstain on the dumpster chute in the dorm building, just like here.

Also the episode where the victim knew her assailant and let him in, re carwash episode **Invisible Evidence** from *CSI* and the CSI:Miami episode from season 2 entitled **Complications** about the anesthesiologist found hanging when the patient's husband was outside the door whilst he was being killed.

CSI season 3 episode **Forever** involved a case of assisted suicides where a teenage victim died from a painkiller overdose and another female victim was killed with the same painkiller patch; a case of assisted suicides or rather murder. Similar to Romeo and Juliet.

Season 5 *CSI* episode **Mea Culpa** where the hair sample was found to not be human and was from a dog.

Compare aspects of this episode with *CSI* **Chaos Theory** where there's a gap on the floor and Gil thinks the rug was used to remove the body. Here the shower curtain was used. Also in the episode **The Finger** (season 2 *CSI*) where a bathroom shower curtain was missing and used to wrap the DB.

Season 3 CSI:Miami episode **Under The Influence** box cutters were used.

Music

Let's Get It started by Black Eye Peas

Did You Know

Scott Lautanen's directing of this episode was mentioned in an article in the Ashtabula Star-Beacon.

Ratings

13.08 million viewers. Rated #19 for the week

Bloops

When the box is opened at the beach, the DB's head is positioned at the right corner. When opened again in the lab for analysis – the head is at the right corner, the arms and legs are seen above. This is the position that is shown in all of the flashback scenes.

1.15 Til Death Do Us Part

Written By Pam Veasey Directed By Nelson McCormick
US Airdate 16 February 2005
UK Airdate 14 May 2005

Guest Stars: Kelly Hu (Det Kylie Macca) Robin Thomas (Abel Bloom) Rick D Wassweman (Walter Lisco) Jim Ortlieb (John Swinton) David DeLuise (Lance Moretti) Neal Matarazzo (Henry Milton)

Story 1

Background

A bride dies at her wedding after witnessing dead doves fall to the floor. Mac comments people here aren't superstitious as it's bad luck for birds to fly indoors. The bridal suite is checked and her father doesn't want an autopsy carried out until she's been blessed by a Rabbi.

Danny tells Della, the bird handler she wanted the birds. Kylie tells her cruelty to animals is a crime. He didn't kill Hannah. It was her idea for the doves, she trained them and the hotel took all the money.

Audrey had access to formaldehyde. The groom, Walter has his hair on the dress. Audrey used to go out with Walter but he left her. They were friends. Walter is worth $50 million. He wanted to surprise Hannah, the bride, but found Audrey in her dress. She brought the dress at a re-sale shop.

Danny and Mac find the re-sale shop, Truman has a receipt but no details for who sold him the dress. The name is John Smith and

Truman doesn't ask questions. He also brought in two other suits. They take these for analysis.

Hawkes examines the body of another dead man on the street, Samuels. He bought a suit and stepped in front of a taxi. There are initials on the handkerchief. He has the same COD as Hannah.

Crime Scene Evidence

Mac notices redness in her eye but no streaks in her make-up. Caused either by external injuries or allergies...slight redness on skin. Mac notices her epidermis is hard showing symptoms of chemical exposure. The bride complained of headaches and dizziness. Mac thinks she could've been poisoned but they don't know how or the motive

Possible Crime Scene Evidence

Danny finds evidence of alcohol use in her suite as there are bottles but no drugs or any signs of poisoning. Mac says they should turn to Plan B: the birds.

Conclusion

Mac tells the suspect desecration of burials, theft, two counts of murder are what he'll be charged with.   He wanted to make money. There's one more suit. Mac stops the wedding to remove the suit from the groom. He's here to save his life.

Story 2

Background

Flack tells Stella and Aiden about an abandoned car and a hand found at a former monastery which is rumoured to be haunted by monks. Aiden calls it an urban legend.

Rick was stabbed in prison. They fought about food; Rick stole his so he cut him. He got off at Queens Plaza after being released from jail. Stella says they know everywhere he went between two places. The first was a diner where the waitress tells them there was fighting and they were thrown out. They drove away in an SUV twenty minutes from here which was taken from outside. This was five minutes away so he was meeting someone.

Connor denies stealing the car. He was placed in foster care after his father died and confesses to killing Rick. Stella doesn't find a photo of his father at his apartment. But Flack finds he collected everything on Rick so any DA would call this proof of premeditation. Stella says he only confessed to killing and not stealing. Flack replies he was confused. He doesn't care what happened after that and so they have enough evidence and he's taking it to the DA. Stella argues that they need more evidence.

Stella goes back to prison and searches the cell. There she finds a pad with the imprint of the map and uses charcoal to highlight it. The victim was lured there and someone killed him. There's evidence of runner on his forehead.

Mac tells Stella he had a call from Flack and Stella loses her temper again. Her phone was off and he called to tell her he wouldn't go to the DA until they both agree. The visitors log at jail has the name Vince Moretti, he visited Robert Lagano.

Crime Scene Evidence

The DB has $1.50 and an NYC bus pass. He was out of prison. Stella finds dermal tissue in his mouth and concludes he chewed his hand off as it was the only way out of the handcuffs. Aiden says he was also trying to dig a hole but there's nothing there. Structural engineers were carrying out a survey to the building and found him. They were here last week too. The SUV was stolen four days ago.

Conclusion

Stella claims you need to know about the structure of the building to know how to fix the shackles to the wall with a two hundred pound man. He took measurements and has traces of rubber on his forehead. Lance hit him. Flack comments the motive was revenge and it started over food. Henry only found the hand, no one found the body. Lance owes Lagano for not getting caught for a robbery.

Stella believes Connor and he confessed to the murder as he wanted it to be true. He tells her he couldn't go through with it. She says he doesn't want to be in the system. Connor tells her she's lucky she never knew her parents because she doesn't know what she's missing. Stella shows his fingerprint and explains he wasn't in the system until now and it's up to him to stay out of trouble.

Notes

Stella is an orphan and never knew her parents. Connor tells her that's a good thing because she's not missing anything but how can it be, she's missing not having or knowing her parents around. She lived at St Basil's orphanage until she was 18. (See season 5 for more on Stella's past and her mother.) In **3.22 Cold reveal** Stella has a foster family. It's revealed Stella was foster daughter of Marilyn Bennet and her foster sister was Mindy Sanchez. The two were "blood sisters". Then how could Stella have lived at an orphanage until she was 18. Clearly someone (plenty of someone's) forgot this in the story/plot line!

Stella loses her temper not once but twice in this episode and both times at Flack over Connor. At least he's one suspect she's actually passionate about and wants to save rather than put him away quick smart.

Lots of jokes in this episode too and one liners.

Another mention of urban legends in season 5's eyeball episode, when the eyeball was dropped in Stella's coffee by a bird.

Hawkes leaves his ME lab once again.

As for wearing other peoples' clothes, didn't they think to wash them or at least get them dry cleaned beforehand, eeew.

It's true, Aiden has a one track mind and if Danny was to say things like that he'd be accused of being sexist etc! See the next episode re bondage, and **1.13 Tanglewood** about the massage parlour. Also Stella and Aiden making fun of Flack at the beginning was rather sexist too. Proving the women in this show try to be one of the guys and don't pull it off too well either!

Eddie Cahill describes Flack as having "impube behind Flack: give and you shall receive. I think helping or being of assistance is rewarding enough...the relationship they have, I don't think so much it's one sided in that, Flack's always giving. They have a great relationship outside of when they're in crisis mode, joking in the hallways and this and that, the little comments in the lab. Then getting into other stuff, I think that's just what Flack does."

Referring to this episode he says, Flack loves food. As in the scene here when Stella says she wants to drive and Flack comments that when she drives they never eat..."that was the beginning of that – I enjoy it because I would be a fan of chow myself. That's the stuff we get on a procedural now. I think our audience is really good at grabbing those and hanging onto those and letting those live, because those are our character beats, outside of **The Fall**, outside of **Consequences** [season 3, a superb episode] – major storylines when you really get into something. That's who we are, that's who those characters are, those brief little moments that speak volumes, that's character."

Which all add up until you get an all-round picture of who they are, what makes them tick, etc, until you think you know a character and out of the blue, they'll go and do something to either completely amaze or totally shock. See Flack in the season 5 finale after, new character, Angell is killed.

Quotes

Mac: "Two dead doves, one dead bride, looks like foul play to me." (Groan!)

Mac stops the wedding on the line: "if anyone here feels...Mac: "I'm here to save your life so you can live happily ever after."

Stella: "I'm driving."
Flack: "Please, Stella, let me drive. Got a cracker or a piece of candy in the glove box because when you drive, we don't eat." Well they were going to a diner after all.

Flack: "Did they continue their big old 'thang' outside?"

Stella: "The evidence is not conclusive." (Hey, that's my line.)
Flack: "His prints were on the car and the gun, you found his DNA under Rick Amadori's nails."
Stella: "Under layers of dirt which proves Amadori was still alive after he scratched Connor. Gives us our timeline."
Flack: "Nice, what's wrong with good old fashioned motive?"
Stella; "Doesn't put him at the crime scene."
Flack: "Car puts him outside."
Stella; "Key word: outside. Not at the crime scene."
On it went, with Stella having to have the last word and the last say! As per usual.

A Danny Moment

Kylie: "Gives new meaning to the words 'cold feet'.
Danny: "You know if I was to say something like that, you'd call me insensitive."
Kylie: "No, I would've asked you if you wanted to grab a drink later. I'm attracted to a man with a dark sense of humour."
Mac: "You two wanna be alone. I'll drag the body outside."

Danny: "She started it." So Kylie had a 'thang' for Danny. From this it's easy to see where they came up with the Flack/Angell romance in season 4.

A Mac and Danny Moment

Mac: "It could happen to you, you know."
Danny: "What marriage?"
Mac: "Love."
Danny: "Don't even say stuff like that Mac, it's not even funny." Why not? It could! And it did in the next season, so did the marriage in season 5, but so not to the right person!!

CSI Deja Vu

This episode, the clothes 'recycling' from DBs at funeral homes *CSI* episode season 1 **Friends and Lovers**: Sara was assigned to a recycling coffins case.

In *CSI* season 1 episode **$35K O.B.O.** a lift from a pad shows notes on the planning of a murder just as it did here. When Stella takes a lift from a pad in the prison cell.

Music

The Outsider by A Perfect Circle. *Air on a G String* Bach

Ratings

14.039 million.   Rated #13 for week

Did You Know

Robin Thomas was also in the *CSI: Miami* episode **Dead Zone.** David DeLuise guest starred in *Stargate SG1* as Amanda Tapping's love interest and is related to the DeLuise brothers see episode **1.13 Tanglewood**

1.16 Hush

Written By Anthony E Zuiker & Timothy J Lea
Directed By Deran Serafian
US Airdate 23 February 2005
UK Airdate 21 May 2005

Guest Stars: Kim Coates (Det. Vicaro) Chad Lindberg (Chad Willingham) Laura Leigh Hughes (Jennifer Stupaine) Albie Selznick (John Stupaine) Mark Sheppard (Kevin Harrington) Bumper Robinson (Mike Prineman) Tory Kittles (Sean Bally) Ted Raimi ("Garage" Joe Strahil) Sonya Walger (Jane)

Story 1

Background

A driver is involved in a shooting in a truck jacking. The police picked up the kids involved. There's blood found on the container. Hawkes brings his spatula. Part of a body is found, compacted. Kevin Harrington, the foreman says they can't shut down the port. Mac wants to look at their tracking databases and says the time of death (TOD) was within 4 hours.

The computer shows where the container was in the last 12 hours. The victim's name was Paddy Golan and Morraga saw him last night but not after 10:30. He looked out for the crew. Mike says the supervisor didn't treat the workers well. They're not meant to be speaking to Mac. All workers have a knife. Sean had an accident courtesy of Paddy.

Mac and Stella check the containers and find a body inside. It's Mike's brother, Jimmy Prineman. Mac claims that Paddy was involved in his death and was in the container but why? Mike is fired. Paddy was stealing electrical goods from the containers. Money is found at his apartment along with brass knuckles. ALS shows blood on the clock and leads them to the Rusty Hook Bar. The bartender tells them Paddy and Jimmy had a fight. Mike followed Paddy out but didn't find him.

Crime Scene Evidence

The rest of the body is found under another container. The container was there at 11pm last night.

Conclusion

The container was from a shipment to Hong Kong. Mac thinks it was moved by someone in authority and with training. Paddy didn't use the equipment but Mac is almost run over at the docks by Kevin. Mac takes his knife. Mac says he wanted to teach him a lesson. Paddy helped with Jimmy's body and then demanded money. The container would make it look like an accident but Kevin stabbed him and then Paddy was crushed.

Mac thanks Stella for saving him and gets Mike his job back.

Story 2

Background

A dead woman is found on the side of the road in the nude. There's blood on the tree bark; headlight glass on the ground and skid marks. Danny and Aiden speak with her husband, Ron Bogda who tells them Debbi and he led separate lives. Danny thinks she was involved in a fetish stunt. His glasses broke.

Danny and Aiden visit a bondage seminar run by Jennifer. The people there are into *Fornaphelia*: the art of human furniture and other contraptions, all manufactured by Garage Joe. He makes a run for it and escapes. Jennifer is wearing base and is concealing a black eye which is a square and she has bruising on her collarbone too. This shows she was on the passenger side of the car. But John, her husband wasn't the driver.

Danny tackles Joe to the ground. He only sells the equipment and he doesn't have any bruising.

Crime Scene Evidence

On the F150 car is found a mile east of Clearview Expressway with a dolly attached to the front. Glass on the passenger side floor and a bag inside containing a latex suit. Straps with teeth impressions and a sign saying 'place shoulders here'. She was strapped upside down.

Conclusion

Danny tells Bob that Debbi was on the 'Scream – a – hitch', he was driving but he didn't slow down. He lost control and crashed into the tree. They planted her body and he wasn't wearing a belt. Danny tells him his children don't have a mother now and he killed her just for fun.

Notes

The first episode where Hawkes actually leaves the safety of the ME's lab to conduct an on site exam.
Aiden missing the hair on the rack. Stella being smug and joking about the DB again. This was going a bit too far in this episode, especially the part about the spatula.

Mac gets 'physical' with a suspect. As does Danny, apprehending another suspect and emotional too when he mentions the children not having a mother now. (See later cab driver episode too.)

Melina: "Our technical advisor Bill, who's a CSI, was in the middle of a story about a guy who he found chopped up in a bag and he described it in the most disgusting way. Then the next second he was talking about how he'd seen his baby kick for the first time on an ultrasound. One moment he's technical and meticulous about describing this hideous scene, then five seconds later he's like the rest of us the first time you hear that heartbeat."

Reference to the Marlon Brando movie *On the Waterfront*.

Another question: why didn't Kevin just remove Jimmy's body from the container and dump it elsewhere after Paddy helped him with it and was blackmailing him. After all if a body can't be found then it can't be proved he killed him (i.e. you need a DB to prove murder) and who'd believe Paddy anyway when no one liked him and he was into stealing too, which Kevin could've used against him. Obviously these criminals have no clue as to how to commit the perfect murder.

The original title for this episode was **Fear.**

Chad Lindberg started acting in Mount Vernon, Washington and in *Black Circle Boys*. As well as going on to *Supernatural* season 2 in a few episodes as MIT geek, Ash.

Kim Coates went on to play H's formidable enemy in Season 5 of *CSI:Miami*, married to H's ex Julia, and then turned police informant.

Carmine comments on the show's hectic schedule, "It's like shooting a movie every night. We have maybe one read through before a scene and it's straight into it. You have to be there and ready to perform. There's nothing glamorous about it. It's 8 days a week, 12-16 hours a day. You do get days off but on them you're just working on your stuff for the next day. It's hard." That's one reason most people prefer to make movies, whereas working on a TV show really takes it out of you. But it's just as hard for the crew.

Quotes

Stella: "That's gonna need a bit more than a bag and tag."
Mac: "Tell him to bring a spatula."

Danny: "First thing you learn on this job is that anybody can do anything to anyone." But it's always the most obvious suspect.

Danny: "Why don't you try it?"
Aiden: "That's sexual harassment, Danny." But if she'd have said it then it wouldn't be. Lots of double standards here, especially as to how Stella and Aiden would get away with such comments but the guys wouldn't and be deemed sexist.

Danny: "Yeah, traffic was murder."

Danny: "Sex, lies and Super 8"

Danny: "You hungry? Get a bite to eat. I'll drive, put you on the hood."
Aiden: "Put you on the hood."

Most Pointless Line

Stella telling Flack he woke them up just to tell them he's solved the truck jacking case! As if he'd bother waking them up if there was no case.

A Danny Moment

Danny: "You take the bottom, I'll take the top."
Aiden: "I like being on top."
Danny: "You getting all free on me because we drew a bondage case."

CSI Déjà Vu

CSI fetish cases season 5 **King** contained the baby fetish of a man: dressing up playing, etc, like a baby.
Bondage cases with Lady Heather, such as season **3 Lady Heather's Box** and **Slaves of Las Vegas** where they examine all the equipment used in bondage, especially the masks and straws.

CSI **6.15 Pirates of the Third Reich** more bondage. **9.5 Leave Out All the Rest** involving the world of domination. (Though these two episodes came later and so strictly speaking can't be called déjà vu; even though this does happen.)

In *CSI* season 2 episode **Anatomy of a Lye,** a suspect has seat belt wounds on his chest. The suspect's wounds of "dicing" glass were from a head-on impact.

As for the insect eggs Gil would have been right at home, such as in *CSI* episodes: **Anatomy of a Lye** where a maggot is found which only lives in a certain temperature. **1.6 Burden of Proof** maggots are found in a decomposing human corpse. Season 2 **Scuba Doobie-Doo,** Gil finds fly egg casings and a Silphid beetle, which feeds on human flesh, thus they can extract human DNA from it.

Ratings

14.305 million viewers. Rated #12 for the week.

1.17 The Fall

Written By Anne McGrail Screenplay By Bill Haynes
Directed By Norberto Barba
US Airdate 23 March 2005
UK Airdate 28 May 2005

Guest Stars: Sonya Walger (Jane) Jack Gwaltney (Sgt Gavin Moran) Stacey Travis (Chandra Heckman) Brad Grunberg (Melvin Heckman) Patrick Fischler (Brent) Erik Gavica (Tomas Perez) Rose Abdoo (Blanca Vasquez) Clark Gregg (DA Allen McShane) Mike Risco (Hector Vasquez)

Story 1

Background

Hooded teens rob and kill a wine store owner, one of them, Hector is reluctant to shoot. Sgt Moran says the owner was shot in the back twice. The gangbangers left on foot.

Sgt Moron describes Flack as the son of an NYPD legend. The teens disposed of the weapons quickly. A hot weapon can't be kept so is thrown away in the alley. The "alpha Maggot" throws it away first in the alley and Moran finds the gun under a dumpster. Flack says, "beta Maggot sees A throw away and does the same thing in the next alley."

The gang's place is searched. Mac tests for GSR on their hands. They're clean. Mac is convinced Perez murdered the owner. The prosecutor tells Mac he needs to make an arrest. Mac doesn't allow politics in his lab if he can help it.
Stella checks the police dispatch log concerning the soda can. The bookstore clerk saw them running around 10:15. The first officer was on the scene at 10:17. Mac says the time-line means there was no retrieval of the can. Flack tells him Moran doesn't forget a thing. Moran can't recall the can. Flack asks for his memo book.
Flack returns to the crime scene. He rode with him for four years and knows how he thinks. Moran dumps the can in a bin across the road, which Flack recovers. Stella comments Moran was on the same beat for twenty years. Mac tells her they don't know anything until the evidence is confirmed. (Isn't this what she said to Flack when she was so eager to keep Connor out of the investigation in an earlier episode.)

Moran was a young man who saved a girl in the Projects. They had a son. He remained on the same beat to keep an eye on him. But the allure of a gang was too much for a Dominican boy with a white father. Blanca Vasquez received cheques from Moran. Hector is with a cousin in Atlanta and told her not to talk to anyone called Perez. Hector failed the initiation.

Crime Scene Evidence

Mac finds footprints through the wine. The gun used was a 9mm. Mac is wearing triple gloves because of the blood. The cold means there's less chance of finding clues and prints or DNA because of their heavy clothing. Glass is swabbed as there may be a second bleeder. Stella finds a lighter and checks the smokes. There's also a surveillance camera.

Mac uses lasers to match the bullet trajectory. The bullet went through the bottle.

The memo pad has scribblings on the entry which Flack asks Stella to examine, off the record.

Conclusion

Mac questions Perez and tells him there could be a way out and he shouldn't throw his life away because of a grudge against his father. Perez shot the owner. He couldn't pull the trigger. Mac says the statement and the can has been compromised so evidence against Perez is needed.

Flack wants to bring Moran in. The DA forced him into retirement; he can keep his pension since he doesn't want too much media attention.

Story 2

Background

A DB is found on a canopy. Hawkes carries out the preliminary exam. Lividity on one side, rigour shows he's been dead four hours. Mrs Hackman always cleans up before the party.
His wife kicked him as he was overweight and was having tantrums. She forbade him from eating chocolate. The wall has silver paint from his cufflinks where she kicked him. She loved him.

Crime Scene Evidence

Danny says there was a party on the third floor and there's an oily stain on his right shoulder. Aiden says he's Melvin Hackman: film royalty. Danny finds the absence of oxidation on the balcony so there's no rust. He finds a fibre on the railing from the victim's shirt so he fell face first. Blood on the ledge is found. Danny says he didn't fall clear of the building so it was suicide or an accident.

Conclusion

Danny finds wrappers in a bird's nest. There are chocolates in a gargoyle above the ledge. He was careless because he'd been drinking. He took one chocolate and went for another, the rail broke and he fell.

Notes

Stella eager to convict again even before the evidence is barely in. She's not judge and jury either.
Also in both the stories, there was the presence of trace on the jackets.

A Flack episode, as he has to bring in an old friend/mentor of his. "On a personal note, "says Eddie, "the one that is going to air this week, [March 23] is my favourite. It's called 'The Fall' and what I loved about it is, it's a real personal story between my character and the guy who brought him along in the department. Who we learned has served as a father figure to Flack. It was a gift to me because I learned a lot more about my character, beyond that he can grab a guy on his way out or do an interrogation."

Flack's notebook will be subject to more 'interrogation' (pardon the pun) in **3.8 Consequences**, where Mac forces him to do exactly the same thing, asking for his memo book – after a consignment of drugs goes missing from the police evidence room and are found in an investigation. An episode where the argument between them is a must-see and ructions from this spill over into some subsequent episodes.

Notice Moran put the can straight into the bin and covered it with paper, yet when Flack retrieves it, it's now in a paper bag. What he's been a cop for over 20 years and he couldn't think of a better place to dispose of the soda can. As usual, the garbage isn't collected until later.

Also couldn't Moran have just tore the page from his memo book and made a fresh entry unless they are specifically numbered.

The title again refers to the producer falling from his balcony and also Moran taking the fall for his son in covering up for him.

A routine episode not many plot twists or a large pool of suspects. But did have some character element in this with Flack having to keep his head whilst bringing in his mentor and friend and a lesson in how not to break rules, a first in this series. As this was definitely a Flack episode, Danny was kept well away from him and the proceedings in this story.

This is one of Eddie's favourite episodes. He says "it's great on a personal level." Says Carmine, Flack watches out for Danny. He's a more caring character, "he's more mature than Danny. Two different ends of a style, of a person in one sense, but both admire the other."

Eddie likes the fact Flack has a legacy in the show. His father was a police officer before him, quite a legend – the tradition to it, as were his grandfather, great grandfather and the stories to grow and learn from. The strong sense of history. "There's some very definite boundaries between the good guys and the bad guys. I think in some respects his life's work is making sure these people who create the most heinous of crimes really don't get to enjoy the rest of their lives. To me that's a worthwhile cause, so I relate to that."

His favourite scene where he talks to Sgt Moran and he says, 'You going to ink me here? Flack replies he isn't, they're going to venture outside. "He [Flack] tends towards the classy in moments of stress. I think he's got a care for people, I think he understands, he's got a protective quality towards the people he cares about. He's aware of more than himself, and I appreciate that. What he wants may not always be the most pressing issue on his mind."

You could say Hackman dies from 'death by chocolate'.
Danny has an uncle who makes canopies in Queens, so he knows canopies run to the kerb. Hawkes describes it as an awning. Aiden has a cousin who is a cobbler.

On Hawkes' character, Hill Harper comments: "What I love about Hawkes [is] he trusts the science and the evidence. If you look at somebody like Gil Grissom – I think there's a lot of similarity between Hawkes and Grissom in that sense. Two characters that love the science and love the evidence...really do it right and then the bad guy gets caught and the good guys go free like they should and you never get that wrong and you can trust that, and you don't have to assume they're guilty because there's no assumption to be made."

Quotes

Mac: "Unfortunately for gangs, they can't intimidate evidence."

Mac: "If there's one speck of dust out there that proves it, I will find it and you will answer for what you did." Which he did.

Mac: "...tampered with evidence, my evidence."
Danny: "Last thing he did."

A Danny Moment

Danny: "Bird's eye view."
Aiden: "You had to say it, right."
Danny: "What you gonna do?"

CSI Déjà Vu

CSI episode 1 season 3 **Revenge Is A Dish Best Served Cold** (the episode Carmine guest starred in) where the gambler known as Candyman dies because of his devotion to chocolate and he also ate poisoned chocolate. The cocoa contained lead. Here Hackman also had an addiction to chocolate and also dies as result of it. Though in both cases, death was accidental and not intentional.

Aiden telling Danny there's no database for women's shoes cf *CSI* again episode season 2 **Cats In The Cradle** where Catherine lifts a shoeprint, possibly from a high heel.

For the cigarette lighter see the episode with the fire in season 5 **Spark Of Life,** where Sara found a partial lighter in the fire residue.
In the season 3 episode of *CSI* **Lady Heather's Box,** a stiletto heel was used to kill with.

CSI season 2 episode, **Scuba Doobie Doo** where a VSC4 machine was used to show ink signatures were from two different pens. Also in *CSI:Miami* season 3 episode **Hell Night,** where the indentation on a note was run through *ESDA* to check the writing.

Bloops

The suspect puts down the can of drink. When the CSIs look at the CCTV video and find it's not there on the screen, so whoever was first on the scene must've removed it. I.e. the police officer. But the actual suspect shot at the security camera before the bodega owner was shot, so the can could've been removed by one of the suspects.

Also when Moran took the can and dumped it, it wasn't in a bag; but in the flashback, when Flack retrieves the can, it's now in a paper bag in the bin. That's one of my own observations. Why is trash collection never on a day when a crime is committed and why dump the can across the road from the crime scene, when he could've taken it with him in his patrol car, assuming he had a patrol car and just dumped it anywhere.

Ratings

13.62 million viewers. Rated #20 for the week.

1.18 The Dove Commission

Written By Anthony E Zuiker & Zachery Reiter
Directed By Emilio Estevez
US Airdate 23 March 2005
UK Airdate 4 June 2005

Guest Stars: Grant Albrecht (Dr Giles) Chad Lindberg (Chad Willingham) Mike Starr (Chief Vince Robinson) Alana Ubach (Constance Briell) David Packer (Morty Sherman) Clay Wilcox (Paul Baxter) Patrice Fisher (Jamie Banks/Savannah) Leslie Bega (Grace Walderson) Jeremy Ray Valdez (Antonio Reyes) Mark Rolston (Inspector Bill Marconi) Diana Lupino (Charlotte DuBois)

Story 1

Background

The Commission releases their report on NYPD police corruption tomorrow. There's a shooting at the bar where Commissioner Stanwyck and a woman are shot and killed. He was the chief investigator. Flack thinks the report is damaging. Charlotte Dubois was collateral damage. Mac starts with the report.

Grace says Charlotte was from Kentucky. Mac assures her every officer in the NYPD is doing what they can to find the killer. Mac gets a preliminary copy of the report. Men under Chief Robinson and he himself are implicated in the report alleging his men were trafficking drugs in police cars. The Chief admits to being on the firing range so he'll have GSR on his hands.

Mac tells Inspector Marconi from IAB that he has evidence pending. He wants to put Robinson away. A mechanical helicopter called 'TAG' is the murder weapon. It has a thermal camera. Mac is concerned by the window. If Jasper used it then he had 4 hours. He was on the late shift from 2am to noon. They have to prove he was the shooter. Officers of the NYPD are given 'Pass and Go' counters so they don't have to pay the toll in cash so they track his movements.

Mac clears everyone. The 'Pass and Go' photo shows Jasper was driving north and didn't have enough time to turn around. They decide it's less about the report and more about something else.

Grace was having an affair with Stanwyck. Mac gives her a tissue which she throws in the bin when she leaves. She can't trust anyone and has to protect herself.

Crime Scene Evidence

The windows are shattered. Stella wants to examine all the bullets herself and also collect them. Flack stops a reporter from filming. Stella finds the bullets went through the glass at a high rate so the glass fell directly down from the windows. She wonders where the shooter was as she can't find any casings but knows the bullets were fired from a rifle. The two bullets have different stria so Stella thinks there were two rifles and two bullets. The bullet went through the glass first so the first shots were fired from the outside, 65 floors up. Mac questions where the sniper was positioned.

Stella and Flack find shell casings on the 65th floor. Flack tells her a sniper couldn't hit the 65th floor.

Conclusion

Marconi also had a 'Pass and Go account'. Five years ago he worked for TARU. He was driving a TARU vehicle without authorization. Marconi threatens their careers. Mac says he killed the wrong woman. It was a crime of passion. Marconi states Stanwyck stole Grace from him. Mac tells him Marconi would be heading the IA investigation and would frame Jasper for the murders.

Story 2

Background

Fernando Reyes, a gypsy cab driver is found dead in his cab. Danny wonders if he had a legitimate licence, whether he'd still be alive. Antonio tells them he's been waiting ten years for them to show up with news about his father. Danny asks forthright questions and asks if he was having an affair, as he could've attacked the woman.
Arnold says he didn't use the cab as he takes a limo service from work. He gave his card to a stripper called Savannah. She tells them Fernando dropped her off and someone attacked from behind. Fernando tried to help and saved her life. She didn't go to the police since they wouldn't believe her. Danny takes the clothes she wore that night.

Crime Scene Evidence

The fare money is missing. The usual M.O is murder with guns but he was stabbed. Perhaps the killer went down the subway. They speak with a transit worker in the crowd. Danny says they should start with the body.

Conclusion

The transit worker was at the crime scene. He watched Savannah come home every night. Paul says he almost got away with it if it wasn't for Fernando. Danny loses his temper and tells him he has a son and was only trying to do his job.

Danny apologizes to Antonio and tells him about how Danny and his father were attacked when they got into a wrong gypsy cab when he was ten and were beaten. He tells him Fernando was a good man and this city needs more men like him. He gives him the photo of his father.

Notes

Flack gives Stella an all important clue when she insists on taking point on the bullets from the scene; when he tells her mid-air is the only place those bullets could've come from. Stella doesn't take any photos of the bullets or casings and just picks them up when everything is supposed to be documented. At least it is most of the time, but not here.

Grace hit the decks pretty fast when the bullets were flying. She and Charlotte also wore similar red dresses.

Hawkes is pickling a brain for 4-10 days so it's easier to dissect.

How could someone like Marconi in IA not think about the cameras on the toll bridges and the 'Pass and Go' counters.

Danny and his father were attacked in the cab and he still bears a grudge and recalls the incident from his childhood. An emotional episode for Danny. Especially when he thinks his father could have ended up dead too, or even Danny himself. But now Antonio doesn't have a father.

A lot of research is being undertaken on the 'Y' chromosome. Another study was carried out on 'XYY Syndrome' where the extra 'Y' chromosome is thought to be associated with male criminality.

This episode was originally entitled **The Mollen Commission**.

Quotes

Flack: "You keep filming, I'm gonna give you rights and lefts."

Hawkes: "...favourite game was *Operation*."

Mac: "His nose didn't buzz red, well done." (Hawkes was a surgeon in a previous life, so why would his nose buzz red anyway, when he has a steady hand, I know it was meant to be a joke.)

Mac: "I can only look where the evidence leads me."

Danny: "Pay it off the rest of your life or pay it off with your life. It's an easy decision in my book."

Danny: "Somebody's gotta ask the questions. It's what you gotta do. I'm reacting to the evidence."
Aiden: "No you're not, you're just reacting."
Aiden: "Holy Boob job Batman."

Danny: "Let me tell you something, you know the subways where you work, you better think one of those opens up when they put you away in prison."

A Danny Moment

Danny: "We need a word in private and I don't mean the champagne room."

CSI Déjà Vu

CSI:Miami sniper episode season 2, **Kill Zone.** Episode **2.1 Blood Brothers** demonstrating close boundaries of legality too, for example, they have access to evidence if it is public property or in plain sight, (as H and Calleigh mention a lot in season 3). In this episode, the dress fibre blown to the floor.

CSI episodes about DNA collection re tissue from the bin. Season **1.18 I-15 Murders** where the security guard licking the envelope inadvertently provided his DNA in his saliva. Then season 3 *CSI* episode **Blood Lust** mentioned the death of a cab driver at the hands of an angry mob, though the two episodes had different storylines and motives.

Music

Sway by Peter Cincotti

Ratings

16.733 million viewers. Rated #5 for the week.

1.19 Crimes & Misdemeanours

Written By Andrew Lipsitz & Eli Talbert Directed By Rob
Bailey
US Airdate 13 April 2005
UK Airdate 11 June 2005

Guest Stars: Sonya Walger (Jane) Chad Lindberg (Chad Willingham)
Dominic Fumusa (Robert Costa) Kevin Alejandro (Tom Martin)
Steven Petrarca (Frank Barrett) Andre Kristoff (Tony Garcia)
Leia Thompson (Paula Reid)

Story 1

Background

A dead woman is found at a laundry wrapped in sheets from a
hotel. Stella will look into missing persons. The sheets have the
name 'Linford Hotel' of which there are 12 in the city. Diplomats
stay at the hotel when the UN is in Special Session.

Flack finds there was one order of caviar to the Trade Delegation
from Tuscarora, an Island in the Mid-Atlantic. Robert Costa is the
diplomat; Tony is his secretary; Tom looks after his transportation
and Frank is his chief aide, he has partial hearing loss.

Ten years ago, Costa was a college student and raped and
murdered Susan Young. She had the same cuts and COD. DNA
analysis revealed an unknown male and Costa. All his friends took

the stand for him. The blood from the bed matches the female Jane Doe. Mac says they'll have to track her back to him. Costa admits he took her back to the hotel with him and that menstrual blood doesn't bother him. (Charming, what about the woman's point of view!! Or doesn't that matter.)

Jenny's roommate says she was dating Europeans and can give a sketch artist a description.

There were two DNA samples on the bottle, one was Jenny's the other is Thomas, he beat his girlfriend. The sketch looks like Thomas. Jenny didn't mean anything to him and he cut himself that night. The whole room was bleached. Thomas had Roofies, prescribed from a doctor in Paris because of a sleeping disorder.

Potential Crime Scene Evidence & Medical Exam

Hawkes finds the laceration transected her carotid artery: difficult to determine the weapon. It looks personal and pathological. The cuts were made to control her body. Mac says there's no bruising and Stella adds there are no ligature marks either.

Mac comments on the uniqueness of the arterial spray. Stella says she was lying on the sheet. There's a void on the area and it appears blood dripped off the side.

Actual Crime Scene Evidence

The bed sheets are all clean. Stella takes a hair from a brush. Mac says sheets are easy to remove. They turn over the mattress and Mac cuts through it revealing a blood stain on the spring coils.
They have a timeline to when the champagne was spiked: the prints on the cork and the Roofies match so they're looking for someone else. Stella thinks the killer didn't leave the room. Mac finds traces of someone else in the room as he finds a hearing aid behind the safe.

Conclusion

Frank's prints were on the bottle and he had access to it. His print is also on the hearing aid. He hid in the closet and waited. He placed Jenny on top of Costa and killed her. He heard blood dripping whilst waiting for Costa to wake and knocked out his hearing aid. He wanted revenge and cut Jenny's arms and legs the way Costa cut Susan. The semen from Susan matches Frank. He waited ten years for Costa to face up to what he did to the woman Frank loved.

Story 2

Background

The DB, a human statue leaning against the wall was found by a Swedish tourist. There is nearby video surveillance. The jar still has money in it. Officer Lilley didn't know him. Danny tells them he had help from support braces to stand up.

Mac tells Danny to hand the case over to precinct detectives. Danny says there are suspicious circumstances as he was redressed. Mac tells him it's a misdemeanour and he shouldn't compromise an active case. Danny goes against Mac and tells Aiden they're still on the case.

Lilley arrested him because he was a homeless man and the weather was so cold.

Conclusion

The man's ulna is 12 inches, femur is 21 so 12 divided by 21 =1.75:1. Scott says it wasn't a joke. John didn't thank him for a tip he left in his jar. He was dead so he took the chance to dress him up and took a day off so he could be a real person and not a statue. He didn't do anything on his free day.

Mac reprimands Danny for disobeying orders. Danny turns around and glances back at Mac.

Notes

See the next episode where Stella goes OTT and Mac doesn't even give her so much as a reprimand. (Also in other seasons, especially season 5.) Stella's been there longer and she hasn't learnt she's not a one woman army! So don't her interrogation techniques, as well as leaving a lot to be desired, affect everyone else too. Danny didn't get any complaints from IA, or anyone else for doing his job and he's just as passionate about it as her.

As this was an episode mentioning the UN, at least we could have got some footage of the UN and perhaps even got a political case. Even if Mac has said his lab isn't political. Would've made the episode a bit different instead of having a personal motive once again.

Stella mentioning they've got a fat chance of finding out where Jenny came from was a bit defeatist for her, usually she's rearing to go and bring in the suspect, any suspect. Also betting on a victim, even if it's just a passing comment isn't nice.

Hawkes got the information about the caviar from Anna, a waitress. Stella later tells Mac this information and takes the credit for it as if she made the discovery.

Danny refusing to leave a tip for the performers etc, so why didn't Aiden leave one?

That's the difference between crimes and misdemeanours: you can investigate a crime as a CSI, but not what is classed a 'misdemeanour', which are only about the little, insignificant people, the underdogs, so don't merit as much attention and are thrown back to the 'ordinary' police officers to solve. Oh and another thing, this was Danny's case, so did Mac really expect him to just turn it over, wasn't as if he was working on anything else; also a crime is a crime irrespective of the victim or the seriousness of the offence! Where's the fairness and justice in not investigating and handing it over to someone else?

You wouldn't see Grissom or H doing something like that. Seems Mac had no qualms with Aiden investigating the death in the pizza restaurant solo (**1.9 Officer Blue** and also the death of the construction worker in **1.12 Triborough.**)

Mac's speech (lecture) to Danny is repeated again in season 2 when Aiden tampers with evidence: he tells her she's messing with the entire lab and its reputation and everything she does affects everyone else there.

Also season 5 - again – when Stella didn't get such a dressing down when she investigates the Greek case for herself and then traipses off to Greece without telling anyone!

So what's going on with Mac and Danny especially when he turns round at the end to see Mac still watching him. I've said it before and I'll say it again, Mac is never fair to the male members of the team, but the women have it easy when they also do so many things wrong!

You know Danny and Mac's confrontation is just a prelude of what's to come in **1.20 On The Job.** Also makes you wonder if there was some fallout from **1.13 Tanglewood**, when Sonny said he knows Danny and vice versa. Was that still playing on Mac's mind? (Not so as we'll ever know.)

Quotes

Stella: "71,000 to 1 chance of finding out where she came from."
Mac: "I'll take those odds."

Mac: "I love the smell of a cover-up in the afternoon, don't you?" Yeah cover up with sheets! (Sorry bad pun.)

Flack: "Crime may not pay, Robert Costa sure does."

Flack"...where I came from, still makes you a foreigner."

Mac: "Not my tactics you need to worry about, it's my results." Oh almost sounds like he's condoning any old bad activity just as long the job gets done and the evidence found, the crime solved!

Danny: "When I say we're good, we're good."
Aiden: "'Cause if I come up dry, Mac's gonna chew you a new one right."

Danny: "You're lucky you and I work together you know."
Aiden: "...Messer, I mean you're cute, but I'm way outta your league." Me thinks it's the other way round, she's out of his league!

A Danny Moment

Danny: "Last time I checked, a misdemeanour was still a crime." Yes!

A Mac and Danny Moment

Mac: "I thought we agreed you were gonna pass your case out."
Danny: "I agreed I'd stay on track, I closed the case."
Mac: "Against my orders. I don't tell you one thing and then you do another...that's not how it works...look you've gotta learn you're not a one man army. We're all connected. What you do affects everyone here. You got it."
Danny: "Loud and clear."

CSI Déjà Vu

CSI Season **5.16 Big Middle** the 'big' ladies convention: re blood spatter on sheet, Gil used Greg as a guinea pig to ascertain how much body weight was on the DB.

Gil and Sara check spatter patterns on a bloodied sheet in a season 4 episode entitled **Invisible Evidence** where Sara tells Gil to pin her down. The body left a void on the sheet. The victim struggled, gave up and the suspect put his hands on the sheet for leverage. Also in this case Gil processes a wine bottle found in the garbage where the prints match the suspect. The victim was also killed in bed, as she was here, and so there was also a bloody mattress present.

Nick and Gil find a broken champagne bottle at the hotel in season 2 episode of *CSI*, **Cool Change**.

CSI season 2 **The Finger** Nick finds two wine glasses stained with lipstick marks and blood spatter and season 3 *CSI* episode **Lady Heather's Box** which had yet another lipstick-stained champagne glass.

In the season 1 CSI:Miami episode **Just One Kiss** a green glass, broken champagne bottle was pieced together from the crime scene and fumed for prints.

In *CSI* season 2 **Chaos Theory** rohypnol was found in the Tox screen. Roofies is another name for rohypnol, the date rape drug.

Nick examines the blood spatter on the floor, where the blood dripped off the edge of the bed in a similar way in *CSI* season 5 episode **Spark Of Life,** when two cases merged.

Season 2 *CSI* **Organ Grinder** where the victim was re-dressed and posed; as well as there being used champagne glasses at the scene.

CSI **4.23 Bloodlines** where the DNA sets a girl's rapist free and Grissom wonders about the conviction being wrong since 'the evidence never lies.'

Here Costa was guilty of rape as a college student but his friends backed him up, even though his DNA was present.

Season 2 *CSI:Miami* episode **Death Grip** where the blood Calleigh found on the mattress was not from an attack but menstrual. Also in the season 1 episode **Entrance Wound** the hotel room was cleaned and the mattress was turned over to hide blood from the murder.

CSI:Miami season 2 episode **A Horrible Mind** where the DB was identified with a hearing aid. Here the killer had the hearing aid which he lost.

In the episode, **1.20 Grave Young Men** where the suspects fingernail was found at the crime scene.

Also the *CSI:Miami* episode **2.10 Extreme** where Delko gets into strife for interfering in a case involving car theft, even though this involvement was inadvertent. Whereas here Danny refuses to give up his case.

Ratings

11 million viewers. Rated #23 for the week

1.20 Supply & Demand

Written By Anne McGrail & Erica Shelton
Directed By Joe Chappelle
US Airdate 27 April 2005
UK Airdate 18 June 2005

Guest Stars: Trent Gill (Billy) Joe Morton (Chief Dwight Hillborne) Chad Lindberg (Chad Willingham) Amy Aquino (Diane Lipstone) Lindsay Parker (Jordan Benson) Matt McCoy (Martin Benson) Taylor Sheridan (Joel Banks)

Background

A student hears gunshots from the apartment next door and discovers the body of another dead student. The lock is broken and the place is trashed; to which Mac adds, so is the victim. Flack says they conducted a thorough search but didn't find his roommate:

Jordon Benson a freshman, didn't attend her classes. The victim is 19 year old Will Nowick from Hoboken, a business major at Chelsea University.

Mac says they have to follow all the leads.

Will's father insists his son is not a dealer. Jordan's father paid the rent for her and Will worked maintenance for the college to pay his fees.

Stella checks out Will's Social Security number: 945-32-9774. His financial records show he didn't deposit any pay cheques since high school. However deposits of $500-3,000 were made.

Will's 'digger' buys tickets for Will, who was a theatre scalper. He saw him yesterday and saw Jordan about a month ago. Will let him keep some tickets in return.

The man in the alley knows his rights and claims the fourth amendment: he doesn't have to be forced into having the bullet removed. Mac takes his mobile.

Flack finds Jordan at her parent's home. She wanted to do the laundry and didn't have her handbag with her. She hardly knew Will. Stella tells her she could be in danger. Flack doesn't believe her story about going to breakfast. The college has its own laundry.

Aiden takes scrapings from under Deroy's fingernails and uses a tazer on him.

Stella checks Jordan's financial records. She was broke and her credit cards haven't been used for weeks. Her credit card bill was paid off by her father and then he froze the cards.

The IA Chief talks to Mac about Stella's behaviour when interviewing Jordan. Mac defends her. Then tells Stella she should have told him about this. She was thinking about Will's father but he tells her she should be thinking about Lipstone, Jordan's lawyer, as she's an expert on trials where police mess up.

Aiden discovers the bag is a designer fake. The stitching on the inside wasn't good so she took it apart and found superglue was used to stick on the fake insignia. So the bag was bought recently. Retail is sometimes a cover for dealing drugs. Stella thinks someone took the wrong bag.

Danny checks out Jordan's student ID. She swiped her card at 11:31am in SC, Special Collections, as did Andrea Alix. Andrea has a campus address. Danny finds her overdosed and gives her mouth to mouth. She wants to avoid a drug possession charge and tells them she got the drugs from Jordan. Mac wants Stella to finish the case.

Mac and Danny raid the warehouse and Danny finds heroin. Mac demands the man's shirt but he refuses so he arrests him for selling fraudulent designer merchandise.

Flack and Stella have a warrant to search Jordan's parents' house. The toilet water checks positive for heroin. The water only diluted the drugs.

Crime Scene Evidence

There's a blood trail and the position of the debris indicates the victim was shot and then dragged near the door. The killer used his body to send a message. Mac says he was beaten before being murdered execution style. No usable prints are found. Mac comments that the blood spatter from the gun came after the place was searched. Stella thinks one beat him whilst the other searched. Mac finds theatre tickets with blood: *King Lear* on Broadway. Stella comments on the 'pricey boys' toys.' There are razor scratches on the glass and a white residue, indicating heroin.

Police Interrogation

Stella questions Jordan and tells her she wants to prevent another fatal overdose. She shows her Paul's photo. Jordan's lawyer warns her and Jordan refuses to talk. Flack says they've built up a Chinese Wall around them.

Secondary Crime Scene Evidence

Jordan's purse is found in an alley with its cash and credit cards inside. The strap is broken so the bag was taken by force. Mac deduces a hunting knife was used in the home invasion and there are synthetic fibres on it, consistent with fillings from a cushion. He also spots fresh blood on the ground. High velocity blood spatter on the wall and Stella notices a gunshot ricochet, but no bullet. The blood trail has gravitational drops and elongated spines facing towards the end of the alley. A man jumps out of the dumpster and attacks Mac.

Tertiary Crime Scene Evidence

Danny finds Paul Collins, 18, a possible OD and white powder in a baggie. He processes the room.

Conclusion

Deroy took her bag and had her address. Jordan didn't tell Will and Stella tells her the jury would have forgiven her the mistakes of a spoilt rich girl but not for failing to warn her friends about the drugs. She's arrested for negligent homicide and drug trafficking.

Mac tells the murderer he was thorough. He disposed of the gloves, shirt, shoes and weapon, but not his T-shirt. This had a drop of stray blood from Will. The DNA on his shirt allowed them a warrant to search his apartment and the warehouse in the Bronx and break up his distribution. In lock-up he'll be taken care of, just like he took care of Will. Mac apologizes to Will's father for doubting his son.

Notes

Another episode in which Stella loses her temper, albeit in the pursuit of justice. This is her fourth complaint within three years. She missed the blood spatter in the alley and the knife.
Buffy the Vampire Slayer gets a mention, paraphrased.

Stella doesn't like to be criticized so she doesn't acknowledge Flack's comment about her losing her head in the interview. Mac does talk with Stella for treating the suspect in a negative way, but it's not as abrupt as he was with Danny in the previous episode. Then he wants Stella on the case regardless!

Melina attended a violent murder scene whilst researching her role. CSIs she was shadowing were called to a scene where a father had shot and killed his two children before killing himself. Melina: "for the first time I felt compelled to get a gun or a knife and bash this guy's head in because I was so angry." She didn't cry or get emotional over this but was shocked at what motivates people to commit such inhumane acts. "I was trying to focus on watching the reaction of the CSIs and the police. Some people were making jokes but one guy, whose wife had just had twins, couldn't handle it and walked out." This was important for her to see so she could work on her character of Stella. She's in awe at the work of real CSIs and how they cope.

The murderer thought he was clever in disposing of all the evidence but why did he keep the T-shirt?
When Jordan flushed the drugs, isn't it usually the case that dealers flush the entire bag and not empty contents.
As a rule all CSIs should tie back long hair. We had to at school and that was only chemistry class, here they're dealing with real evidence.

Melina also commented that Stella "would put her whole heart and soul into something and get extremely connected from the beginning." Usually Stella enjoys going after the suspect full throttle and then finding out she needs help in solving the case and not be swayed by anyone or anything in her determination to solve the case.

Quotes

Flack: "Well, I'm the cooler head, you knew you blew it."
Stella: "I blew it – what about 'Buffy the Friend Slayer.'"

Flack: "There's nothing more depressing than looking at a rich kid's money line."

Mac: "I don't need management tips from an IA chief. You run your staff, I'll run mine." Mac and this show have always had some Chief or another on his case in practically every season.

Stella: "I know how trials work, Mac."
Mac: "Good, act like it."

Stella: "That's why evidence collecting is so important, people lie." This is paraphrasing Gil form *CSI* when he says "the evidence never lies."

Most Pointless Line

Stella: "What are you doing at this number?" Well, obviously the phone has been found.

A Danny Moment

Even when he's not fully on a case, like here, he still manages to save a life.

CSI Déjà Vu

There was a missing roommate in *CSI* episode **Chaos Theory**.
CSI: Miami episode from season **1.18 Dispo Day**.

Gil was always getting into trouble for his team not doing the job right and him not keeping proper reports, especially season 5 episode **Mea Culpa** when the team was broken up.

In *CSI* season 3 episode **Play With Fire**, Gil defends Catherine just as Mac defends Stella here after she's had another complaint against her. This time round it's Mac who tells her that she needs to pull her head in.

As Gil says about protecting the integrity of the lab, if there are no people, then there's no lab. In **Burden of Proof**, Catherine tells Gil as supervisor, he needs to be more personally involved with his team and he orders a plant for Sara by way of apology.

1.21 On the Job

Written By Timothy J Lea Directed By David Von Ancken
US Airdate 4 May 2005
UK Airdate 25 June 2005

Guest Stars: Joe Morton (Chief Hillborne) Chad Lindberg (Chad Willingham) Alana Ubach (Constance Briell) Nick Damici (Det Patrick Colton) Kimberly Dooley (Glenda Wallace) Noureen DeWulf (Matrice Singh) Octavia Spencer (Child Welfare representative) Maurice Compte (Michael Armstrong) Gilbert Rosales (Det Rodney Minhas) Chris Tardio (Steve Dark)

Story 1

Background

Danny and Mac process a crime scene. Mac says the killer wanted money. Jan Knight is the DB and a gun is found. Danny finds high velocity blood spatter on the wall next to the window. He checks the rest of the apartment and hears a sound from the closet. He's hit by an assailant and pursues, identifying himself as NYPD.

He follows him to the subway where a shoot out ensues...Danny fires from behind the pillar and fires the last shot. The dead man is a policeman. Mac takes Danny's gun. Danny's pretty sure he was the man he was chasing. Flack identifies the man as Detective Rodney Minhas. There were six witnesses and their stories are all consistent: a man came down the stairs and ran to the middle of the platform; he hides behind the pillar, sees Danny and fires twice. Minhas came down the north stairs and shoots at the same man being chased by Danny.

Flack comments three people were shooting. Danny is certain Minhas fired at him first.

Mac asks Danny for his version: he chased the Perp into the subway from the apartment onto the platform and he shot at him. The Perp then turns and runs at him and fires. Danny fired twice but isn't certain he hit him with both rounds. Danny insists he followed his training by the book: Minhas didn't identify himself; was an imminent threat and so he took him out.

Mac tells Danny IAB will want to question him and tells him to keep quiet until he issues a preliminary report. IAB Chief demands a statement from Danny and Mac tells him he has 48 hours before he has to do this. That only applies to uniformed officers and not detectives. Mac orders Danny to the hospital. But Danny's willing to talk as he's got nothing to hide.

Mac tells Danny he's off the case but he wants to help. Mac tells him he's assigned to a desk where he would be if he were Danny. The audio tape means his story doesn't match Danny's version of events. Danny insists he didn't hear anything. A bullet is still missing. Mac gives him a card to call a lawyer and he should talk to someone if it helps.

Danny talks to Flack and tells him he's not going to call the lawyer. Flack advises him to not take matters into his own hands as

Mac is watching out for him. Danny has to do something because no one else is; and if they were, then all they had to do was to tell him.

Danny tells his story to IAB. He didn't know he was a policeman; just that an armed man fired at him. He wanted his side of the story on record. Chief Heilborne says it's on tape. He informs Danny, a preliminary investigation shows the account of his statement is inaccurate. Witnesses say he wasn't turning when he fired and identified himself. The suspect didn't fire until he instigated the shoot out. Minhas's behaviour is irrelevant. They'll review if Danny is fit to be an officer.

Mac is furious at Danny, since he ordered him not to talk. His findings on the shooting clear Danny of any responsibility in Minhas's death. If IAB has a statement contradicting their findings then their CSI information will be useless in his defence.

Primary Crime Scene Evidence

The blood spatter was the only blood found in the apartment. Flack says the man bled heavily. There were three men in the room. Knight pulled a gun and the Perp was shot. Aiden sees the window was open from the plan when the room was first processed. The bullet is found outside lodged in a tree.

Minhas was the mystery man from the apartment. He was shot there so Danny didn't kill him. Aiden says he had to stop the bleeding so he took another route to the subway: there's another entrance down the block. A car parked across the road has parking tickets. There's blood on the pavement and a bloody rag on the wheel arch. Minhas got to the car and waited. There's blood on the door handle. He couldn't get in because his partner, the Perp was still in the apartment with keys. Flack runs the VIN.

Secondary Crime Scene Evidence

Aiden retrieves a message recorder from an injured civillian standing next to the male Perp. She informs Flack the bullet skip marked the ground and the directionality shows it came from the south end of the platform. Flack thinks it could have been fired by Danny or the Perp. Aiden finds a bullet lodged in a stair. It's negative for blood.

Conclusion

Michael Armstrong is the registered owner of the car. The gun found in the apartment had his prints. All the rounds were from his gun. He hid in the closet. Minhas was his partner and wanted money from Knight. Minhas was in the subway and witnesses saw Armstrong fire. He wasn't trying to help him but wanted to kill him so he wouldn't talk.

Danny tells Mac the DA refused to prosecute. Mac explains it's because they don't have enough evidence for a case against him. Mac reveals he was opposed by people to hire him but went ahead. Mac tells him he can't account for the eighth bullet; it is missing and could have hit a civilian. Danny "fired wild" and his story about Minhas turning, he examined every bit of that platform and he couldn't have seen Minhas until Danny's field of vision, running at Armstrong, running at him. Mac tells Danny to take his gun and they won't talk about this again. He's no longer in line for promotion. Mac gets a call from Chief Heilborn.

Story 2

Background

Stella processes a DB in the toilets in Central Park. Sandra Lopez, 19. Matrice, Glenda and Sandra were all nannies. EMS says the Bureau of Child Welfare is locating the baby's parents. She processes her.

The Myerson's butler says Sandra was acting strangely. The Myserson's are away on business. There was a robbery about a month ago when a nesting doll was stolen, before being returned anonymously. She was seeing a bartender. There's fire breathing at the bar where he works. His name is Steve Dark. She came onto him and wanted to breathe fire. Stella takes a DNA sample from his hands.

Chad tells Stella he has an address and finds Glenda there. Sandra's prints were on the jewellery box and a blue sapphire necklace was stolen. Glenda says they tried it on. The jewellery went missing and Glenda was blamed. Stella takes her prints.
Matrice asks for a lawyer. Stella also takes her prints.

Conclusion

Stella tells Matrice they were stealing from each other's houses and leaving their prints behind. All the prints had been wiped clean except for hers. Matrice took the doll. Glenda wiped it down but Sandra put the doll back. She confronted her and she got cold feet so she hit her. She was only making money for health insurance.

Stella tells Mac the baby has everything a child could want. Stella holds Daniella before saying goodbye.

Notes

Since episode **1.19,** there's been a build-up to this story with Danny and Mac. Excellent writing and continuity in this episode. Mac saw promising work from Danny for the past five years and was on the promotion ladder (episode **1.6**). Then Danny begins to defy orders since episode **1.19** when he refused to hand over the misdemeanour case of the homeless man to the officers. With Mac having to reprimand him for disobeying orders. Then this episode when Danny defies his orders again when his neck is on the line and this time his actions are to his own detriment.

When Mac told him in **1.19** that Danny was to think of the entire unit and his actions affect everyone, is what probably prompted

Danny to tell Flack Mac hasn't got his back; that he's only interested in the good of this unit: well, hey, that includes Danny too. Mac did have his back – that's why he told him to go home and call the lawyer. As for not consulting him, if Mac recommended him, he must be good, otherwise why would he have bothered hiring him.

Mac tells the Chief that Danny has 48 hours before he has to talk to IAB and he's told that only applies to uniforms and not to detectives, so why didn't Mac know this before? (See the season 5 episode where Flack is interrogated by IAB and that's done immediately.)

Everyone was giving Danny advice which he obstinately, stubbornly ignored and went head first to IAB, including Flack who told him not to hang himself, which is exactly what Danny did. Even Flack would've been speaking with years of experience 'on the job', from his father and what he's seen over the years.

As for Danny saying he's already hung, well he wasn't: Mac's findings cleared him of any wrong doing so Danny tied the noose around his own neck when he readily and freely spoke to IAB. Like Warrick bawling out Gil in *CSI* but Gil has to have the last word, just like here, where Mac always has the last word whenever he argues with Danny.

As for being in the system again, we'd like to know what Danny meant by this. If he's already been in the system once, then he should've known when to stay quiet and when not to. Also Mac saying he was discouraged from hiring him raises more questions than answers, we want to know who and why? Was it because of his past, his background etc, in which case why didn't Mac realize something wasn't quite right when Sonny mentioned Danny in episode **1.13 Tanglewood** and why did it surprise him when he talked about Danny? There are a lot of blanks to fill – hopefully next season we may get some answers!

Ah, sorry, we didn't get any answers in any season, sadly for us, the writers didn't pursue this line any further in the show, they either forgot about it, or didn't want to mention it again! Which is a shame as it could have given us some more character background on Danny, which is what this show was meant to have been about.

Unfortunately we won't. (As I said.) D'oh! As shortly after writing this, Carmine said in an interview; "we're moving along now but for Danny, it is 'just don't screw up'. Hopefully I do screw up, but right now [season 2] we're just pleasing everybody by making a solid show all around. I was told just to be patient and we'll get into the stuff I think people love, which is that personal emotion." That's true. But let's hope we won't have to wait 5 seasons for it either! Again I was right, we didn't get any of the personal background stuff which would have made for great viewing, instead they made Danny go all mushy and soppy over new girl Lindsay!!

Carmine comments on this episode: "I knew they always had that episode where I do accidentally shoot a cop. Anthony Zuiker had always talked to me about that particular point and thankfully it came into play. To me it was satisfying just because that is why I am an actor. It was quite a silent episode too. There wasn't a lot of dialogue but he was put in this corner and couldn't do a lot about it. That last scene between Gary and I where he lets me have speech was a great moment."

Aiden and Flack were the only ones who asked about Danny. Not even Stella was concerned about one of the team and didn't ask about him once, even when Mac was giving her advice about parents. So much for her caring attitude.

Says Carmine: "Flack he's kind of that opposing voice somewhat even though he's on my tears and tries to calm me down. I think that just reflects the characters more than it reflects our relationship. They had him doing the right thing as far as being a detective is concerned and not feeling how I'm feeling which is more emotionally. It made for a good minor conflict." Flack will come to Danny's aid in many more episodes to come, you'll be glad to know. As well as everyone else's too.

Comments Eddie, "Carmine's character was at a moment where the second he got up from that table, something was going to be done either way and it looked like he was going to go the bad way...fun to play that moment and it was the first time on the show that I felt like it and it was an interesting feeling for a character on a crime show where we tend to get the bad guy all the time – in that moment in time, [Flack] lost a little bit or wasn't quite sure if he got what he wanted. When Danny got up and took off, it left a little bit of unfinished business and that was real – [Flack] was at a loss."

This is another of Eddie's favourite episodes, for the 'Danny moment.' "I liked that it came home to the department [the NYPD]. I like when it comes home to the Department or me personally. Those were excellent, they were great fun." (His other favourite episodes include, **2.23/24**, **3.8**, all about Flack.)

Continues Carmine, "I remember being so excited about that scene in the diner when we kind of went off each other and got a little heated up. Unless they disagree – somebody's got to disagree with somebody. I was the guy disagreeing with Mac for a long time and then Lindsay and I [in seasons to come]. So for Flack it's a good way to deal with [Danny] because we are good friends and have this cool relationship. So it's nice to have us disagree on something and find how far you go with that. It's great."

Flack appears to be the stabilizing force in all of their lives, always the one there for them.

Carmine on this episode: "[Eddie] telling me how monumental doing that scene in the diner was at the time and how challenging and emotional and nice it was to do that and how enlightening and how much we learned. It was the first time we got to do that. It's weird because in these kinds of TV shows, a lot goes down in one scene – a lot has to go down in small doses because those are the only chances you get to do them. We definitely love doing those scenes." Just like we love watching them.

Eddie truly believes in his character of Flack. "I think that Don has a strong sense of justice, he believed in Danny...he believed his friend...he believed his colleague and also believes in the system. So it was nice to try to bring all that together in communicating with somebody in that one scene because Danny came from the total opposite – 'I don't trust the system...anything.' Fun to sit down and say, 'trust me if you are good, will take care of you'...on a show like *New York*, it's great to be able to have those moments and develop those relationships amongst the characters." It is good to see what motivates characters, especially in what is termed a procedural show, like all the *CSI* shows are. It gives for more three dimensional characters, that you can actually feel something for.

Mac thinks Stella's a strong person.

Hawkes wanted to be a sculptor at one time.

Re the shots in the opening in the subway; the first shot is fired even before Danny fires back so naturally he'd assume he was being fired at. But come on, how can they expect him to have heard Minhas identify himself as a police officer from that distance and commotion. On the recording Minhas doesn't even sound like he's shouting but he's barely audible and was only heard on the recorder because he was right next to the civillian.

Also, there were two policemen, at least, running behind Danny when he entered the subway, what happened to them, since they didn't run in after Danny, but only entered when Mac came in.
Maybe I'm missing something, but Danny didn't instigate the shoot out as Heilborn tells him. A shot was fired and heard by us, even before Danny fired. Minhas was a dirty cop so that was nicely swept under the carpet by IAB. Probably another reason why IAB wasn't pursuing an internal investigation. Did no one think of this, aside from using the excuse that they just didn't have enough evidence to go ahead.

The subway scenes were filmed in San Pedro, California in a building which actually houses a subway.

As for the witnesses, they're always correct in such a situation when everyone's diving for cover and thinking about their own personal safety, but not everyone will keep a cool head and recall every little detail; so they never 'lie' in the sense of getting facts wrong. So no laser stringing in this episode to determine the bullet trajectories.

Stella only getting the names of the nannies and not their addresses. Also Chad has to tell her she has the address so she can go there to investigate.

The title **On the Job** refers to the police officer as well as Danny and also the nannies stealing whilst also working.

N.B There's a character in this episode called Steve Dark. Incidentally, this is the name Anthony Zuiker has given to his character in the digi-novel, *Dark Origins*.

Quotes

Flack: "I don't want anybody making their minds up about this until we know the facts."

Danny: "I followed my training by the book, Mac."
Mac: "...evidence is damaging to you."

Flack: "Don't start taking things into your own hands okay. Listen to me..."
Danny: "It was a good shoot Don. And I feel like I gotta do something about it."
Flack: "Listen to me, you don't have to do anything but keep your mouth shut and let Mac handle it."
Danny: "Mac's worried about the reputation of the unit."
Flack: "You're wrong. He's got your back."
Flack: "Don't hang yourself Danny."

Danny: "You know what, it feels like – I feel like I'm already being hung." Poor Flack could only tell Danny to listen to him and he didn't.

Mac: "...don't win in this kind of situation, Danny."
Danny: "Mac, I'm not saying I won anything, IAB's calling it a good shoot."
Mac: "...they're only saying there's not enough evidence to go forward with an internal investigation – it's not exoneration – it's a pass. Something like this comes up again."
Danny: "Never again." Until the next time then...

Danny: "You made no mistake. I made no mistake. I can account for every second of that shooting, every breath, every shot."
Mac: "No you can't...I can't...you're off the promotional grid."

Mac: "A lot of bad parents out there...not our job to fix it."
Here's Mac saying they shouldn't get personally involved in their cases, but he's going to do exactly that in future cases too, when Claire's son Reid, turns up as well as in season 5 with his female 'stalker'.

A Flack and Danny Moment

Danny: "I feel very alone in this. I feel like there's people out there talking about me and I got no chance to defend myself." (That's what the lawyer was for.)
Flack: "You gotta trust the system."
Danny: "I know what it's like when the system gets you in their sights and I'm not gonna let that happen again...you think that I can just shut this off ...why didn't somebody step up to me and say, 'Danny I got your back'?"
A pity they didn't have Flack ask what he meant by this!

A Mac and Danny Moment

Mac: "There's two things I wanna say to you that you should know. One, I thought I'd never tell you. I was strongly discouraged against hiring you but I followed my gut and for the last five years I thought I made the right decision."

Danny: "Who's bad mouthing me?"

Mac: "Doesn't matter but they said the decision to hire you was mine and one day I'd realize I'd made a mistake."

(No it doesn't matter, because no one even knew at the time, nor did we get anymore on this aspect of the storyline either. Another wasted storyline for future episodes.)

CSI Déjà Vu

IAB rears its ugly head again in another *CSI* episode as it does in *CSI: Miami* also frequently. IAB is not so clean cut either. So again these two shows are where the CSIs are either part of the police department or work closely with them as opposed to *CSI*: Vegas where they're civillians and don't have to deal with IAB but the Sheriff and with Ecklie, who's a stickler for the books, but not as bad!

CSI season 3 episode **Play With Fire** where Gil defends Catherine who is suspended. He is accused of kicking back her reports. Her actions affected everyone in the building and Director Cavelle tells him it's not his job to protect his people but the integrity of the crime lab. He replies, "without the people there is no lab." (See earlier on in the previous episode when mentioned in the context of Stella.) Here Mac attempts to defend Danny to the best of his abilities and under scrutiny from IAB. Though Danny doesn't really believe Mac has his back.

CSI season 2 episode **A Little Murder,** when Catherine is processing a CS and detects movement before being attacked by a Perp and in the pilot episode, this was one of the first things covered; which Warrick painfully learned when Holly was killed as the crime scene, as it was left unattended by him. Which begs the question of why it wasn't properly secured in the first place, and in this episode of *CSI:NY* too.

In season 4 *CSI* episode **Play With Fire**, Sara tries to clear a room and she's warned not to do it, but helps in the capture of the suspect after having a gun pointed at her.

Nesting dolls also the subject of an investigation in season 5 episode of *CSI* **Nesting Dolls.** Or to give them their proper name: 'Matrushka'

CSI season 2 episode **The Finger,** where the wound had fragments also from a smooth stone.

CSI season 5 opening episode **Viva Las Vegas,** when Greg contaminated the crime scene at the nightclub by using the toilet there. Gil, of course, was not so impressed and for this he failed his first proficiency test. However was given a second chance because he found a replacement in the lab for himself, but even she didn't stay long, because she "wasn't him" and everyone wanted someone like Greg around in the lab. Although the situation was a little different with Danny, it stresses the importance of following orders and never letting your guard down as a CSI.

CSI Miami from season 2 onwards, Rick Stetler is introduced from IAB and looks ever so smug, reinforcing that IAB is smarmy anyway. But his addition was good as a potential foe for H and to keep them on their toes.

Music

Somedays by Regina Spektor

Ratings

13.416 million viewers. Rated #16 for the week.

1.22 The Closer

Written By Pam Veasey Directed By Emilio Estevez

Us Airdate 11 May 2005
UK Airdate 2 July 2005

Guest Stars: Sonya Walger (Jane) Raphael Sbarge (DA Latham) Kathryn Harrold (Judge Beverly Fulton) Amaury Nolasco (Ruben deRosa) Andre Bowan (Bryce sweet) Jason Cerbone (Tony Reanetti) Petros Papadakis (Rico Savalas) Michael Clarke Duncan (Quinn Sullivan)

Story 1

Background

A woman comes running out of nowhere and is run over by a truck. She has no shoes, handbag or many clothes on.

Possible Crime Scene Evidence

She has bruising on her wrist, laceration on her cheekbone. Mac says her injuries are not consistent with a car accident trauma. The speedometer of the truck stopped at impact on 20 mph. Stella notices the inverted number plate: '73X' imprinted on her body.

Story 2

Background

Gilbert Novotny, a Boston fan is found dead in his car in the Bronx. Danny explains his theories: theory number 2 with the baseball found on the ground with ink on it which umpires rub on the ball to remove the "new." Perhaps the killer thought the ball belonged to them. [Stories 1 & 2 could be connected.]

Mac says they need to find what Margo was doing an hour before the match. He and Flack check out her apartment which is owned by a sports management firm. There's a hole in the door and an open bathroom window. She climbed out of the window and got puncture wounds on her feet from the pigeon spikes outside. Flack finds a baseball in the bath.

Gilbert's ticket was bought by a radio station in New York. They have a tape with Gilbert talking to an angry fan named Tony. Danny tells Aiden Jane's results from the kernel DNA was run on CODIS and came up with an 'Anthony'. He runs when he sees Aiden and Danny. She has a photo of him. Danny gives chase. He admits to throwing the Crackerjacks at Gilbert but didn't kill him. He was thrown out of the stadium by security.

On the footage there's a man between Margo and Gilbert who wasn't there before. He looks at Gilbert angrily. Reuben is a baseball player and Margo wanted to be his agent. Reuben pitches and the speed gun measures his throw at 94 mph. He also puts his spit on the ball. Danny catches the ball from the stand for analysis.

Possible Crime Scene Evidence

There's dry blood in his nose; lividity in his lower body. Aiden finds his ticket which reveals he had an expensive seat. Stella says he died in his car and was dead at least 12 hours. There's a brown hair on the ball.

Danny and Aiden check out the stadium. Aiden processes his seat whilst Danny finds blood on the ground. Gil got his bloody nose at his seat.

Conclusion

Danny tells Reuben he threw the ball into Gilbert's gut and at Margo's door. He's facing charges for assault and murder. He says there's a section on the Jumbotron on close up and Gilbert kissed him on his mouth. Margo laughed at him over the kiss.

Story 3

Background

Mac receives a call from a man he sent to prison. He doesn't want to spend the rest of his life there for something he didn't do. The murder weapon had a mix of the defendant: Sullivan's and the victim's, Alyssa Danville's DNA. He should check and review the evidence.

Mac tells Stella he thinks he made a mistake in the case. The defendant knows something they don't. He made a call to Mac and he testified in court on Friday. Stella says they processed the scene together and Sullivan claimed he didn't own the hammer. Stella doesn't make mistakes. Mac looks at the evidence from the case.

Stella sees the evidence on Mac's desk. He tells Sullivan he tracked all the evidence and no mistakes were made by anyone. He looks him in the eye. Mac tells him he collates the evidence but he doesn't decide if he committed the crime or not. Mac tells Sullivan he's accusing the prosecution of profiling. As Sullivan says he would be the main suspect since he's got big hands, a deep voice. He fits the description. Mac tells him the DNA looks for a match. He admits the hammer belonged to him, but he lost it. If he told the truth, he'd be pleading guilty.

Stella finds Mac in the coffee shop and tells him she wants to be told if he's looking into the case. Mac tells her there was no control sample for the murder weapon. Stella says because the weapon wasn't his so it's not standard procedure. Mac thinks this should be changed, since if you don't find a suspect's DNA on a murder weapon, it doesn't mean they're guilty.

Mac wants to believe him. If the hammer belonged to Sullivan then his DNA from his epithelia was already on it. Alyssa's blood was spattered on top. So there was a match for both of them when it was tested. Stella thinks this could have altered their conclusions about the case. Mac must prove the blood only belonged to Alyssa. (Thought Stella doesn't make mistakes!)

Mac tells her about his wife, Claire and that he needs to do this.

Stella tells him she hasn't seen him this happy in a long time and asks him why he hasn't taken his ring off? Stella says to prove his findings; Mac will have to show the hammer belonged to Sullivan. Mac tells her that's where reasonable doubt comes in. The DA refuses to give the defence this evidence.

Conclusion

Mac testifies on behalf of the defence. There was doubt as to guilt so he re-tested the evidence. Sullivan is released. Mac tells him he told him the truth. There'll be a civil trial but the evidence will help him. Mac liked the chance to change things.

Notes

Mac leaving the evidence lying around in his office where anything could've happened to it: contamination, lost, misplaced, tampered with etc. Stella always convinced she's always right and doesn't do anything wrong, not even in her over zealousness to convict the suspect. She always wants to be told about everything but doesn't like to be on the receiving end when things don't go her own way.

Opening her 'big' mouth telling Mac she hasn't seen him so happy since his wife died, bad timing and tactless. He doesn't have to take his wedding ring off already. Why was she so interested in this anyway?

She knows nothing about baseball or what happens at matches. Then she also tells Mac not to worry about the evidence since they did everything right even if it means convicting an innocent man, or having the conviction of an innocent man not be overturned. She'd just go home and have a good night's sleep, having forgotten that Mac doesn't sleep anyway.

They left it a little late checking out Margo's apartment. (But then do a lot of this in other seasons too, then they're too late and somebody already steals the evidence or gets away with hiding out there etc. Bit too lax for CSIs.)

Danny played Little League when he was seven and also played baseball at college and was in the minors; until he broke his wrist in a fight.
We get to know a little more about Mac's feelings when his wife died and his final line of the episode probably sums up what he really wanted to do on 9/11; along with everyone else in the world: to change everything back then and now, for the better.

As for not hoping anyone is guilty or innocent, well he has shown some bias towards victims and suspects in past episodes, such as (**Officer Blue, Night Mother, On the Job** etc and will do so in future episodes too.)

An episode which clearly would've contradicted Gil's fave line in *CSI*: "the evidence never lies." Well, it may not lie, but it does conceal the truth, on occasions.

Quotes

Stella: "Well, if this is the new look for spring, you can count me out." (Then Stella's fashion sense always leaves a lot to be desired! And not much to the imagination either!)

Stella: "Wanna switch jobs."
Hawkes: "This is where you two take over." (Until he too became a CSI next season.)

Danny: "There's one thing I hate more than running. Leaping." (But he seems to do an awful lot of running lately. Besides if he played baseball professionally, he'd have to do a whole lot more running. Anyway, we always love Flack and Danny in a good chase scene and there are plenty more to come in other seasons too! Lucky us!)

Danny: "...before we even had a chance to flash our badges."

Mac: "...because a small mistake can be significant enough to change the dynamic of everything that happens."
Stella: "We don't make mistakes. Hell, I don't make mistakes, not with evidence. Don't worry about it." She would say that.

Mac: "I gather the evidence, analyze it and the results tell me the probability of your actions." Isn't that like gambling with peoples' lives because if you're wrong...look what happened here...aren't the miscarriages of justice great enough already in many cases.

Mac: "Something more than just the truth and sincerity I see in Quinn Sullivan's eyes, is driving me to find another answer here. When the Towers fell and Claire died; it was the closest definition of what is unjust and unfair in this world and I was powerless to do anything about it. All those innocent lives, but here I just need to do this."

Mac: "...job is to collect evidence without bias or expectation, to provide an answer. I don't usually hope the suspect is innocent or guilty...liked the possibility of changing everything."

A Danny Moment

Danny: "...and the graduate from the Police Academy top of my class."
Aiden: "You're dangerous, Danny Messer."

Danny: "Very dangerous." Yeah, in more ways than one!

Another Danny Moment

Danny: "You got all hot under the collar because of a little smooch."

A Mac & Danny Moment

Danny: "I get the hard part."

Mac: "You're the baseball player and I'm the boss." (Someone should tell Stella that.)

Most pointless Line

Stella: "Don't tell me you're gonna make me hold something else."
CSI Déjà Vu

CSI season 2 episode **Cool Change** in which Catherine and Warrick find a partial licence plate number seen in a bruise on the DB.

CSI season 1episode **Fahrenheit 932** an inmate awaiting trial for his family's murder in a fire, calls Gil before the trial and pleads his innocence and his case. He lies about the third degree burn on his palm, the same way that Sullivan lied about not owning the hammer, the murder weapon.

CSI episode **Mea Culpa** (season 5) trace blood was found in the grooves of the wrench and the suspect's prints were found on the handle.

CSI:Miami season 3 episode **Speed Kills** shows sports matches can be dangerous events as people tend to get attacked sometimes for no reason.

CSI:Miami season 2 episode **A Horrible Mind,** the professor's dead body has puncture wounds on his feet.

Ratings

14.551 million viewers. Rated #16 for the week.

Did You Know

Carmine wanted to be a baseball player until a back injury put paid to that. Here it's mentioned Danny had a wrist injury and the fact

Danny's into baseball and a baseball player is mentioned many times.

Bloops

Stella calls the DB "Gilbert Novotny" as George Novotney", his name is actually Gilbert and he's called this throughout the episode.
The DB in the truck investigation should put them in Yankee Stadium, instead the seat colours and numbers aren't right, clearly they appear to be in the LA Coliseum. (Obviously since most of the show is filmed in LA.)

1.23 What You See Is What You See

Written By Andrew Lipsitz Directed By Duane Clark
US Airdate 18 May 2005
UK Airdate 9 July 2005

Guest Stars: Raphael Sbarge (DA Latham) Garret Dillahunt (Steve Collins) Wil Hornef (Dennis Sporco) Emily Harrison (Amy Madoff) Sandy Martin (Mrs Collins) Dave Power (James Madoff)
Ben Bode (Professor Newlin) Penelope Ann Miller (Rose Whitley)
Jesse Colliver (Paramedic)

Background

Mac arrives at his coffeeshop for breakfast and comments on the waitress Amy's new boyfriend. A woman already there speaks with him. He's an oatmeal person. Amy accidentally takes the newspaper from another man and a gun drops out. She drops the plate of bacon and he holds the gun on everyone. Another man pulls out a gun and is shot, so is Amy. Mac helps her.

Mac tells Flack what happened: three shots were fired; the first ricocheted off a metal chair, through a pastry tray and into the wall. The second hit Amy and the third hit the other man. His prints are on the mobile as he called 911. The killer was alone and left his DNA. There was another man alone in a booth and he left $20 for his bill.

Stella questions the woman at the counter but she doesn't know what she saw and was distracted. She tells Stella to talk to the man in the white shirt, i.e. Mac. The woman, Rose, gives Mac the address of a bar she goes to on Mondays. She wants to buy him a drink for saving her life.

Aiden asks if Danny wants to tell her about his mandatory psych evaluation. He replies she's not his mother. She's just looking out for him.

Mac identifies the killer as Photo number 5: Steve Collins. He spent one and a half years in Rikers that's why there was no activity on the gun. They check out his apartment and find the blooded shirt and a rent money envelope on the floor he left behind. There's a piece of tape on his shirt.

His mother doesn't know where he is. There's a chewed swizzle stick inside a cup of hot coffee and shoe prints on the carpet leading to the trailer outside. She tells them where he is and gives Stella her permission to look for him. There's a gun inside the trailer.

Amy's brother, James asks about the case and Mac tells him to go back to the hospital.

Stella and Mac need more evidence but ballistics confirms he was the killer in the coffeeshop. Steve is released and is shot at by a helmeted biker. The gunshot came from across the street. Mac rides in the ambulance with Collins and tells him he's being 'handled.' Collins is working as a confidential informant and that's why there was tape on his shirt. He was wired when he was in the shop.

James brought the gun as protection for Amy. He sold his bike for cash. Flack canvassed the neighbourhood but there was no sign of the gun. The department is having a 'turf battle' and he hasn't been able to find out who's handling Collins. Aiden says they're looking for a Metzler MEZ Y tyre.

Collins' mother is found beaten at her home.

The DA tells Mac that Collins is no longer a valuable asset. He has nothing to offer the FBI in exchange for information and they still don't know who he's an informant for. He meets his wife and Mac watches them.

Research on the CLCs is carried out by a university. The doctor's assistants don't work for money. A list of his former students shows

Amy's boyfriend from the coffeeshop: Dennis Sporco. He lives on Avenue C, but that's not his real address. Mac talks to Amy. She gave the gun to Dennis because she didn't want it. She calls Dennis on his mobile which is traced to a warehouse. There's a bike outside and a printing press inside.

Crime Scene Evidence

Danny finds the first bullet in the wall. Aiden finds a swizzle stick in the killer's glass with his DNA.

Secondary Crime Scene Evidence

The bullet was from a .40 calibre. There's a bike tyre tread, a footprint and some sort of substance inside this, left behind by the biker.

Tertiary Crime Scene Evidence

Hawkes's preliminary examination shows she was beaten and then strangled. A metal object is found in a garbage bin down the street. There's also a blank piece of paper in her mouth.

Conclusion

Mac tells Dennis he needed US Treasury paper for printing and so was meeting Collins. He sent Clark in first and waited outside. He got the information from Amy. It would've gone down as planned, but Mac came in and Clark coughed alerting him to the fact he was a police officer. He's going to give Dennis to the Secret Service and in exchange they'll give him Collins. The tyre treads match the bike and he has the gun. Clark missed Collins when he shot him so killed the other instead with the printing press component.

Mac tells Collins they no longer need him so he's all his. He'll be tried for the murder of Adam Baxter.

Mac looks at Rose's card. Danny tells him he went to the evaluation. Stella asks Mac if he talked to Danny about the evaluation. She has a date. Mac says he's trying, but now Hawkes wants to be in the field. They both should've seen that coming. Stella removes Mac's tie. He meets Rose who didn't think he'd come. She asks him his name.

Notes

Mac orders oatmeal, raisins and maple syrup.

It would have been good to have actually seen Danny in his psych evaluation as you'd have seen what was happening and added another dimension to his character since this show was meant to be more character driven. Danny, in true Danny style wants to handle it on his own and doesn't want to talk about it. Though he felt it was "all good." Oh Danny was sent for psych evaluation because he was involved in a shooting (**On the Job**) and its departmental procedure when this happens.

Stella analyzes the paper using the *Michael – Levy Birefringence Chart*.

Birefringence (n2-n1)

First Center.........Sixth Center

238

Birefringence……….Thickness Interference Path   Cotton &
Flax
                                  Colour   Difference

Application   Sheldon Hawkes
N.Y.P.D.   Badge # 9786
C.S.U.   DOB 1973   FIELD INVESTIGATOR

Funny how Stella gets a date when Mac decides to move on and go out too! In contrast to the Pilot, where he's still mourning the loss of his wife and throughout most of the season. This episode was also less darker than the opening. Only leaving us with the dilemma of whether Hawkes will leave the ME's office for good and if Danny will get back into Mac's good graces: stay tuned. (Well Hawkes became a permanent CSI and Danny does get into Mac's good books again. As everyone forgot about the tension between the two of them and that side wasn't pursued in future episodes.)

As for Stella never mentioning her personal life and going on a date, seemed rather hurriedly attached to the finale as if to show she doesn't spend all her waking hours rushing to the lab! As for that outfit – one can only say: recall her quote about the lingerie – springtime look in the episode **1.22 The Closer**, which seemed a bit false just like they were packing up shop at the end of the season and she can now find time to leave her lab.

Stella didn't ask about Danny when he was suspended after the shooting and now asks if Mac spoke to him about it his evaluation. Apparently Danny didn't have much to do in the season finale and he didn't want to tell Aiden about the evaluation either. At least Aiden asked about him again in this episode.

Flack and boys toys re the bike. Hawkes wants to be a field investigator now just like Greg in *CSI* and wants to leave the lab but why? He was good as an ME, but he was also good as a CSI. The number of times he will help Stella and Lindsay break their cases in the upcoming seasons and not to mention getting into Mac's bad books too.

Once again suspects leave evidence lying around. Mac getting heavy handed again. Also in contrast to **On the Job**, notice how Mac recalled every single piece of the shooting, how it happened, who was doing what etc, yet in that episode with Danny, he tells him he couldn't account for the shooting in the subway and the bullets like Danny could, but that's conveniently forgotten here, as Mac noticed everything!

Eddie Cahill said, "working with Gary has been awesome with a capital awesome. It is great. I am the kind of guy who likes mentors. I'm a young guy. I am 27 years old [back in 2005] and I like having mentors and he's somebody I am proud to follow at work. He's a generous man, incredibly talented, and the same can be said for Melina. They both have so much valuable experience which they are more than willing to hand down."

Plenty of other things happen too in other seasons like Danny and Flack stepping into a metrosexual moment or two. Such as admiring each other's clothes and shoes. Ha! You have to watch that episode **Necrophilia Americana**. Not to mention Danny losing his cowboy boots and turning to trainers, okay not so much cowboy, but biker-type; and his glasses disappear too in seasons 4/5. 'Oi Lindsay what have you done to our Danny Boy?!!' Also in season 2, there were new wardrobes for the men, new, shorter hair for Eddie and his leather jacket disappeared. In came more subtle shades in suits, and ties. Out went the suits and ties for Mac and the suit for Danny.

Eddie Cahill's thoughts on seasons 1 and 2; season 2: "we're certainly lighter. It's hard to put an exact dial on New York. In one respect, I stand by this empirically, I think it could be argued New York is a far lighter city than it's ever been, since probably about 1993 – when Giuliani got in there and Jack Maple started to turn the Police Department around. It became a relatively safe [place] compared to what had been. Times Square now looks like a theme park. Yes it's dark, let's not forget it's still a big metropolis but it's not a dark, gloomy place. I think it could be just as much of an injustice to the city to paint it in an entirely grey and blue light. I think what we did do in the second season was; there is by virtue of lining and trying to accomplish anything in New York – there's an energy that takes place, and I think in brightening up we've picked up the pace of the show a bit, which is more accurate...I don't think you can look specifically to one or the other and say one is more New York and one is not."

The show could've been cancelled after season 1, but commented Carmine, "I think we came out with a bang. It was visually edgier the first season. But it's all about the characters' involvement and the writers knowing exactly who these guys are and how to write them." He wished Danny had a romantic interlude with "Jane from DNA."

On season 2, with everything involving more light and a radical change of tone and content, Eddie says, "they've scraped the sets. They've built this really beautiful very workable, aesthetically pleasing lab set. Each room plays into the next so it opens up the show to have a lot of movement and a good place which I think will add to the feeling of New York."

Hill Harper on the new sets in season 2: "I think it's great. Rather than being down below the city in a basement; we're above the city now, we're in a high rise and we're looking down on the city – it's like there's a protector out there that's looking out over Manhattan and the five boroughs and looking out for people. New York City is a city of skyscrapers, so to be high and to be able to look out on the city is fantastic."

Carmine says he's in the show until the end – since it's a great job and he likes working with everyone else and it's changed his life in a number of ways. We're glad to hear that!!

Quotes

Mac: "Save it for your new boyfriend Amy, you're gonna tell him about how you survived all this." Profound words too because she did survive and helped in his arrest.

Flack: "I'm never gonna get a better eye witness account than this." (From Mac, see my comments above.)
Mac: "Not just a nickel and dime robbery." No, it involved counterfeit money.

Stella: "You're free to go." Stella talking to Rose as if she's a suspect and not a witness.

Aiden: "You go in, you say the right thing and that's that."
Danny: "Don't worry about it. I can handle it."
(Aiden sounds like she's speaking from experience.)

Aiden: "It's all about the tyres, Flack, not the bike."
Flack: "Speak for yourself."

Mac: "That's why we don't rely on eye witness testimony. I saw what I saw, but the evidence knows what was really going on."
(An inadvertent reversion to **1.20 On the Job**, when Danny was convinced he saw what he saw and that's why he fired his gun. Which is why Mac told him he can only rely on the evidence. Again see comments above.)

Mac: "I know someone who does." Probably Mac's favourite line as he said that about Danny too in **1.13. Tanglewood**.

Mac: "I think it's time"…to move on. What about his ring?

A Mac and Danny Moment

Danny: "What about me and you? We good?"
Mac: "We'll see." Kind of left us hanging for next season!

CSI Déjà Vu

CSI episode **Table Stakes** where the suspect's drinking straw was analyzed for DNA, the swizzle stick was used to identify the suspect.

CSI:Miami **3.14 One Night Stand** where a complex counterfeiting operation is uncovered.

CSI season **2.10 Ellie** involved counterfeit money when Sara investigates and refers it to Questionable Documents, where she notices the money doesn't have a line of engraved letters, which are normally found on Ben Franklin's collar. Also it's all a type of 'sting' operation, initiated by Treasury Agents: the money is given to criminals and traced back to law enforcement personnel, who may be tempted to take it. Sara passes the temptation with flying colours!

CSI:Miami season 2 episode **Witness to Murder** Horatio said, "DNA is a funny thing, it has a tendency to hang around. He just put you away for life." Here she also put the suspect away after surviving from the gunshot.

CSI:Miami season 3 opener **Lost Son,** H loses his temper at a suspect physically, as does Mac here.

Bloopers

Amy's brother calls her Aiden and not Amy!

Music

Beautiful Day by U2

Ratings

12.301 million viewers. Rated #18 for the week.

Leadership Qualities/Contrasts

A good leader excels in leadership qualities. William Petersen says Gil gives Warrick more leeway because he reminds him of himself, as shown in the pilot episode. Gil is based on the real life CSI Daniel Holstein whom William met on the Pilot of *CSI*. A lot of his research was done then. Gil is relentlessly curious and he gives Catherine equal treatment because of their relationship and how it "defies characterization." She has a different life experience.

When Brass led the CSI unit he came down tough on Warrick for prematurely leaving a crime scene, leading to the subsequent death of newcomer Holly Gribbs. Gil stood by him because he thinks Warrick follows his own path. "A unique character needs to be uniquely supported."

This is in contrast to Mac: when Danny wanted to follow his own path, he told him he should follow one where the evidence leads him; to not be subjective or think too much about the case. (Episodes: **A Man A Mile, Crimes and Misdemeanours, On the Job**.) Though he stood by Danny in this episode, he didn't say this in so many words. Mac shows more support for Stella and treats her as his equal as Gil does with Catherine.

Horatio on the other hand seems to treat his team as a team and treats everyone on an equal par. In fact he has little cause to discipline them and allows them to make their own mistakes as long as they don't affect the job, but if they do, he knows they'll turn to him in the end, such as Delko in the episode where his investigation led to one of their own and he kept this from H.

Mac doesn't appear to show his support to his team too readily though maybe he doesn't need to, it's implied from the outset, unless you go flouting and disobeying orders. See Danny in **On the Job.** H cares about his team in a more obvious practical way. He actually tells them if they've done something wrong and should know by now they can be honest with him.

William Petersen, "we know little of Gil because his work defines him." The same thing can be said about Mac and H. Work shapes their personality and the men they are to a certain degree. William comments "[Gil] manifests a certain seamless element because he loves what he does and couldn't imagine doing anything else."

"The Evidence Never Lies"

The *CSI* shows are known for choice catchphrases, relating to the show and more importantly, the evidence. Here's some I came up with they should use, on occasion.

The evidence is only as good as the CSI.
Don't let the evidence cloud your judgement.
When the evidence is so overwhelming, you have to separate that which has probative value, from that which is misleading.
Gathering evidence is a gamble.
There is bias in evidence, it either clears one defendant/suspect in favour of another.
Evidence is like gambling, a fixed outcome with a number of probables.
Evidence is a number of variables with a fixed outcome.
Everyone is guilty until the evidence proves otherwise.

Evidence speaks volumes.
In evidence there is truth and vice versa.
Evidence is not the be all and end all but can itself be contaminated.
Processing evidence is a three ended prong: collect, analyze, apply it to the facts.
Evidence bridges gaps.
Theories assume facts not in evidence.
When in doubt, question the evidence.

CSI: Similarities and Differences Between the Shows

CSI

Not police officers, but carry guns. (Except Grissom.) They are criminalists, therefore civilians, carry ids but no shields. Initially headed by a police officer in Captain Brass, Grissom replaced him. Grissom is also a doctor (not medical.) Heads the night shift until the team was broken up in season 5. They meticulously document evidence, including photos of everything. Also have the day shift and the swing shift. Grissom writes evaluation reports. As to Promotion, there are grades 1,2,3 of CSI. More years on the job mean more seniority, therefore more choices and chances of getting the 'better' cases.

The DB is normally viewed by the next of kin, whilst it's under a sheet.

And Then There were None: not all CSIs are civilians and in some states in the US, such as Oklahoma, criminalists are commissioned and so they can carry guns and badges.

CSI:Miami

The crime lab doesn't all consist of police officers but do carry shields and guns. Calleigh graduated from the Academy, as did Ryan. Headed by Lt Horatio Caine, originally in the bomb squad. Horatio, or H, is CSI Level 3 Supervisor. He's more in the field than the lab and they work closely or are connected to the Miami Dade PD. H mentions the evidence a lot in some episodes, as if to remind viewers what the show's all about and to "educate" new fans: "it's all about the evidence". He also says he's not a police officer, but a CSI, which most people won't know. Hardly show H spending much time in the lab/office, or writing reports on his team. But at least he does venture back into the lab on occasions and when he needs to process a piece of evidence for himself. Have a different approach to solving cases and don't carry out all evidence processing at the crime scene, but at the lab.

Stories they can't do in the other two shows, such as tsunami episodes, crocodiles/alligators and the everglades. Due to the location, there's more action orientated storylines; more special effects and more action filming, therefore the scenes are more expensive.

Calleigh is CSI Level 3 Assistant Supervisor. Delko is a CSI Level 3 and Wolfe is CSI Level 1.

CSI:NY

All police officers (aside from Hawkes) and all carry shields and guns. Part of the NYPD and thus are called detectives and have ranks. Promotion is earned by showing initiative and being placed on the promotion grid as a result of this and Mac's recommendation. Don't photograph all documents or evidence at the crime scene all the time.

Used to bag evidence and process there at the crime scene, especially early on. Tougher tactics like forcibly taking samples from a suspect and not just that in the public domain. Working within close boundaries of the law, bordering on 'entrapment' at times and are legally able to lie to suspects.

As in the other shows, must be accompanied to the scene by another officer, in most cases, or another CSI. (As with the other two shows.)

How/Why Not to Get Fired/Leave…a *CSI* Show

The story behind those firings: in May 2005, just before season 5 *CSI* was due to be filmed, all the actors were meant to be on set for filming, promptly on July 14. Also everyone was given a pay rise, described as "fair and equitable". Everyone signed and faxed in their responses, but Jorja apparently sent her letter by post – hence CBS said it arrived late. She was fired.

When she was fired in July 2005 Jorga Fox received a tremendous amount of support from fans. "I've never been fired from anything in my life, not even from a coat-check job…our show is still trying to pick up the pieces from that." She was fired alongside George Eads allegedly over a pay dispute.

Temporarily sacked from *CSI*, Jorga Fox thought it was a joke at first, "then after about 4/5 days I started to realize it was serious. I think that I probably feel a lot less safe about anything having to do with the show than I did, but I think that's probably a good thing. I think change is inevitable in life but the reality of what happened was half of the cast is working with a pay rise and half the cast is not. I think that's not necessarily good for anybody on the show."

George Eads claimed to have overslept after he was fired, three hours after not turning up for his 6.30am roll call on July 15th. Many people told CBS that he was just late – but he was fired anyway and he has never been fired from anything. Whereas Jorga said there was a misunderstanding in signing contracts. CBS saw their actions as a means of re-negotiating their pay rises. However the rest of the cast were behind them. Gary Dourdan even said he'd leave the series in support. George said, "I poured everything I had into this show, and I have since day one. But after it happened [the firing] I thought everything happens for a reason. I didn't realize what a great friend I had in Gary until then. I didn't realize how he would go to bat for me and say, 'I quit if he doesn't come back.' That's kind of a friendship you don't find between actors working together on shows." He also commented on the show when it began saying, "we

[*CSI*] were always the underdogs. We were the last pilot to be picked up – then all the money was going into another series and they were hardly even publicizing our show."

Eric Szmanda was on set when they were fired and he got a call from his lawyer. "It was heartbreaking. I knew things were going to get ugly but I didn't expect them to get that ugly. It was kind of ridiculous we can laugh about it now, but it was very serious at the time. I always had faith things would work out because I knew William [Petersen] wouldn't come to work without them." Eric also commented, "our show makes millions of dollars an episode and you would think a piece of the pie would be shared with all the people who are involved. But that's not necessarily true anymore." Jorga was re-hired at the same pay before negotiations and George was re-hired after he apologized over the phone to Les Moonves.

Rory Cochrane who played Tim Speedle in *CSI:Miami* decided to leave the show in 2004 – the question being asked – did he commit professional suicide? He became weary from the terminology used on the show and wanted to be released from his contract, to which CBS agreed but not without conditions and consequences. Allowing him to leave came at a price, such as not being able to work on TV for a number of years.

Subsequently Speed was killed off in season 3 episode **Lost Son**: a bit of a cop out from the show/writers as he was killed in a jewellery store, shot, whilst attempting to discharge his weapon. This was again his 'fault' as he kept it dirty. A continuation, if you like, of the story from the season 2 episode **2.17 Money For Nothing** where he was shot in the armoured car robbery when transporting heroin to be destroyed. His gun was found to have jammed when Speed didn't keep it clean. So H bought him a birthday present – a gun cleaning kit – and it wasn't even his birthday. So once bitten twice shy, we really don't think Speed would've been so careless second time round, since the weapon comes with the job. To misquote H in Season 3 episode, **Speed Kills**: "Speed Kills" or how about, dating Speed kills"

Didn't think much thought or imagination went into Speed's exit – it looked as if they wanted him out as soon as possible. Also there was no interaction between H and Speed's family as is usually the case in *CSI:Miami,* as H readily comforts victims' families, but unbelievably, not when it came to one of their own. Delko, his friend, showed little or no emotion. It was left to Speed's replacement, Ryan Wolfe, to remove his name from his locker. (Everytime H calls him "Mr Wolfe", we always add, "what's the time Mr Wolfe?" A game played by UK school children.)

Though Alexx said Speed was her good friend she didn't have much to say about his loss either. Killing him off was such an indignity and he didn't really go out in a blaze of glory either – if the episode was heading that way – or his demise - we thought it would have been better if he became disillusioned with the job - as he was in many episodes, for example, season 2 episode **Blood Brothers** when he questioned why they do this work if the suspects aren't bought to book. Hence his decision to leave: because of that one suspect too many who got away, would have been more plausible.

It almost appeared as if the writers were embarrassed with his entire character and wanted to exit him quick smart. There was a lot of potential to develop his character in season 3, as we always said, such as he didn't really do the job for money.
Now we'll never know the inner workings of the Speedle mind.

Said Rory, "they have all these creative ways that people die. A main character on the show, I thought they could have come up with something a little more imaginative. Getting shot, anybody can come up with that." He suggested some outs for Speed but they wouldn't go along with those and he didn't even get to shoot anyone. Not cleaning his gun, he described as "lame" too. He was not allowed to work in TV for four years since he was 'let out' of his contract – his obligation still was with them for another four years. (Compare this with Vanessa Ferlito's decision to leave.)
Perhaps there's a lesson to be learnt here somewhere.

On zap2it Rory said of Speed: "originally the character was supposed to be a quarterback or something for Miami, so obviously I'm not fitting that profile. It seems like some people on the show have history. He's supposed to be a trace expert, but it seems everybody knows all the different dimensions of what we do. We all sort of share it. It seems like nobody's one thing or the other, except Alexx. She's the coroner and you don't want to get into that."

Also when Vanessa Ferlito wanted to leave *CSI:NY* and her character of Aiden, she didn't have any bars on appearing in other TV shows and wasn't held to her contract completely or at all. On starring on the show and getting the part she commented, "it was *CSI:NY* – you don't say 'no' to that." On leaving: "I have no regrets. It was a great experience and everybody was very good to me, but I really wanted to be home in New York. I wanted to still do movies and theatre. That's why I got into the business in the first place."

When she left she had her manager and agent inform of her intention to do so. "I really love and admire Anthony. I don't want to say it went over so smoothly, but after they told him, I called him personally. I'm not good with drama but he handled it so well."

Vanessa also comments on the way Aiden was written out of the show. "I had no idea that was coming. I knew they couldn't shoot me or kill me, because when Rory Cochran left *CSI:Miami* they shot him. It was sort of ironic in a way because they "fire me" after, are they trying to tell me something."

Also Warrick in *CSI* was killed off too, that makes one character from each of the shows who were written out in that way, leaving no possibility for them to return. Especially as Khandi Alexander, William Petersen and Jorga Fox's characters didn't suffer the same fate either. Imagine the uproar if Gil Grissom was killed off in *CSI* or even Jorga. The three are set to appear in episodes from time to time, as Khandi has done so in season 7 and 8 of *CSI:Miami* and Jorga in season 10 of *CSI*.

The first casualty of a CSI actor was that of Kim Delaney who played CSI Level 3 Assistant Supervisor, Lt. Megan Donner. She was written out as she and David Caruso shared absolutely no on-screen chemistry. Not just with David, but with other cast members too. Kim was a last minute addition to the cast as the producers wanted to replicate the chemistry between co-stars William Petersen and Marg Helgenberger on *CSI*. Kim's last appearance in the show was on November 25 2002.

Kim starred alongside David when he was in *NYPD Blue;* which also had Melina and Hill make guest appearances.

From What We've Been Told of the Characters' Qualities

Mac Taylor

All of the qualities Zuiker maintained about the character, Mac Taylor and Gary too can be seen throughout the season: an integrity about his work: he doesn't let anyone play him for a fool; never deviates from his goal: find the evidence – prove the crime or guilt. Mac is a Detective First grade. His wife was Claire Conrad, killed in 9/11 and this still affects him. He's a chronic insomniac. A beach ball is all he has left of his wife's breath. It is important for him to serve his country more than anything else. He has a scar over his heart. His goals are: to protect the honour of his country and the safety of his city; the integrity of his lab. Therefore he fired Aiden for tampering with evidence to prove the guilt of a suspect.

He does seem to exhibit some biasness towards the characters. As for the integrity of the lab, in season 4 he didn't have anything to say about Lindsay when his lab was being inspected, and how she shouldn't mix business with pleasure. Also Lindsay compromising evidence in this episode, anything could've happened and she wasn't punished for this.

From What We've Seen

*What about his own integrity, see **3.33** where he 'got away' with being an accessory to a shooting, and covering it up, even if he was only little.*

*Honesty: maintains objectivity whilst dealing with victims and suspects alike – not judging until the facts are in. Maintains the same with his team, encouraging them to figure out the evidence rather than hasty decision making. His main episode: **1. Blink:** keeping vigil with the victim at the same time being affected deeply still by the death of his wife. In **1.10 Night Mother**: an affinity with the woman who appears to be the main suspect, who turns out to be innocent but is grieving in her own way for her lost family too. **1.5 A Man A Mile**: showing Danny the error of his ways and finally moving* on from his loss, to some degree, in the season finale **23. What You See Is What You See**.

Directness: he never minces words with suspects, especially when he has all the evidence cards to play up his sleeve. Seen in **Officer Blue** arguing with Stella over the horse. He doesn't give in his ground – experience is the key and patience is paramount rather than jumping headstrong into making the wrong decision.

1.13 Tanglewood consulting Danny for information and help where he's no expert or needs it. **On The Job,** confronting Danny about going against his order and being on his side after all.

There's also a slight deviousness or edge to his character. He likes to play/operate on the boundaries of the law at times: coercing suspects as in **23. What You See Is What You See**. Telling Aiden to use the rule of being able to lie to suspects when questioning a potential killer in **1.9 Officer Blue**.

As a leader he must balance this with looking after the interests and well being of his entire team. Though he carries out his investigations on the basis of Veneziano's Theory of Quantum Physics which states "everything is connected."

Originally from Chicago. Due to his heroic military career in the marines he garnered a place amongst the NYPD elite. His work: he likes to involve himself in the 'how' and the 'why' of a crime. As well as struggling to come to terms with the loss of his wife during 9/11. He also appears to give Stella more leeway and benefit of the doubt than he did to Danny or would most likely give to anyone else, except perhaps Aiden. (Until season 2.)

Mac plays bass guitar at jazz clubs: as Lindsay says he knows how to hold the instrument, so what does this prove? Also in **4.5 Down the Rabbit Hole** he actually admits to Flack he has sleeping problems. Thought I'd mention that since it wasn't really pondered again until then after being said in season 1.

255

Stella Bonasera

Melina Kanakaredes: "Stella's father was murdered by an unknown assailant, leaving her to find out why." This wasn't actually mentioned in any episode in season 1 and could have been altered for the actual show.

All we know as mentioned in **1.15 'Til death Do Us Part** episode is that she's an orphan and never knew her parents.

Anthony Zuiker: "She is the Statue of liberty walking around, the show's pillar of strength."

Stella is Detective First Grade; is meant to be devoted to the job. She has been described as having a strong personal determination to be one of the boys and intelligent (debatable) as she always needs help when on solo cases. She is an orphan. (But she was also fostered.) Both Mac and Stella are co—heads of the lab, but Mac is always the one in charge, though Stella likes throwing her weight around, most especially when he's not around.

From What We've Seen

*Stella walks tall and aims high. Though she likes to think of herself as a strong character/role model – or strong willed – she's not so in real life. She does the job, usually without compromises and doesn't portray compassion towards anyone, especially not a potential suspect who may be a victim of circumstance. See **1.10 Night Mother**.*

She usually wants to get the last word in and believes she never gets the evidence wrong or makes mistakes: which she does, she's human but doesn't like to admit it too readily.

*Key episodes: **1.2 Creatures of the Night** though she appeared sympathetic towards the victim she got too bogged down in wanting to find the assailant; missing vital clues in the process – as well as* *appearing as if the only thing on her agenda was finding the offender.*

Some of her lines and interview techniques with her "tough-guy" attitude make her come across as smug.

Half-Greek, half Italian. Direct and sharp-tongued. Her life in "the system" has in part, made her how she is – can't help but wonder if she sees a potential suspect or criminal in everyone; as she displays little or no emotion or sympathy towards anyone she meets, well hardly ever. Ability to differentiate between victim/assailant but doesn't exhibit it.

She may be seen as the Statue of Liberty but hasn't really demonstrated she's a shining beacon of neutrality and hope; as more often than not, she's more interested in solving the case, which is good and right but it's not the be all and end all of being a CSI. In contrast to Mac, she doesn't seem to be interested in the 'why or the how' but the collar.

*In a rare role reversal she displayed more sympathy towards the baby than her colleague, Danny in **1.20 On the Job.** Which is understandable, but not so much as 'how you doing?' from her.*

*Stella is abrasive and volatile, a ticking time bomb with little control over her temper. Cf episodes **Night Mother**, unduly brash and abrupt when she was processing the female suspect. Rather eager and mean in **Officer Blue** and she has had complaints against her already in the past. Cocky and wanting to prove her point that she's always right after her confrontation with Mac, wanting the horse put down just to recover a bullet – a piece of evidence which may or may not have helped in the case and with hindsight didn't.*

Stella was named for Stella in Tennessee Williams' A Streetcar Named Desire. (Which is what I figured even before I found this out.)

Danny Messer

Carmine Giovinazzo: calls Danny, "a street smart energetic, young detective, having family mob connections and a 'don't bull**** me' attitude."

Anthony Zuiker: "Danny's the Sonny Corleone of the show. He has a temper, a mouth and that can get him into trouble."

Danny has also been described as "passionate with an urge to question all that is corrupt...a kid from the streets who studied and made good for himself..."

Danny is Detective Third Grade: his family has been under surveillance and has both "lawbreakers and law makers." He had a short-lived business career and was a baseball player. He broke his wrist in a fight and was first in his class at the Police Academy. He was personally selected by Mac Taylor to be in his team.

From What We've Seen

Danny actually lives up to this accurate description. He is hot-tempered; does mouth off and consequently has to pay the price and suffer the consequences. Dedicated to the job; has a sense of justice and underneath it all, is vulnerable. A good guy who's struggling to prove his worth and make sense of the world. He also studied to get to where he is and from what we know, his father and he travelled in cabs too.

*Temper in the interrogation of suspects; even towards victims and their families, though unintentionally or mistakenly. See **1.18 The Dove Commission**, the gypsy cab episode. Fights for the underdog and doesn't give up too easily especially when it comes to finding evidence and speaking up for victims without voices: those who can't fight for themselves. Though at times, he needs help from Mac to steer him in the right direction and to keep him focused.*

Impressed with his work, leading him on the path of promotion – cruelly ripped away due to a fatal mistake on his part: getting involved in shooting an officer and then talking to IA against Mac's advice. Thus he can give up on himself and on Mac too readily, believing no one was on his side.

*We haven't really stumbled across any family mob connections yet: though in **1.13 Tanglewood** this was hinted at, with Danny worried about what may come out about his past. Other key episodes include: **Night Mother, Tri-Borough, A Man A Mile, Outside Man, Crimes and Misdemeanours,** where Mac reprimanded him for not dropping a misdemeanour case and things just went downhill from there for him and their friendship won't be the same again.*

An avid sports fan, baseball player, working in various cases has given him street smarts as well as the experience necessary to make decisions concerning investigations and evidence.

*Born Staten Island and grew up in the spotlight: re his family though there's no mention of this in the entire season which begs the question if this is the case, why didn't Mac know about him in **13. Tanglewood** which then contradicted itself in sorts, in **21. On the Job,** with Mac telling him how he was told not to hire Danny and this is something he always meant to keep secret. But personally took him on anyway.*

Danny does look up to and respect Mac, hence easy to understand why he thought Mac wasn't in his corner batting for him when he told him not to talk to IAB. Though in fairness – a word of support from Mac wouldn't have gone astray, even if we knew he was working to clear him.

Mac now has doubts about his integrity and whether he can really trust Danny or will he let Mac down again if he does. Can they go back to where they were in the beginning? (See later seasons.)

Aiden Burn

Vanessa Ferlito: "A tough, young criminologist rolling with the best of them."

Anthony Zuiker: "we call Aiden the chameleon. She can put on any face, play uptown or down – professionally and personally."

Aiden is a Detective Third Grade: she has a love of the job, similar to Sara Sidle in *CSI*.

From What We've Seen

Aiden is probably the rookie – not much experience on the crime scene front and is probably still learning on the job, seen when Danny has to tell her things about crimes or criminals on the street, eg, pickpocketing episode, **10. Night Mother.**
Like Stella she never fails to get in a one liner, but unlike Stella, can be sympathetic and show concern about her colleagues and friends, victims and their families.

*Sees herself as one of the guys, although with some jokes and comments bordering on blatant sexism re Danny and Flack, which if her male counterparts would have made would have caused them to be called misogynists or sexist. Eg the fetish episode, **1.16 Hush** when she told Danny he was on the verge of sexual harassment but made jokes along with Stella in the monastery episode about Flack being chicken.*
Naïve at times which almost got her into strife when she turned up to investigate a potential crime scene on her own.

*Another CSI who's streetwise or tries to be. Born and raised in Red Hook, Brooklyn. Her specialties are anthropological skills; facial reconstruction and skeletal identity demonstrated in episode **3. American Dreamers**. Though her skills were only utilized once in this aspect in the entire season.*

Dr Sheldon Hawkes

Anthony Zuiker; "after 9/11 happened, he doesn't like to leave the morgue. He's socially inept but brilliant."

Hawkes is Detective Third Grade and part of the New York City Office of the Medical Examiner (OCMG). He was a child prodigy and graduated at 18. By 24 he was a surgeon and an experienced ER doctor. To achieve Third Grade he would have had to do a proficiency test and train/practice using firearms.

From What We've Seen

He doesn't come across as socially inept in the sense of being young and put upon or finding himself in a world where he had to deal with not only his primary task of saving lives but the bureaucracy and red tape surrounding this. He is rather clued up on the world and reality, what's happening outside his domain in the real city. He does leave the morgue on occasion for work and play since he's had conversations with a waitress about caviar of all things, so presumably dines out.

However is brilliant as an ME: thinking laterally including ways of preserving evidence and retrieving it intact. He did eventually get out as the season progressed and finally applied for field status, perhaps actually venturing out may have influenced this decision.

Key episodes didn't come about until later seasons, such as 3 and 5. especially season 5, when lots of events from his past come back to haunt him, such as his ex-girlfriend's rape and how he was going to propose to her, not to mention Mac's put downs.

Returned to the ME's office after losing a patient. Although we're not actually told this in the show and we don't know why he stays in the morgue, aside from Anthony saying it's because of 9/11 (so unless you've read it you wouldn't really know.) In 1. Blink he just said that Mac's Jane Doe wore him out and thus he had to sleep there. Hence the presence of his bunk in a corner of the morgue.

Either that or some may argue he prefers the company of dead people. Which he probably does in a way, at least a DB can't be menacing or be repugnant.

Det. Don Flack Jnr

Eddie Cahill: "It's not that he's not by the book, but he's got a bigger book and he's written some new pages."

Anthony Zuiker; "he's very edgy and very sexy with great wit. He's not the typical NYPD cop."

Flack is Detective First Grade and hails from a long line of police officers. He's part old school and new school. He uses borderline, but effective investigative methods.

NB: if Flack is a First Grade Detective, like Mac and Stella, why isn't he treated as their equal, as he's always seen as being subordinate to them. He always has to check things with them, or with Stella when Mac's indisposed. Whereas Detective Angell in later seasons was Third Grade and yet she was treated like his equal.

From What We've Seen

Taken to extremes Anthony's description could mean he doesn't get to do much in the show per episode. Flack was not in the cross-over episode and hence was yet to be written or cast.

He's very young, trying to do the right thing, ends up arguing with Stella for his troubles, more often than not. To the point he's even teased by Aiden and Stella.

A friend at times of need – Danny turned to him for his heart to heart when he was suspended; advising Danny from his own experiences, advice Danny subsequently chose to ignore.

His father was also in the NYPD. Exhibits staunch loyalty to friends and fellow officers. From a line of police officers. Streetwise and is aware of the need to question defendants effectively, even if this borders on the edges of not being 'by the book'. A bit over zealous in some of his tactics which usually produce the desired results.

Never misses an excuse to have a quip at the expense of a suspect – along with Danny. Though to be fair all the others do too.

Also hot-tempered (like Danny) and the both of them enjoy throwing their weight around in interrogations. Their behaviour in their quest to gather evidence sometimes invariably borders on the thin blue line. Crossed in episode **1 Blink** when Danny gathered evidence, a DNA swab from a suspect during questioning. Hence Eddie's description of Flack and his 'bigger book'.

Anthony's description of Flack not being a typical NYPD cop could have many interpretations, such as not being in an episode long enough to achieve results and follow an investigation to its conclusion. A case of one too may CSIs perhaps. He also respects Mac intensely as well as his role model/mentor, Sgt Moran, in the episode **17. The Fall**.

Stella and Aiden probably see him as a bit of a 'newbie' thus giving them the opportunity to have a laugh or two at his expense in **15. Til Death Do Us Part.** Though millions of women would (and do) see him as inevitable eye candy.

Cast Biographies

Gary Sinise

Born March 17 1955 in Blue Island, Illinois. Also known as Gary Alan Sinise. His family relocated to Highland Park and he attended high school there.

First performed in his high school production of *West Side Story* which gave him his first taste of acting and he relished the experience. On acting he says, "I only started acting because of the band I was in as a kid..." he was dragged to auditions for *West Side Story,* they tried to look tough so "...the drama teacher thought we looked like gang members I guess. "At 17 he made his first stage appearance in *The Physicist*.

He founded the Steppenwolf Theater Company in Chicago (which started life in a church basement) with some of his friends in 1974 and starred in many of its productions, including Sam Shepard's *True West*, alongside John Malkovich. *True West* also marked the theatre company's off Broadway debut in 1982. Gary was co-artistic director here from 1980-82, then again from 1985-86.

William Petersen also worked with the Steppenwolf Theater Company; hence he and Gary becoming friends.

In the late 1980's he directed two episodes of the TV series *Crime Story, thirtysomething* (1987) and *China Beach* (which also starred Marg Helgenberger.) Also the feature *Miles From Home* (1988) marked his directorial debut. Starring in the World War II drama *A Midnight Clear* in 1992, this was his debut as an actor in a feature film. He also starred in the critically acclaimed *Of Mice and Men* again alongside John Malkovich. He went on to star in other well known feature films, including *Forrest Gump,* for which he was Oscar nominated as Best Actor in a Supporting Role. He has also been nominated for the Golden Globe on three occasions and won a Golden Globe in 1998 for his leading role in *George Wallace*. As well as a SAG, Golden Sat, Cable ACE, an EMMY for Best Actor in A Mini-Series Motion Picture made for TV.

He has received nominations for the Tony Award four times and has won the Screen Actors Guild twice for *Truman* and *George Wallace*, as well as winning many other awards, these include a Best Supporting Actor Award from the National Board of Review, for *Forrest Gump* and the Commander's Award from Disabled American Veterans for the same movie. In 1980 he won a Joseph Jefferson Award for Supporting Actor for *Getting Out*.

1983 OBIE for directing *True West*. A Joseph Jefferson Award 1985 for Best Director for *Orphans*.

Joseph Jefferson Award 1996 for Best Director for *Buried Child* and also a Tony Nomination for this. In 1994 he won National Board of Review Best Supporting Actor for his role as Lt Dan in *Forrest Gump*. In 1996 he won the Chicago Film Critics' Commitment to Chicago Prize.

He's been in *Stephen King's The Stand* (1994) alongside Rob Lowe.

Apollo 13 (1995) and TV movies such as *Imposter* with Vincent D'Onoforio and *CSI*'s Gary Dourdan. Other features include, *The Green Mile* again with Tom Hanks, *Ransom* (1996), where he played a bad cop. *The Human Stain, Snake Eyes* (1998), *All the Rage* (1999), *Reindeer Games,* with Cameron Diaz, *The Forgotten, Fallen Angel, Mission to Mars.* He starred and was executive producer of *The Championship Season* (1999). More recently he can be seen in *Scheherazade* with Laurence Fishburne.

Gary married Moira Harris in 1981, who was an original member of the Steppenwolf Theater Company and they have three children, Sophie, McCanna and Ella. He received an Honourary Doctorate from Amhearst College in 2003.

On his character of Mac Taylor, Gary comments: "he enjoys the science part of it...Mac has a real sense of justice. A person with high moral integrity, somebody who's determined and dedicated to do the right thing." He enjoys the actual doing of the experiments or the processing." He also adds "our show can be pretty gruesome." On *CSI:NY*: "I was afraid I'd feel really stuck and penned in on a TV series, but the truth is, I've never felt so free knowing I'm in one of these hit TV franchises means I don't have to constantly worry about where the next job's coming from,...I can donate money to things I never could have before. I'm into a lot of humanitarian efforts and charities now. I'm in a new phase of life as somebody who wants to give back and has the ability to do that. It's a real blessing." Also he's a dab hand with the ol' rubber gloves on the show.

Gary does own a gun in real life, although the show doesn't use real firearms. He once pulled over a drunk driver who rammed his car from behind. The driver was a fan of the show and begged him not to turn him in – but was arrested. Says Gary, I sped down the freeway trying to get this guy and he's 90 miles an hour and I went into Mac Taylor – cop-chase-the-bad-guy- mode."

Although he does admit he didn't jump into playing the role. "I hadn't really considered settling into a TV series, but I sat around for about three and a half hours and just talked and it sounded very intriguing. After a couple of weeks of mulling it over, it became clear it would be a positive step...there's a security in playing the same character and a freedom to try a lot of different things in a successful series."

Gary has eleven weeks off from the show which he likes to spend with his family, play in his band (*Lt Dan Band*) or undertake charity work. He doesn't spend time looking for movie roles in his hiatus. His wish is to play in front of a huge crowd somewhere like Madison Square Gardens, which just may come true as the band has such a large audience now; thanks in part to the show.

He entertained troops in Iraq in May 2007 three times and in Kuwait, as part of USO and finds it rewarding to help them out. The second or third time was in November 2003-May 2007, it was for high morale and the troops say, "hi" to him and thank him for coming. He says it makes them feel good and vice versa. On his work for troops Gary comments, "the work that I've been doing on behalf of the troops and the children by offering them supplies – that's more of a socially-conscious-American-citizen than a political thing. If doing the right thing today means you're an activist, then I guess I am one, but I'd rather be called active than an activist."

Gary was awarded the *Presidential Citizens' Medal* for his work with Lt Dan Band, for performing for soldiers in Afghanistan and Iraq. He co-founded the charity, *OIC Operation Iraqi Children* with Laura Hillenbrand – collecting supplies, such as clothes and school equipment, like books, so that the US soldiers over there can hand them out to children.

Melina Kanakaredes

Born on 23 April 1967 in Akron, Ohio, USA. Her full name is Melina Eleni Kanakaredes. When she started out, people wanted her name changed to those like Melina Lynne, Lina Kane, Melina Karedes, but she refused.

Melina is a second generation Greek American and was the youngest of three sisters. Her father retired as an insurance salesman and her mother is a homemaker. As a child she spent long hours in her family's candy store. She always wanted to be an actress but she was fascinated by how people are motivated to do the job of a CSI. She is also the third member of *NYPD Blue* who has joined a *CSI* series.

Her stage debut was at eight when she starred in an Ohio Community Theatre production of *Tom Sawyer.*

As a teen she loved dance and theatrical productions and was involved in many of these.

When she was in Junior High she won a science fair.

In 1985 she graduated from Firestone High School in Akron, Ohio and attended Ohio State University studying music, dance and theatre. Competed as a synchronized swimmer at Ohio State University.

As there was no unity between the theatre and music departments, she chose a more conservatory education and left for Point Park College, Pittsburgh, affiliated with Playhouse, from where she was recently awarded an Honourary Doctorate. This led to appearances in commercials, industrial films and on stage at the Pittsburgh Playhouse and Pittsburgh Public Theatre. She graduated Magna Cum Lauda with a BA of Fine Arts in Theatre and left for New York. Here she supplemented her income by working on a dinner boat, World Yacht Elegant Dining Afloat, to pay for her to pursue an acting career and in off-Broadway plays. She played Sally Bowles in the stage production of *Cabaret.*

Melina was first runner up for *Miss Ohio*. She was seen by a William Morris agent and went on to play Greek immigrant Eleni Andros Cooper in the soap *Guiding Light* earning two Emmy Award nominations. She had a recurring role as Jimmy Smits' girlfriend, Benita in *NYPD Blue*.

In 1995 she co-starred with Gregory Harrison in the TV series *New York News,* as well as the short-lived *Leaving LA*. Also *The Guiding Light*. Guest starred in many TV Series including, *The Practice, Oz, Due South*. She was the lead in TV series *Providence*. Also the TV movie, *Saint Maybe*. Features include *Rounders, Dangerous Beauty, Into the Fire,* where she played twins, Katrina/Sabrina, *15 Minutes and The Long Kiss Goodnight*.

Melina is into researching her roles and did a stint at a coroner's office for *Leaving LA* and with surgeons for *Providence*. When she was cast for *Providence* she didn't undergo an audition and other cast members were cast on the basis of their chemistry with her. In this she played a plastic surgeon, Dr Sydney Harrison for five years. She won a TV Guide Award for Actress of the Year in a Drama series in 1999, for her role in this. She was also nominated in 2000 for a TV Guide award for Favourite Actress in a Drama and won. Of *Leaving LA* she says, "I don't think TV was ready for a show involving death then" not until *Six Feet Under*. She commented, "when a woman plays the role of a forensic detective and that year the enrollment for young women in the sciences and forensics goes up over 50%, then I know I've done something really cool."

She turned down a part in *Law & Order* as too formulaic. Her husband reads all her scripts. She's a fan of *CSI* but he told her to do the show only if viewers got to experience the show's character. Says Melina: "*Law & Order* was a great success but at the same time it wasn't a fire for me. *CSI:NY* we're really going to delve into the characters. It hasn't happened straight off the bat because when you've got a successful franchise you don't want to alienate the audience by shoving this whole new thing in. But once you gain the audience's trust you can start adding new things. It's a slow process based on months and years of adjusting, but we're moving in that direction." Her favourite episode from season 1 is **1.20 On The Job** where Stella's maternal instincts kicked in to look after the baby.

She wasn't sure about acting on TV and told her husband whilst working in *Cabaret* on Broadway they should sell everything in LA and she'd do theatre. She had lunch with Anthony Zuiker and he persuaded her to come on board *CSI:NY*.

She was up for the lead in the movie *My Big Fat Greek Wedding*.

Melina comments how they sing show tunes to stay awake with their hectic schedules. "I keep threatening to pitch an all-musical *CSI:NY* – 'I've got the hair! He's got the *NY* fiber. You've got the evi-de-e-ence!"

To keep the show fresh, she relished the chance to write an episode, **5.24** – she has directed before but found "writing was an incredibly new experience and it gave me the chance to put in a little Greek Plain, I put in a weapon buried in Alexander The Great's hidden tomb. The freshness is when all the talent in the room thinks outside the box and I was a beneficiary of the executive producer doing so." Melina also said more recently, "it has always been my hope that we'd be able to reveal more questions about Stella's life outside work and since I'm so proud of my Greek heritage, I thought, 'hey, let's go there.'"

She enjoys visiting her family in Ohio when not working and working out with Pilates as well as travelling to Greece; listening to music and is an avid fan of the Cleveland Indians and Chicago Bulls.

She met her husband, Peter Constantinides, a professional chef, whilst at Ohio State Phi: a group for Greek-American students. She has a large extended family so her husband had to invite 550 guests to their wedding in 1992. She has two daughters, Zoe and Karina Eleni. She resides in the San Fernando Valley region of LA.

More recently she will be seen as Athena in a film with Pierce Brosnan and Uma Thurman, entitled, *Percy Jackson and the Lightning Thief,* based on a series of books, which is set for release in 2010. She has also visited the Vatican with her family.

Carmine Giovinazzo

Born August 24 1973 Staten Island, New York. Also known as Carmine D Giovinazzo. The 'D' is for Dominik, after his father. He is 5' 9" tall.

Carmine: "I'm half Italian from Calabria and on my mother's side we come from Norway. I think there's a bit of Bristol, England, in there on my mother's side. It's a great mix. I love it – the fiery Mediterranean temperament with the ice cold Viking. I think it's the balance of life."

Carmine grew up playing most sports on the streets of Staten Island but enjoyed baseball and hockey. He wanted to be a professional baseball player and played baseball at Port Richmond High School and three years of college ball at Wagner College, Grymes Hill, Staten Island and also got to have a workout with the Chicago Cubs at Wrigley Field; but due to a back injury he gave up baseball and began a career in acting. Carmine was a former shortstop in baseball and said, "Baseball threw me for such a loop. I was that passionate about it." He slipped a disc in 1993, describing it as "probably the worst time of my life. I died in that period. I went through a lot. I walked around the room for six months banging into corners."

As a child he made his own short films but doesn't remember when he particularly wanted to go into acting. "Before I knew it, I was running around Manhattan with a headshot and taking classes at HBO Studios." He undertook several short films at NYU, SUNY Purchase and other independent films. He had the support of his family who were happy he found another avenue for his talents.
He said "I put aside business and decided this was what I was going to do." Also saying, he narrowed his career down to sports or theatre and opted for the former.

In 1997 he moved to LA and got a manager. His first audition was for the pilot of *Buffy the Vampire Slayer* where he was credited in the end as 'Boy.' A role in which Darla happened to get her teeth into, subsequently turning up in the girl's locker room! Says Carmine; "they called me Teaser Boy'. I had to break into the school and I was supposed to knock on the window and I put my hand through the glass in my second take. It took an hour before we shot again. It was a good experience and I had no idea it was going to be so huge. You do a pilot and all of a sudden it turns out to be such a hit." Though he wasn't part of the hit on a regular basis.

To Carmine, moving to California was just about work and for work. He has never been on stage and was an extra in the Woody Allen movie, *Radio Days*, when he was aged only ten: in a scene set in a zoo. (Now don't everyone go rushing out to find it! Well, you won't have to venture out such is the marvel of the World Wide Web.)

Carmine had to audition for the role of Danny Messer and describes "the process of getting a television series is miserable, miserable. You have to audition in front of 30 or 40 people. You feel like a dog on a leash. Then they make you wait eight days, you go back to smoking after quitting and then they say, 'Maybe'!"

On getting the part of Danny he said, "I think I was cleaning up some leaves in my backyard and I'll never forget it, I got the call on my phone and I was so relieved to have a job and a good one at that...the best part is getting to work with Gary Sinise every week and getting to act everyday. It's good, as an actor, to be able to do that."

His father, Dominik and sister, Alise Varela were both NYPD police officers, his father was on the NYPD for fifteen years. Alise was a police officer in the DARE programme, aimed at discouraging children from using drugs. Carmine looks upon them for advice. "With that kind of background I really felt I was right for the job. It means I was able to be myself in the role. I know the nicks and ticks of being a police officer."

274

His brother in law, Will Varela, was a detective assigned to former New York Mayor, Rudy Giuliani for eight years and worked with gangs. "He'll cut me with 'grab your gun like this – you wouldn't put that guy there when interrogating etc.'" His father was so excited to see Carmine on TV, as was his entire family, saying, "to know that's my son is incredible." Will commented that "cops will be the biggest critics." And also how Carmine called him for advice on interrogations, like where to sit the perpetrator and how to approach them."

Alise said they "love to say that he's following in our footsteps in a way." She gave him tips on fingerprinting.

His uncle, also named Carmine, was proud to see his name in the credits. "I've been watching since the first one [CSI] started. [Carmine] is doing a great job, he's very talented." Carmine's mother, Nancy, also loves the original CSI too and comments "it's a wonderful opportunity for him...I was delighted when I heard that he read for it. It's an opportunity to be seen by millions of viewers and be part of a great franchise." (And millions just in the US alone.)

"I'm on board indefinitely and I'm so appreciative, it's a great vehicle. But film is what I really want to do." Once in a show, it provides greater security than leaving to pursue a career in movies, which really boil down to the luck of the draw or pot luck as to whether you win the role. Carmine said back in 2004, "I'm not as excited as everyone else yet – I can't feel good until I get a response. This business is too whimsical but I'm totally embracing that."

On Danny he comments: "when the character came through, it was first and foremost being a Native New Yorker. You'd be surprised how rarely those parts come along for me. When that came through, it was very exciting to see it. I couldn't wait to meet for it after I saw the character description. You're rarely in a position to pick and choose. I was up for a couple of things around that time, so I was just looking for a job and this one was the most appropriate." His street in Staten Island was very culturally diverse, with Italians, Blacks and Puerto Ricans, he said it was an exceptional place to be raised, "the people are just real."

CSI:NY gave Carmine his big break but he starred in many roles on TV and films including: *U*-Boat (2004), Learning Curve (2001), Billy's *Hollywood Screen Kiss* (1998), *For The Love of the Game* (1999), *The Brass Ring* (1999) and *Black Hawk Down* (1999). Here he spent filming four months in Africa. He trained for a few weeks but missed the Boot Camp training for the movie in the US. Got to fly in actual helicopters and how to use an M16, as well as 'fast roping' buildings. They were coached by an ex navy Seal. Other roles were in *Conception* (1996), *No Way Home* (1996), *Locomotive* (1997), *Fallen Arches* (1998), *Terror Tract (Segment Nightmare)* (2000), *Big Shot: Confessions of a Campus Bookie* (2002), *Pledge of Allegiance* (2002), *Columbo Likes the Nightlife* (2003), *In Enemy Hands* (2004.)

He played lead for two seasons in his sitcom *Shasty McNasty*. Where he said, this show "gave me stability and I managed to fool them into thinking I could be a sitcom actor."

His other TV roles include guest starring spots in:
The Guardian (Glen Lightstone)
CSI (Thumpy G)
UC: Undercover (Clarence 'CE' Peters) in *Nobody Rides For Free*
Providence (Kit) in the episode *Heaven Can Wait* alongside his current co-star Melina Kanakaredes.
Pacific Blue (Cody Fisher) in *Matters of the Heart*

He has a great passion for cinema and stars in films whenever the opportunity presents itself. He co-stars with William H Macy in *In Enemy Hands* and alongside Freddy Rodriguez and Peter Dobson in the Indie movie *Red Zone.* Also in a film by his co-star Hill Harper, alongside Eddie Cahill, *This Is Not A Test*, where he played a Brit but didn't get any scenes with Eddie.

He enjoys painting, poetry and plays guitar. As well as roller hockey, basketball and baseball. He has been drawing since he was little and says he was inspired by everyone, including all of his fans. He had an art show in LA in 1997 and is waiting for enough material before having another show. He had twenty-one pieces in a celebrity artist show and has used pastels, oils, acrylics in his works, including spray paint. (I've used nail varnish – that's a totally different medium, but hey no one wants to know about me!!)

Carmine launched his official website carminegiovinazzo.com in September 2004, which is unavailable at the moment, at least everytime someone I know has tried to find it. Carmine initially went for the role of Danny Messer, what appealed to him about it (as mentioned already), was Danny being a native of New York and those parts are difficult to come across. He's learning a lot of science from the forensics in the show, as he was never really a science buff. He was recognized more when he was in Venezuela than he was in LA and admits he never used to watch *CSI* until he got the role of Danny; he thought the Vegas cast was cool. So does that mean Carmine didn't watch his own performance on the show when he guested in season 3 and thought – "yo, cool dude!" Er, let's leave it at that!

Writing and directing are two of his other talents he hopes to realize. Eventually. He is working on a project *The Brink of Black* which has been in the pipeline for years, since 2006, says Carmine, "a film that has a Cassavetes feel and Tarantino colour." He describes it as "a character film about friends from New York, a love story, realizing that where you grew up may not be where you belong. I'm always writing and have several other things in motion." He wrote this and will also act in it. He's been trying to raise money for this project. Said Carmine, "If I allow myself to have a moment, it may become the most important job of my career as far as the opportunity it can bring. I guess it's not what I had in mind. I thought I was going to go the film route. But maybe this will allow me to get my film going."

This film, as already stated was *Brink of Black* and Carmine also described it as being "about a Staten Island kid realizing he doesn't belong where he lives surrounded by wise guys, and he makes a move to get out of New York." That sounds very familiar to Danny's personal life in the show and to episode **1.13 Tanglewood**, from the show – but Danny didn't want to get out of New York, he only wanted to be better than those he grew up with and leave behind the lure to be tempted into a gang life – one of crime and nothing but trouble. However, Carmine wrote his film many years previously, even before this episode was ever conceived. Wonder if the writers of *CSI:NY* had an insight into this, i.e. Carmine's writing as a backdrop to his character, Danny. Well, one can but ask!

Seems like he has an appropriate name for such an artistic career!

As for writing, Carmine has achieved his writing debut for the show, episode **6.14 Sanguine Love.** This will air in February 2010 in the US and around April here in the UK. The episode is about a modern day vampire cult which involves blood sharing as part of a religion. A dead woman is found in Central park with a puncture wound on her neck and a hacked off earlobe. A must for vampire lovers everywhere and finally *CSY:NY* gets its own episode too. (*CSI* had a vampire episode too, of sorts in its earlier seasons.)

On Twitter, Hill's page, he's posted: *On set-shooting Carmine's episode. Just finished stabbing a pig!! It started to smell under the hot lights!! I may become a vegetarian!! Lol Hill Harper December 14th 2009.* He then continues in response to other Twitters: *Yes Carmine wrote this episode. Melina wrote one last year. Carmine this year. It's called "Sanguine Love" and it's great!! He's talented!*

Yes something already known!! Well, that was well and truly kept under wraps and close to his chest!

When asked about how he feels being an actor, his chosen career, Carmine: "to tell you the truth, I always have such a boring answer for these questions which is why my family is just so happy I'm employed and ironically, I am playing what they knew I would never become but what they all are!" He's so glad to be on such a show. "I'm now waking in the morning, putting on a suit and tie and grabbing the briefcase and going to work – that lifestyle, that's probably the biggest change I'm adjusting to. It's kind of a claustrophobic feeling for me, the idea of committing to [that lifestyle] it's not even 9-5. It's 6am to 6 at night. There's a grind and a lot of waiting." He applauds everyone in the world for doing what they do everyday, but for him they have to do that for TV and then viewers have to watch them. "We have to do it and we can't hide the fact if we're having a bad day. So it's kind of a trip. It's a nice challenge for an irresponsible guy like me." Yes, but then do people on TV really have bad days?

He also says of acting "I probably could not have picked a more difficult profession. I wouldn't recommend it, but it's one of those things where you have to do it, you don't plan it. You have to have an obsessive nature." His uncle filmed videos for 'Sweet Sixteen' parties and his cousin, Buddy Giovinazzo is also into acting.

Carmine commented on acting and music: "I'm trying to figure out how to have balance rather than work, work, work." But he likes acting since he enjoys "reading people's stories. I like telling other people about it. My kick is recreating realness. That trips me out – it's a complete release, exposing your [creative] self to the fullest. It's unbelievable."

On the subject of being a sex symbol, he doesn't really care about his appearance much on the show. "I have a great pair of boots that I wear on the show [which disappear in later seasons]. It's a great pair of black zip up boots that I wear on the show [from season 3]." He wears them home and forgets to bring them back! Yes, Carmine, we've noticed the boots. In fact that was the talk back when we first saw them and even Flack got a comment about them. Wonder if that comment was ad libbed. Then they disappeared or were they taken away because towards the end of season 4 and throughout season 5, Danny now sports a pair of plimsole/trainers. Did the heels play havoc in the running/chase scenes? His glasses vanish too. Carmine came up with the decision to remove his glasses since season 5, as he thought his character needed to "feel different."

Also he said, "I don't really mix into the Hollywood scene – I'm kind of a loner."

He also describes how they went to the morgue in New York City, "which I couldn't stomach. It was horrible. We were in the basement where they put a mask over your face because of the smell and you're in with the corpses. We were shown parts of bodies. It's a job I just couldn't do."

On the subject of symbols, Carmine had this to say, "a lot of Hollywood crap people are symbols because they're pretty or they do this...but I think that cats you find attractive that aren't really conventionally or typically attractive is because they got balls and passion and come from a gut kind of place and what they do...like the old De Niros – and the Johnny Depps.

They commit so much to what they do that's ...when you see a person be honest – that's sexy...I don't really think about playing that role too much on that surface sense if I am that guy."

Favourite characters he's played include: Gundy from *Billy's Hollywood Screen Kiss*, Frankie in *Fallen Arches* and Danny Messer, naturally. On being similar to Danny Carmine feels, "we have many of the same quirks and idiosyncrasies. I think the people who write have utilized who I am and what I brought to the character. I'd say 40% of me is in him and his passion and righteous ways, his frustration towards criminals."

Carmine says: "I'm not a 'Johnny Sports Talker' but there's something hot about a girl at a game with a hat on just sitting there enjoying it."

Carmine also started his own band, *Ceesau* and released an album *Era of the Exposed*. He would like some of his music to be featured in the show, but so far producers have refused. On Ceesau he comments: "it's something that I started over 10-15 years ago, about racial unity and equality, about a drawing that I had had done."

Mike Brasic says Carmine was behind the spelling of the band's name. I personally think it can have a more exotic meaning – *Ceesau* looks like having an international flavour behind it too, especially if you're new to the band and the name and see it written without the image it represents, i.e. two persons (one black, one white) on a seesaw, hence *Ceesau*: "the world in balance." Carmine: "*Ceesau* was just a word that I came up with using when I was at Wagner College." In his time off he does work on other things. He's read books on philosophy, "it's about balance, equality and universalism and the way the world ticks...with the way the world has gone. With a Black President, is exactly where *Ceesau* came from."

Carmine: "my roommate in college, Keith, kind of took part in that. We had made shirts and hats initially and had really wanted to do that, but then it kind of always used that title for things I'd done." He continues: "I've always been writing music and kind of messing around. I consider myself a real average – f****ing guitar player. I just write songs and I've played with a bunch of different people over the years. I play with this drummer who's in my band now, Mike Brasic, and playing with John Amedori, who's the lead guitar player. I just want to put something together more than just acoustic, more than just myself. I've always wanted to bring a couple of people together, make something happen."

Michael Brasic on how the band came about: "Carmine and I are old friends and on occasion [we] would get together and just play music, never serious, just for fun. Carmine started writings songs with John about two years ago {2006}, then he brought all of us together and it just clicked. It actually happened pretty innocently, having a band was nothing we decided upon, it just happened." They also recruited Stephen Tecci after their CD *Era of the Exposed* came out. He calls the band, philosophical in meaning and deed, says Mike, "we love life, music, people and culture. Art and music and all flavours from around the world. We are all one race, the Human race. Love it and love it. It's all good.

We represent no borders – one world."

He gives Carmine credit, he understands people and has "great abs!" Carmine has also been a great influence on him in the band, musically – as he feels Carmine "challenges" his playing and wants him to "think outside the realms of my room."

Carmine loves his music, "...music is a little bit more personal because I can do it myself. You can control music to a certain extent. It all came out of an interest in making something from nothing, just creating. Growing up on Staten Island...I was listening to ...disco...I went through that phase in high school. I wasn't listening to the good stuff until later...Also grew up on rap and *KISS*."

On the album coming about, Carmine says, "John is unbelievable on guitars – as far as I'm concerned. He's a little busy right now. We did lose it for the whole hiatus last year [2007] and just played and played...and we got to the point where I was like – 'let's record.' We wrote 10-12 songs and then we were like 'let's pick 3' and then we were going to do 6 and decided we were getting closer to an album. We decided to just do 5. We recorded it in a day and a half and it was really kind of raw. (See their website on myspace. *Era of the Exposed*. www.ceesau.com) The CD was released mid-March 2008 and is huge in the UK, France, Sweden, Denmark and Japan.

There's a meaning behind the title of his album, *Era of the Exposed* which Carmine says means it's "been this way for a while but everything is just being exposed now, whether it's corrupt people or whether it's the media or peoples' lives, or how things work out or how things tick, who did this wrong or did that wrong – everything's being unravelled. It's the era of being exposed. It's kind of sickening and also over-do. It's a little heavy. I'm trying not to be too heavy – there's so many things you could say, or a title of a book, or say in one line, and you have to kind of come up with five words. That was something that happened and does reflect our time."

Carmine being on such a high profile and prolific show as *CSI:NY* also has an impact on the band. Comments Mike, "without it, he's Carmine from the block. The show lends a certain cache that allows us to separate the band on our terms – something most bands don't get to do." As well as getting more fans and listeners, as Carmine's brought over his fandom with him, or at least most it. Mike sees *Ceesau* as a band as Carmine's vision backed "by my foundation. Anything more is just icing on the cake."

As for other aspects of Carmine's musical side, such as recording he says, "it's sometimes overwhelming and too much because it is complicated when you want to do the recording and really get it together and make a finished product – what goes into it when that's not [the only thing] you're doing. If I was just doing music right now, that would be a different story, but to uphold this job and keep that going and keep these guys [from the band] together and everybody happy and excited it's tough. So this is what we got. It's not bad. People that have listened to it have thought it was alright. I'm just more excited about making something from nothing. That is totally amazing for me to do that."

Mike attributes the influence for their ideas, music, lyrics, as being solely Carmine, who saw peoples' lives influenced by the media, hence Carmine came up with the quote, "living in the era of the exposed" and so went with the name for the album.

Carmine and Mike came up with the basic versions of the songs, then Stephen has to "tie the vocals and guitar back to the drums of course the big pressure is not to screw that up." Carmine comes up with a riff and then they carry on from there. *Nirvana* is an inspiration for Carmine's music and lyrics. Especially the early stuff. Explains Carmine: "our music is not heavy and hard punk rock – like the *Germs* but it comes from that world."

It's not easy putting together something from scratch when you're juggling other things and to finance your projects yourself, which is exactly what Carmine has done with his album. He has had no financial backing from anyone at all.

Carmine's thoughts on what the song *Wrote the Longest Word* is all about "how everything is everything, everybody is everybody, everybody's the same in a sense, in a philosophical, ideological [way.] The sense of if we could all start back from zero and just be like what makes us segregate and separate and get all screwed up. Just all these little bubbles that we come from and these things were taught and we think are right, the way people should be or shouldn't be or what we should believe in. That's my voice in that sense and my remedial guitar playing with everyone else's kickass lead guitar and drums. I'm happy about it."

On other songs from the album, like, *Wishing*, "that things were a little better, wishing we could rewind from the chaos and the ultra, ultra, technologically modern world that we've become fast-paced; and we're all running too fast. I'm trying to pull back from being so affected by all of those things. It's something I feel – it's more about how I feel and I see things. Then there's a song about my perspective, me looking through other peoples' perspectives having gone through something – that [song is] *She Will Get Over This*. It's kind of whimsical in a sense, that song [had] different kind of lyrics when I first wrote it and then it ended up becoming this little story I wrote about from the point of view of somebody losing someone. – Insomnia and losing sleep and wanting to be happy and accepting that things are good and not worrying so much. *Tear to Spare*.

Carmine calls his band members very talented, musically and John is a superb guitar player, "he's got that gift for the guitar that makes you want to break yours." Rehearsals for the band revolve around unusual hours – such as midnight, noon or even 6am.

He is very modest too commenting that artists like Queens of the Stone Age, David Bowie, Tom Waites all write music and they're extremely gifted and talented. Then people like Jimi Hendrix, Eric Clapton or Zeppelin are "just so ridiculously on another planet. But for me it's kind of like a certain art. I don't discount art that's somewhere in between abstract and insane realism. You look at art like that and it's like, 'well, f***, I'm not going to pick up a brush again'. It's just music that's about the right thing. I'm not doing it to put on black nail polish [prefer purple myself!] and dye my hair and become a rock star. I would love to be playing around, and if I could keep the band together [oh Carmine! Sorry] right now it's just more like another outlet."

For the creative side to him is very apparent in everything that he's done and does, not just in his artwork but also his music and acting.

Carmine is into Iggy Pop, Henry Rollins, The Pixies, Nirvana, Velvet Underground, Lou Reed and Mean Streets. He has a varied taste in music and likes various genres. He grew up on rap and other music. "I feel like lots of these songs were passed down in one way, way shape or form and what John took on to it and what we [brought to it] – has a decent range of styles. Some of it's sad; some of it's kind of rocking. It's all kind of about something. It's always interesting writing lyrics when you're only doing 5 songs, you kind of get crazy about it and it's just five songs. I like it to be about anything. This is mostly about universal kind of things and what everybody writes about looking at the world and how you see it and think you need to do with yourself and as well as what you think might be a better thing for everybody else. It's angry. It's kind of uplifting."

Offers Carmine, "I don't worry about the result, whether my stuff will be good, bad...when you're trying to act – you're trying to get a job...we picked five songs...people don't know I have a thousand songs. Mikey Drum [his name for drummer Mike Brasic] keeps me focus on that stuff. He's like, 'dude, I feel good at playing with you because you don't really care about wearing cut off gloves and eye-liner or whatever.'"

Carmine is very set and definite in his views about not only his music, but also his acting life. He doesn't like how in the acting world, people want to get to know him, everything about him. He understands it, but he also hates it, at the same time. He doesn't mind it so much with the musical side, since it's more personal and a part of his own creation. He comments about this as being, "like a great episode of *iconoclast* this great show of *IFC*, where they take two fascinating people, say Mikhail Baryshnikov and the woman who revolutionized organic food in San Francisco, or Paul Newman and Robert Redford...I think Newman said something interesting like, 'what the f*** are these kids doing now?' We know if they're drinking, wearing out. It's the truth. As an actor you want to play a character and that's how you want people to see you. Johnny Depp keeps it under wraps and so did De Niro, back in the day...You want to keep that, but in this day and age, it's all about publicity and that's what gets the job and these are the people that people want to hire and that's who you're talking about."

Carmine doesn't really believe that today, a great actor can be discovered, since everybody is just the same as the next person. There are so many people out there, 'wannabees' who want to be somebody, but it's not based on acting ability. He comments, "we have a Black guy and a woman running for President [and he won] cool movies are being made like *La Vie En Rose*. I think we're going through that shift, going back towards doing things that are more for everybody and about the right reasons and not just about making money. The people in power have that way of thinking, but they're controlling the situation. It's hard to have an album or an unemployed actor or a low-budget writer getting this stuff out there, because you have to have a movie star in it."

Which is all true begging the question of who and what defines what a movie star is? Obviously the looks, but also the studio, since what the shallow public wants, is exactly what the shallow public gets. It's all about conspicuous consumption and obviously the first thing anybody looks at isn't talent but looks. If you don't have the looks, you don't have a career.

Case in point to what Carmine said above is in reference to his own band. "This *Ceesau* thing it's about all that I'm talking about. I would like to make it big enough so that I can do something with it and it says it on the site and I will do this, certain charities that I've been involved in and have dealt with, I'll use this money if I make any [for them]. I'm doing this completely independently – I don't have a record label, I produced it myself, I put up my money, I put up my time, I designed the shirts, I talked to the people that made the shirts; I found a place where I'm going to print the shirts. I'm just trying to get it up and running, so all money that I make is going to go to a charity in Staten Island and different things here and there. I don't want to be another actor jumping on the charity 'f***ing' bandwagon like everybody's doing, but you know it's definitely something I'd like to be able to do and I am doing in my own little way right now; so hopefully people can catch on to *Ceesau* about an idea that's positive, that happens to have an actor underneath it, music underneath it, shirts underneath it."

There you go folks, you heard it straight from the man himself, so take an active part in *Ceesau* and help to save somebody, make a difference in others' lives.

Some producers are interested in the band, but Carmine is too busy to pursue certain avenues that would be available to them and for that reason, can't play live shows either.

Carmine's good friend, and co-star, AJ Buckley comments, "...he's really talented. I don't know if Carmine realizes what he did [with the band.] That's not easy to do, to write it and to produce it. It's really good stuff." On the song, *Wrote the Longest word,* AJ calls it, "cinematic. He's so talented."

This Is Not A Test in which he co-stars with Hill Harper and Eddie Cahill is an Indie film, by Hill. Carmine plays an English (that should read British) artist, but he only had scenes with Hill.

Also *Life is Hot in Cracktown* written by his cousin Buddy Giovinazzo, who is a writer/director. Also stars Kerry Washington, Lara Flynn Boyle. Carmine has a cameo as a homeless junkie.

He is instrumental in charities, such as those for abandoned children in Staten Island. Autism, the Dodgers who are building parks etc, and for others like Gary Sinise raising money to keep his theatre company running. Showing up, giving money to support others. Also there's *New York Foundling* which is connected to September 11 and in the *Save Ellis Island Campaign*. This is another campaign that Carmine is very passionate about. Mentioning his grandfather was from Naples, Italy who arrived in New York in 1923 and his other grandfather who arrived here from Oslo in May 1921. They both had a delicatessen, called *Sunshine*. Also his grandmother arrived in New York when she was only seven. Upon arrival forms had to be filled out, asking questions about 'where you are going, why you are here?' Says Carmine, "We are all part of Ellis Island. We are all a part of each other." [See Carmine's *Ellis Island* interview online. As well as the *Save Ellis Island Campaign* and get involved for yourself.]

Once *CSI:NY* is over with; Carmine would love to travel with his band, but admits he's hard on himself and his capabilities. "It's more of a passion, but I have worked hard at it. I would like to have it out there for a lot of people to hear and to be appreciated and to be heard." You are appreciated, of course you are and there are many of us out there who recognize what you're doing and trying to achieve. So selflessly!

On places to visit, "Prague is a good place because I'm calm there and everything is beautiful to look at...I like a nice balance of what it is that you want to do...just roaming around, going at your own pace, it kind of felt easy there. I wasn't rushed and it didn't seem hectic like Paris might have been."

He would also love to get back to movies and do nothing but just make movies after *CSI:NY*, as TV is a hard slog. He would love to coach a baseball team. And would love to play Johnny Boy in the movie *Mean Street*, Martin Scorsese's second movie. It's low budget, "De Niro's young, funny, crazy and a cool character." Carmine admires Viggo Mortensen who is also a musician, he also writes and "he's got soul."

He believes *CSI:NY* "...turned out to be something that's actually a lot better than half the movies you read these days and it's good job for many reasons." Saying, "for me Staten Island was a telephone pole and a schoolyard. Now I'm in a fantasyland [LA] staring at mountains. Staten Island has so many wicked places that I took for granted when I was there and I'm hoping we'll utilize them [in *CSI:NY*.]

In the season 2 opener, Carmine opens the scene running on a rooftop in downtown LA. Poor Carmine, he was clearly exhausted "...running...for like twelve hours in a pair of boots and jeans, chasing down this guy and tackling him. As the action guy they put me in these scenes, which is fun but it was 6:30am and I ran all day. It felt like 100 degrees. I'm in boots, a jacket, sweating, and I had smoked a couple of cigarettes." The crew weren't too sympathetic either. Perhaps you should give up on the smokes Carmie. "It was like, 'old man' and they told him, 'you're the athletic one who said they could do this and run full throttle.'" And he said, "Yeah, yeah, but come on spread it out. And I'm puffing and some guy has me doing calisthenics on the side going, 'loosen up Carmine. Stay loose.' The next four days I felt like such an old man with my claves and hamstrings, I am limping into work going 'hey guys, do you think you could get me a massage here or somebody to rub me out?' Didn't hear anything back on that one!"

No dramatic scenes to come in season 2 though. (But of course that was far from the case.) Carmine: "We really want to create some humour and lighten it up, but we definitely intend on dealing with **Tanglewood** and what is going on with that."

Grand Murder at Central Station (in season 2) marks Vanessa Ferlito [Aiden's] last episode. Carmine comments, "it is going to be very different. Mine and Vanessa's dynamic was really coming together. It is going to change just from who the actor is and what they are going for. In a sense, the whole show has changed with the new, brighter sets."

She is replaced, or rather her character is replaced by Lindsay Hamilton, as she was named at the time [Lindsay Monroe.] Says Carmine "a new detective from another city that has been called in to join our group based on her expertise. [Re Sara Sidle here perhaps. She was called in from another city because of her experience and being a friend of Gil's and former student, but Sara has real presence and pizzazz.] She's [Lindsay's] done some really good work and comes in to fill a hole. It is going to be a fun dynamic because it is something I can play on, her being an outsider and not from New York. I have an opportunity to have a good banter with her and give her a hard time in a light-hearted way." Mac wasn't from New York either so that's nothing new which the writer's have added.

Also in this episode, Carmine is the unaccredited public announcer at the opening of the episode, as I also said this and no one listened!

The first quarter of the new season will concentrate on crimes in Grand Central Station, the Bronx Zoo and the Empire State Building. Carmine says, "it is *CSI* in the valley due to the ramifications of moving everyone to New York. A lot of people are here and Anthony goes to Vegas to see his wife and kids every weekend...our intention is to go back three or four times so I hope they hold up to that."

Hopefully this has whetted your appetite to go watch season 2 if you haven't seen it, but no matter if you have, go watch it again.

Some Carmine shorts:

On 15th May 2009 Carmine was awarded the *Arts and Letters Award* during the Annual Neptune Ball on Staten Island.

26 October 2008, he was part of the *Annual Love Ride* in California – raising more than $1 million for Southern California charities.

1996 he won the *Grand Special Prize of the Deauville Film Festival* for *No Way Home*. He can't drink caffeine saying, I'm just a tea guy, if it's a rainy day, I'm just gonna stay in, I like tea."

In 2006 *People Magazine*'s *Sexiest Man Alive* named him *Sexiest DNA Dude*.

Chicago Sun Times had a 'heart-throbs on TV which make readers swoon' in an issue and Carmine was on the list of TV boyfriends.

TV Guide Magazine 2006 named him *the Hottest Guy from CSI:NY*.

Carmine rides a Harley, also his character Danny, rode a bike for a while in season 4. His fave baseball team is the New York Mets. He played at Yankee Stadium twice in his senior High School year.

At a celebrity baseball game, he was the only actor to hit a home run right out of Dodger Stadium, Los Angeles.

His favourite junk food is chocolate. Hey, that's not junk food, well not if you eat the really bitter, dark variety, that's supposed to be good for you. Not that many people do.

He calls himself a "certified groupie of the Lt Dan Band. I'm running out of words to say [you're a writer, you never run out of words! Ha.] about Gary. As an actor, as a boss to employees, he treats everybody the same. He is easy to work with…he comes in and you think he was there to repair the plumbing."

His advice to budding actors: "first you have to love it. Like baseball, you can't be good unless you want it. Immerse yourself in the business side of things, find a manager who is apt to work with you…do student films. Work for free. I did extras working in New York. You do whatever you can do until you can do what you want to do." Advice he credits to Clarence Clemens from Bruce Springsteen's E Street Band, given to him around 1992.

Vanessa Ferlito

Born 28 December 1977 in Brooklyn, New York. She is 5' 6"
Her father died when she was three. Her mother and stepfather own a hair salon in Brooklyn. Her son was born 21st September 2007.

Vanessa is a vegetarian and her fave dish is chickpeas and spaghetti, as made by her Mom. Shaun Monson's documentary *Earthlings* (2003) encouraged her to become a vegetarian.

Vanessa also used to work in her parent's shop, at a washing counter. She is close to her family which is important to her and she insists on paying her mother whenever she baby sits.

Vanessa was signed up as an actor even before she auditioned or got to do a show reel, she was spotted outside a club.

Also in 2003, she was nominated for an Image Award for her role in the TV movie, *Undefeated*.

Her most famous role to date has been *CSI:NY*. Vanessa's big break came in the movie, *On_Line* as Internet sex worker, Jordan Nash in 2002. She also guest starred in *The Sopranos* as Tina Francesco in the episode Rat Pack, (2004) Another Toothpick (2001)

As Claudia Salazar in *24* in the episodes: Day 3: 10-11pm; 9-10pm; (2004) 8-9pm; 7-8pm; 6-7pm; 5-6pm; 4-5pm; 3-4pm; 2-3pm; 1-2pm. (2003). She loved working on this as it gave her "such a depth of character and was such an edgy, exciting place to work."

She played Tina Montoya in *Law and Order* in the episode Star Crossed (2003).

Val in *Thirdwatch* in the episode Blackout (2002)

Her movie roles include: *Man of the House* which she filmed at the same time as *24*. As well as Spike Lee's *25th Hour* (2002) as Lindsay Jamison, with Ed Norton.

Wall Street 2: Money Never Sleeps (2010) (Audrey) (to be released.)

Julie & Julia (2009) (Cassie) with Meryl Streep

Madea Goes to Jail (2009) (Donna)

Nothing Like the Holidays (2008) (Roxanna Rodriguez). Where she starred in the comedy alongside Debra Messing and Alfred Molina.

Grindhouse (2007) (Arlene/Butterfly) [Vanessa means *Butterfly*]

Quentin Tarantino's *Deathproof* (2007)

Descent (2007)

Shadowboxer: (Vicki) (2005)

*Cheer Up (*2004) with Tommy Lee Jones

The Toll Booth (2004) Gina

The Tollbooth: Gina (2003)

Undeafeted: Lizette Sanchez (2003) which earned her a nomination for Outstanding Actress in a TV Movie.

Her role in 2004's *Spiderman 2* ended up on the cutting room floor.

On *Grindhouse* she says Quentin Tarentino actually wrote the part for her.

For her role of Aiden Burn, she didn't have to read for the network and so got the role with plenty of ease – all she had was a meeting with the casting director. Begging the question of why she found it so easy to leave the show after one season! Especially since being in such a highly rated show would've given her prime time exposure. (Okay I for one, would've liked to have seen where her character would've gone on the show and to develop further! As Aiden was more interesting to watch than Lindsay, in my opinion!) She also wanted to work with Gary since he's huge in movies. Hence he was going to be a major presence on any set.

CSI:NY is filmed at CBS Radford Studio City, LA and *CSI* is filmed at the Universal Studios lot. One of her main reasons for leaving the show, primarily she cites as not filming in New York more often, or as much as she would've liked at the time of season 1 and perhaps this would've made her stay on the show longer. "I could've taken my friends from the show around my neighborhood." Now the show shoots more frequently in New York and she's disappointed and a little envious that this wasn't the case before.

293

On *NY* Vanessa comments: "I had a taste for movies before this show. I had just wrapped one before I started the show – so it was hard to make that transformation and be on a procedural show like that. They were all great to me. Anthony Zuiker is a doll, a gem and I love him dearly." Anthony called her "a really talented and sweet woman who I think I'll work with in the future."

Continues Vanessa: "there's no bad blood because I was so honest with him. I went to him and told him exactly how I was feeling and he got it. We're great friends and I'd love to work with him again. I actually invited him to the premiere [of *Grindhouse*] but he just had a baby."

Vanessa got on great with all the cast especially her fellow 'New Yawkers', Eddie and Carmine, who still visits her whenever he's in New York.

Vanessa says "I'm weird with stuff like blood. I get grossed out." She's very different to her character.

She divides her time between New York, she now lives in Staten Island, and LA. She's looking to set down roots because of her son and eventually find a regular role – pity *NY* passed her by! Maybe she could return as a completely different character, or how about Aiden's twin sister/look-alike! That'd be cool.

Hill Harper

Francis 'Frank Harper' Harper was born 17 May 1966 in Iowa. Also known as F Hill Harper.

Hill has an MPA: Masters in Public Administration from the Kennedy School of Government. Joint degrees from Brown Undergraduate, then Harvard, to get his JD (Diploma in Jurisprudence, equivalent of a UK LLB i.e. Batchelor of Laws) and MPA at the same time. He studied Theatre at Brown and won an Alfred P Sloan Fellowship, as he was Magna Cum Laude and Valedictorian in his department at Brown. He joined the Repertory Company in Boston whilst at Harvard. Whilst at the Kennedy School of Government and Harvard Law School, he was fellow classmate with future President, Barak Obama. For whom he campaigned on the Presidential trail.

His mother is Dr Marilyn Hill Harper – retired – anesthesiologist. His father, Dr Harry Harper, passed away in 2000 (sadly didn't get to see Hill in the show.) Both his parents and grandfather were doctors. He calls on his mother for help with some of the terminology. He says if there's something he needs to find out about he'll use the Internet. "If it's something that's much more medical that I don't know about or want a better understanding of – that one simple definition of death, I can call my mother and ask her about it, or ask our on-set consultant who worked in the Sheriff's Department for years. You do the research and you ask the questions so you understand exactly what the process is, exactly what you're going for." Hill also gets onto the net as soon as he gets his script to research all the medical lines and has also been on a visit to a body farm for two days, but prefers the fake DBs on set.

He's sat in on autopsies with the Chief Medical Examiner's Office in New York. "These people are heroes. They deal with things society needs done but doesn't want to do – that's why I'm really proud, because talking to them, these people are heroes when September 11 happened they had to individually bag and barcode

27,000 individuals...the DNA analysis on each [body part] to try to piece them together like a jigsaw puzzle. That's why I'm really proud to be playing one of them in the greatest city in the world."

He was the winner of Image Awards for Outstanding Actor in a Drama Series for *CSI:NY* 2008/09 and nominated in 2005-07. Method Festival: Winner 2000 for Best Actor in a feature film for *The Visit*. Urban World Film Festival 2008 he won Best Film for *This Is Not A Test*. He was honoured with W.E.B. DuBois Scholar Award at the Thirteenth Annual Inner City Awards. His book, *Letters to a Young Brother* won him an American Library Associations Prize in 2007 for Best Book for Young Adults.

Roles include in such movies and shows as:

Lackawanna Blue

Mama Flora's Family.

I Love the Nineties Part Deux as Himself (2005)
    The Handler Darnell (2003)   where he played an undercover cop.
    The Court Christopher Bell (2002)
    City of Angels Dr Wesley Williams (2000)
    Live Shot Tommy Greer (1995)

He guest starred in:
Soul Food Klevin Chadway; Angelitos Aegros (2004)
    The Sopranos Stokely Davenport MD in the episode Irregular Around the Margins (2004)
    The Twlight Zone John Woodrell in the episode *Shades of Guilt* (2002)
    Preston in *Men are from Mars, Women are from Astoria.* (1998)
    ER Mr Jackson in Obstruction of Justice (1997)
    Dangerous Minds
    Cosby
    Darryl in *Family Ties* (1996)
    NYPD Blue Bo-Bo Thomas in *The Backboard Jungle* (1996)

The Fresh Prince of Bel Air Dana in *Will Steps Out* (1994)

M.A.N.T.I.S.: in the episode *Tango Blue* (1994)

Married With Children Arron in the episodes: *The Legend of Ironhead Haynes; Field of Screams; Honey, I Blew Up Myself; A little off the Top; Scared Single.* (1994-1993)

Other movie roles include:

Love, Sex and Eating the Bones, America Brown, In Too Deep, Hav Plenty, Zooman, Full Court Press

The Badge Gizmo Herbert (2002)

The Skulls Will Beckford (2000)

Loving Jezebel Theodus (1999)

*Beloved Halle (*1998*)*

The Nephew Chad Egan Washington (1998)

He Got Game

Get On the Bus X (1996)

Zooman

Full Court Press

One Red Rose co-written by Hill. Pumpkinhead II: Bold Wings Peter *(1994)*

The Visit for which he was nominated for an Independent Spirit Award.

The Breed Filmed in Cape Town, South Africa in 2005.

Received a 2004 Golden Satellite Award Nomination as Outstanding Supporting Actor in a Drama Series. For his role in *City of Angels* on CBS he was nominated for an NAACP Image Award for Best Supporting Actor. Hill's favourite actors are Daniel Day Lewis, Morgan Freeman, Jeffrey Pierce, Emily Watson and Meryl Streep. He would love to play Marvin Gaye, Bob Marley and Smokey Robinson.

Hill's third book was out on September 8th 2009 called, *The Conversation*: an adult romantic fiction from the perspective of a single man. His first book was entitled, *Letters to a Young Brother* and his follow-on, *Letters to a Young Sister*: DeFINE Your Destiny, a new motivational book was out June 2008.

He has a non-profit foundation, *Manifest Your Destiny Foundation* and has been sent to Italy and Turkey by the State Department to give talks to young people, due to his relationship with President Obama. That's why he enjoys the appeal of *CSI*, "it has such an international reach that it offers me a platform to speak to young people around the world."

He states many of Hawkes' mannerisms, his character traits are similar to his own. "Dr Sheldon Hawkes is a probably a better man than Hill Harper, is all around but that doesn't mean I don't aspire to be a better person...I love that my character breaks many stereotypes. He's the most intelligent character on the show – all the other characters have to come to my character for answers. It's not the typical portrayal of the African/American male in the media in general. I like breaking stereotypes." He also feels Hawkes is reclusive and booksmart and Hill is educated by Hawkes, who is a genius.

Hill didn't have to audition for the show, the part was offered to him – all due to his role on *The Handler,* a short-lived CBS show. CBS suggested him for the role of Hawkes to Anthony Zuiker and Jerry Bruckheimer. When auditioning for a Network show – *The Handler*, for which he did have to audition, the Network President, others under him, producers and the production company all get their input. The final audition is called *the test*, where you test against others – the contract has been signed already, they watch you. He says "if you're a writer rejection is tough because it's something you created, when you're an actor you feel like they're rejecting you."

On the other two *CSI* shows he comments, "I think it's [*CSI:NY*] is better acted, not to take anything away from their shows, but I know our actors are the best, in my opinion." But doesn't everyone say that about their own show.

He thinks the quality of US movies is on the slide whilst the quality of US TV is much higher. *CSI:NY* stories are very interesting to him and that's because of the standard of writing. He would prefer to direct an episode rather than write, since they have great writers anyway. He'd like to stay on the show a few more seasons – but is unsure what will happen in this changing climate. "The days of sitting back on a show, thinking that your character is not getting killed off, are over." (In the season 5 finale, the entire cast were shot at in a bar) "the creative and business side are getting too much more linked in a way that I don't think is necessarily good." He concedes that what makes *CSI:NY* so good is the writing. "All television begins with the writing period. We have the best writers in my opinion."

They get a day off or time off during filming, which is eight days, but he says Gary is there all the time since he's in most of the episodes: Monday-Friday 05.30/06.00 – until 20.00. During the week, he sometimes ends up finishing about 5am on a Saturday morning. He calls Gary "a master at the craft and I have so much respect for him – he's a wonderful actor. We have a ball. Everyone has different acting styles so I respect his style and hopefully he respects my style. He has a focus and a stillness that's really nice when he acts."

Eddie Cahill

Born January 15 1978 in New York. He is 6' 2". He graduated Byram Hills High School, Armonk, New York in 1996. Other attendees at his school included Eyal Podell and Sean Maher.

Eddie is the only son of an Italian mother and Irish father. He has an older sister and a younger sister. In kindergarten Eddie wanted to be a farmer and still has aspirations of this, one day maybe when he's no longer acting. He attended acting school at The Atlantic Theater School in Manhattan and he caught his break in the Summer Theater Festival at Vassar College.

He sent over 'sides' call, after call. He has a great personality, sarcasm and it was a dream come true to be able to play a New Yorker "for real" and readily came on board *CSI:NY*.

Eddie moved to Brooklyn after dropping out of NYU to follow acting full time, he was going to become a teacher. He wanted to go into acting after watching *Les Miserables* when he was 17.

Says Eddie, "I was drawn to acting because I have a fascination with truth and understanding. The challenge is not to put out a judgement in your portrayal. We all have opinions when we read these characters. Even if we like them, you don't want to put it out that you like the character. You want to find out what motivates them. I like to act anything. The trick is to find what motivates them."

In July 2000, after getting hold of $300, he went to LA but returned to New York shortly after. It had turned out to be a wasted trip. He was all packed and ready to leave when he was called and told the good news of landing a part on *Friends*. "I had $19.50 in my bank account – no – I had $19.50 in each, so I had $39." He played the part of Rachel's younger boyfriend (as we all know by now) Tag Jones. After his appearance in this, the door opened up for him to make many other guest appearances in shows such as, *Charmed*, *Felicity*, where he had a recurring role as James – a bad guy role of drug dealer.

Whilst on stage in a New York play, he was spotted by Sarah Jessica Parker and subsequently landed a role as Carrie's bisexual boyfriend in *Sex and the City*.

Marlon Brando inspires him. He practices Anasura yoga five days a week. He is eight years younger than his girlfriend. Whilst in the past, he rented a house in Silverdale with Eliza Dushku and her brother, Nate.

Eddie is good friends with David Schwimmer and recalls him since he was 15. David directed Eddie's first episode of *Friends*. When he first got this part, he used to wonder what he was doing there and how everything was so new. Also Sarah Jessica Parker was so nice to him. Eddie says he's not as naïve as Tag, but identifies with his character of Mike in *Glory Days*. "One thing I identify with him is the identity crisis you have in your early 20's. You want to know who you are, definitely looking to home as a way to identify yourself, Mike and I have that in common. I'm a bit of a sceptic. I can appreciate that."

Eddie's favourite music ranges from Meredith Monk, Brian Eno, to Bach. He loves to spend time with family and friends when he's in New York and even cleans, sometimes. As well as reading in his free time. His favourite soccer (that's football to the rest of us) team is Glasgow Celtic Football Club. When he was filming in Vancouver, Eddie used to like driving and he loves meeting people.

On being called a 'hottie' he replies, "the short answer is it's better than being called an asshole. It's a bit of a giggle, and dare I say an irony because for the first half of my life I was a very heavy kid. I did not grow up hearing that stuff, so I dieted. When I hit the seventh grade I was like, 'everyone is getting girlfriends I'm sick of being the fat, funny guy.' So I committed to losing weight. It is part release and part of a giggle, but at the end of the day it doesn't mean anything."

Eddie's ideal in a woman is "a strong value system, loyalty and directness – a woman who isn't so concerned with being everybody's friend." His pet hates include, "impoliteness, rudeness and anyone mean." He also hates teasers.

In June 2005 he starred in *Lords of Dogtown*.

His feature film debut was in 2004 in Disney's *Miracle* where he portrayed one of his real life heroes, Jim Craig, a 1980 US Olympic hockey team goalkeeper. Eddie had never played goal before and comments, "you have to be incredibly focused and relaxed, fast. It's more than I ever sweated in my life." For this, he attended a six week hockey camp. In 2000 he appeared in an off Broadway production of *The Altruists*. His first off- Broadway role was at the Vineyard Theater. He was paid $206.57 a week for playing a 'handsome male prostitute'.

He would love to have Edward Norton's career, combined with that of Peter Falk, as well as wanting to work with Gena Rowlands (John Cassevete's widow), Kevin Spacey and Ang Lee.

In 2001 he was named one of *E! Entertainment*'s *Sizzling Sixteen*: one of the brightest up and coming stars of 2001. (Others on the list included, Elijah Wood, Kevin Kline and Colin Farrell.) Eddie admitted to not owning a suit at the time. *E! Online* interviewed Eddie at a breakfast meeting and he arrived wearing clothes to the value of $4. His attire was faded jeans; camouflage hunting cap that he found; T-shirt, Levis; dusty cowboy boots he picked up from a flea market.

His grandfather was a police sergeant in the same borough and great grandfather was an Inspector in the Bronx. His father also wanted to join the force but his eyesight was too poorly; and "I am playing a homicide detective. I was a big *Law and Order* fan. I am a big fan of the true crime stories. It's just a part of something I am fascinated with." His grandfather passed away when he was in the fourth grade so he says he didn't get his heritage or street smarts from him.

His best friend's father was commander of the Homicide Squad for Manhattan South and is retired now. "Growing up with friends who are cops and talking to them, that is truthfully where it comes from. It gives me something to smile about. My mom always says, 'I wish your Grandpa was around to see this. He'd get a kick out of it.' On the non-technical side, having it in my family, having it something my mother was raised so closely with, there's a value system that gets passed down."

He has his grandfather's police badge, which he inherited.

Commenting on his accent, he doesn't think it's very thick in real life as it is on the show but it depends on the circumstances. "If I go back home or if I am with friends I grew up with, it is a lot thicker. I remember one of my first auditions ever, I forgot what it was for, the kid was from Wichita and I got nervous so my accent got thicker and the only thing the casting director said to me was, 'Eddie where are you from?' We were in New York at the time and I said, 'I am from New York.' 'So where is this character from?' I said, 'Wichitaw.' She goes, 'thank you.' That was it. Baptism by fire. Who said they are not friendly in Hollywood?"

Eddie beefs up his accent for the show, just as in the episode of *Friends* when he found it tough to say [hot] "dog", instead of his usual "dawg". He almost felt like asking if he could change the word to Frankfurter instead.

His most famous role to date is Donald Flack in *CSI:NY*. He says, "it brings me back home and I get to play a person who belongs to a group of people I adore. To go to New York under these circumstances is great. People congratulate you for being a part of something great. You can only appreciate those kinds of comments when they come from home."

He calls New York, "the best city in the world." That you can cheat the idea of a place when featuring a city but you can't cheat New York entirely. Eddie describes his audition for the role of Flack, as a meeting with Anthony Zuiker. He says Flack is the one everybody turns to in times of trouble, which is what I've been saying since season 1.

As for Eddie's long hair in season 1, he had just finished filming *Miracles* so they didn't want him cutting his hair short all in one go.

Eddie also admits to being insecure whenever he turns up for work on the first day. He tells himself the people he works with, his co-stars are those he wants to be when he grows up."

Eddie had spent two years doing theatre work and attended a meeting with WB bosses, winning a deal for his own show, *Glory Days*: playing Mike Dolan (2002) alongside Poppy Montgomery. (Originally Julie Benz was to play Poppy's role.) This was created by producer Kevin Williamson of *Dawson's Creek* fame and also the *Scream* films and based on the novel *Glory Days* by Mike Dolan, based on his own life. In this, Mike writes a warts'n'all book about his hometown and now suffering from burn out he returns home to Glory, wanting to prove his father was murdered and didn't commit suicide. He ends up investigating every crazy crime committed there. He finds no one there is impressed with the book. Eddie loved the cast and crew on this show and they all spent plenty of time together.

This show was filmed in Vancouver and whilst he was there, Eddie also took up ice hockey. He is an official NHL Blogger.

He knows how lucky he is to be part of a successful franchise, "I get to have a gig – what I like to do for a stretch of time. It's great."

To Eddie, "Hollywood was a big scary world. I am inspired by people who understand teamwork and who understand that one person can't make or break something – from craft services to actors. They have been the most inspiring...if you can't connect to pleasure, you have no business doing it." Someone he worked with said that to him. "If I acted to watch myself I'd sit home with a camera. You owe people. You must be responsible."

Guest starring roles:

Best Ever as Himself (2004) four times

Dawson's Creek Max Winter in the episode Everything Put Together (where it was murder on the dancefloor, literally!) A must-see episode just to see Eddie strut his stuff as a disco-dancer. Catch it if you can!!

Law & Order: Special Victims Unit Tommy Dowd in Folly (2001). Here he played a male escort victimized and brutally attacked and disfigured by the head of the escort agency. She threw boiling pasta over his face when she discovered he was wearing a wire.

Friends Tag in episodes: The One with the Red Sweater; The One Where They All Turn Thirty; The One Where They're Up All Night; The One with All the Candy; The One where Chandler Doesn't like Dogs; The One With The Engagement Picture; The One with Rachel's Assistant (2001-2000)

Felicity James in the episodes: And To All A Goodnight; Final Touches, aka Let's Get it On; James and The Giant Peach (2000)

Charmed Sean in the episode **Sight Unseen**

Sex and the City in *Boy, Girl, Boy, Girl* (2000)
Haunted Simon in *Redux*

More recently Eddie filmed *The Narrows* (2008) based on a Tim McLoughlin novel, where he played Nicky Shades, alongside Vincent D'Onofrio.

Eddie thinks *Haunted* was a good show and he was surprised it didn't last long. "It was a nice mix of a cop drama and a supernatural show. When I did *Charmed* I was just happy to have a job. I do like that stuff; my preference is the kind of show that has its roots in what actually happens but I had a great time on them."

"I wish I could say I have a preference. If I could muster up a career I would like that a lot. I love television because I get work every week and as a young guy that is very helpful. I would love to have a career of film/television/theatre. That would be ideal for me."

Eddie used to feel uncomfortable working with Gary on the show, and having worked with other stars like Sarah Jessica Parker, and especially since they're stars, in his eyes. As for the success of *CSI:NY*, he tries to ignore it as far as possible, "it makes me paranoid and crazy."

Eddie has plenty to say about Flack and especially his character in season 2 episode **All Access** where he says, in reference to Stella bumping off her unstable boyfriend, Frankie, that "had it been any old broad who shot her boyfriend, there would have been a much different tone in the room. He can get a little on the high horse. So I think that was an interesting position for him to be in because it eliminates a bit of that, dare I say, cockiness when he walks in the room and that's a tool I think the character uses. That's something that became very clear to me in the last season [1] because they gave me such nice quality moments to play with my colleagues, that I realize you see the difference when Flack's up against a stranger or somebody he thinks is guilty of a murder; he will take the tone as a tool, but it's not who he is necessarily. It's a game he knows how to play and it's his approach."

That's very noticeable about Flack's character: Flack the cop and Flack the man; loyal friend. He will dig his heels in, throw his weight around and display limitless sarcasm when 'interviewing' a suspect to the point of almost erring on the side of not doing things by the book, until this turns around on him in season 5 episode **5.13 Rush to Judgement** – whereas for his friends he will always be displaying a more humane, softer side. Though on the flip side, some suspects do clearly deserve his wrath, again season 5 episode, **5.22 Yahrzeit** when interrogating the Neo-Nazi and Flack's curt and exceptionally cool response: "I don't talk ignorant." No judgement, no outward show of racism, but a simple reply! Showing how much his character will evolve through the seasons and has done so already.

Another is Flack: the ladies' man – not only getting his own love interest in season 4/5, but the way he "eyes the female suspects during interrogations/interviews, throughout the seasons is always good for a laugh. Eddie didn't think much of his leather jacket as he admits he wore it more often than not – it was almost a second skin and very uncomfortable so he was happy when he didn't have to wear it anymore.

On Flack and Danny he feels they have more of a brotherly relationship as they're closer in age.

Eddie says Flack didn't get involved and interact with other characters much in season 1; I commented that's because he wasn't in many of the episodes, or even for long – his scenes were quite short until later on in season 1. He thought of Flack being on the outside – the police guy – no scientific knowledge, he felt Mac was more of a father figure to everyone. So when they argue in later seasons, they actually worked together in the end and so no one was exclusively right or wrong. [See especially later episodes, such as season **3.8 Consequences** – a great Flack episode, which continues on in **3.10 Sweet 16, 3.11 Raising Shane** and **3.21 Past Imperfect** which are all related plot-wise, in some respects and particularly character-wise for Flack.

He divides his time between New York and LA. Eddie has a tattoo on his shoulder – his girlfriend's name in a heart with an arrow through it and a swallow atop. It was cut out of the season 2 finale scene in the hospital, when Eddie was shirtless, after Flack bears the brunt of an explosion.

Eddie said it was even great for him when he survived the season 2 finale **Charge of this Post**. No we can't lose our Flack!

Eddie also likes the episodes with the story arcs – such as in season 4 with the **333** and the cab killer episodes, as it draws out the characters' feelings and motivation.

Eddie on staying with the show, "as long as they'll have me [great news for us!] I envision staying with the show as long as the show goes and I hope it goes a long time. It's fun. I love it. It's the first time in my young career that I've had that sort of 9 to 5 feeling and I dig it. I like having a place to go to work. I feel very fortunate for that."

Eddie will watch the show when it is on, otherwise he will use his TIVO. He says, "that's where you learn. Think of it this way, if I were to watch season 1 and not watch season 2, I'd be doing a totally different show. You get the conversations, you get the insight, you get the scripts, the final product is the result."

His stunt double, Sean Taylor taught him to surf and he says he makes Flack look good on screen.

Eddie is into the more intellectual reading books, such as James Joyce's *Portrait of the Artist as a Young Man, Nor Meekly Serve My Time* which are first-hand accounts of prisoners in Northern Ireland. It's heavy reading and he's not into other less serious, gossipy stuff. Eddie comments that he was "born at the tail end [1978] of a generation that didn't come up with the idea of computers in the classroom [same here, though there was one computer in my school available for teaching purposes, bummer being only four students could pick Computer Studies as a subject. No I'm not that old either!] Or the idea of DNA; I think that may remain surprising to me for the rest of my life. It's amazing." He's in awe about how much can be discovered from DNA about a person, especially a strand of hair.

As for not acting, he says he put pressure on himself to make this happen and it took a long time to come about. So he hasn't thought about what he'd be doing if he wasn't acting. "Seeing them [his family] react has been one of the coolest things – to bring that joy home. It excites them. They're on a different cloud than I am. It's a dream come true for me. It's a real dream world, but it's not something we all thought about when I was a kid. It's been a nice surprise."

To end on wise words from Eddie: "when I feel stressed I think, you are all you have, and you are enough. I learned that in school and I try to learn and re-learn that everyday. Do your thing." (Or as Flack would say, "your thang."

Not everyone will know this, but Eddie needs to have his feet powdered before he can begin to film.

If you can, go see Eddie in *seventeen.com* March 2002 when he took them around Vancouver, whilst filming *Glory Days*. Eddie commented, "it's weird to meet a bunch of strangers and have them follow you around with cameras and a tape recorder. I had fun. On a normal Sunday I would just be by myself." Some great photos there too.

References

Buck V Bell 274 US 200 (1927)

American Way 9 August 2009
TVCalling.com 2 July 2009
What's On TV.co.uk 24 June 2009
The Sun News 15 May 2009
SILive.com 12 May 2009
The Independent 16 January 2009
Futoncritic 23 September 2009
Futoncritic 21 September 2009
Hollywood Chicago.com July 2009
Cultfollowing.com 19 June 2009
TV Guide 8-14 December 2008
SpoilerTV New York Post 4 October 2009
TV Guide 30 September 2008
Radio Times 2-8 February 2008
CBS Watch The Who's Who! 10 January 2008
Grand Rapids Entertainment Grand Rapids Press MLive.com 21 April 2008
Snippets of cast interviews: Carmine Giovinazzo, Eddie Cahill, Gary Sinise *Five US* 2007
DVD Monthly July 2007
The Works June 2007
Hill Harper's Twitter page
CSI files.com 4 December 2007
Maureen Ryan Tribune Tower Gets Airtime on CSI:NY Metromix Chicago 28 November 2007
CSI files.com 29 October 2007
CSI files.com 26 October 2007
Marissa Gutherie Location Shots Have the N.Y into CSI Daily News 2 April 2007
CSI files.com 29 June 2007
TVGuide.com 6 April 2007
National Post 14 October 2006 (Canada.com)
TV Guide 6 December 2006

TV Guide 4 December 2006
CSI:The Inside Story five US 29 December 2006
The Independent 19 December 2006
Men's Daily News 14 October 2006
newscred.com
nwHerald.com May 2006
CSIfiles.com 24 April 2006
Cosmopolitan 2005
TV Guide September 25-October 1 2005
       May 1-7 2005
       February 27-March 5 2005
CSIfiles.com 8 August 2005
Entertainment Weekly 5 August 2005
TVSA 25 May 2005
TV Guide 27 February-5 March 2005
Teletext 'CSI's Cosmopolitan Cop Carmine' 13 May 2005
Carmine Giovinazzo llvechat @ CSifiles.com 29 June 2005
Cult Times #121 October 2005
Cult Times #116 May 2005
Cult Times #114 March 2005
JoBlo.com
TeenHollywood.com
Goveg.com
TIME 8 November 2004
CSIfiles.com 21 October 2004
Entertainment Weekly 1 October 2004
          10 October 2004
Sllive.com September 2004
LA Times 10 September 2004
TV Guide September 26-October 2 2004
TVGuideonline 25 September 2004
Eddiecahillonline.com 22 September 2004
Entertainment Weekly 10 September 2004
Sllive.com May 2004
VenturaCountyStar.com May 2004
Playboy March 2004
TVGuideonline 9 February 2004

Eddiecahillonline.com 30 January 2002

The Colour of Rape: Gender and Race in Television's Public Spheres by Sujata Moore Barrett   State University of New York 2001

WB Transcript December 2000

CSI and its sister shows are great shows which provide lots of insight into the workings of science and to a lesser extent, the workings of the criminal mind. I wrote this as already said since CSI:NY was the show no one really bothered writing about.

Writing guides seems to be in my nature, as well as this one I also have written about Supernatural (all unofficially of course) and a few other books, lots of serious articles and fun stuff too.

So if you enjoyed this little guide, my own little production why not e- mail me and tell me your thoughts, did I cover enough on your fave characters from the show; anything omitted and who knows I may cover the remaining seasons, depending on the feedback I get...it's over to you...

mila123h@yahoo.com

Printed in Great Britain
by Amazon